Aspiration, Desire and the Drivers of Migration

This book throws new light on the drivers of migration and explores the different ways in which aspiration and desire are involved in the generation, experiences, and outcomes of migration.

The authors propose novel approaches to advancing collective understanding of migration, including reassessments of classical push and pull theory; explorations of the lexicon of aspiration, desire and voluntariness in migration; and reflections on the relationships between migration and modernity, youth and expectation, and anti-immigrant discourses. The chapters have a broad geographical scope, spanning migration on different continents and in diverse socio-economic and cultural settings.

At a time when migration has become one of the most prominent areas of national and international political debate, this volume provides the tools for researchers to reconsider how we understand the forces and outcomes of global mobility.

This book was originally published as a special issue of the *Journal of Ethnic and Migration Studies*.

Francis L. Collins is Professor of Geography in the National Institute of Demographic and Economic Analysis at the University of Waikato, New Zealand. His research focuses on international migration and cities with a particular emphasis on the experiences, mobility patterns, and government regulation of temporary migrants in urban contexts.

Jørgen Carling is a Research Professor at the Peace Research Institute Oslo, Norway. His research addresses migration theory, transnational practices, and the links between migration and development. He has a particular interest in the thoughts and feelings that precede migration, and in the experience of involuntary immobility.

Research in Ethnic and Migration Studies

Series editor: Paul Statham, *Director, Sussex Centre for Migration Research (SCMR), University of Sussex, UK*

The *Research in Ethnic and Migration Studies* series publishes the results of high-quality, cutting-edge research that addresses key questions relating to ethnic relations, diversity and migration. The series is open to a range of disciplines and brings together research collaborations on specific defined topics on all aspects of migration and its consequences, including migration processes, migrants and their experiences, ethnic relations, discrimination, integration, racism, transnationalism, citizenship, identity and cultural diversity. Contributions are especially welcome when they are the result of comparative research, either across countries, cities or groups. All articles have previously been published in the *Journal of Ethnic and Migration Studies (JEMS)*, which has a rigorous peer review system. Collective volumes in this series are either the product of Special Issues published in the journal or published articles that the Editor has selected from individual submissions.

Titles in the series:

Regulation of Speech in Multicultural Societies
Edited by Marcel Maussen and Ralph Grillo

Deportation, Anxiety, Justice
New Ethnographic Perspectives
Edited by Heike Drotbohm and Ines Hasselberg

Migrants, Minorities, and the Media
Information, Representations, and Participation in the Public Sphere
Edited by Erik Bleich, Irene Bloemraad and Els de Graauw

The Global Economic Crisis and Migration
Edited by Christof Roos and Natascha Zaun

Muslims in Europe
Comparative Perspectives on Socio-cultural Integration
Edited by Paul Statham and Jean Tillie

Ageing as a Migrant
Vulnerabilities, Agency and Policy Implications
Edited by Ruxandra Oana Ciobanu, Tineke Fokkema and Mihaela Nedelcu

Asian Migration and Education Cultures in the Anglosphere
Edited by Megan Watkins, Christina Ho and Rose Butler

Exploring the Migration Industries
New Perspectives on Facilitating and Constraining Migration
Edited by Sophie Cranston, Joris Schapendonk and Ernst Spaan

Aspiration, Desire and the Drivers of Migration
Edited by Francis L. Collins and Jørgen Carling

For a full list of titles please visit:
https://www.routledge.com/Research-in-Ethnic-and-Migration-Studies/book-series/REMS

Aspiration, Desire and the Drivers of Migration

Edited by
Francis L. Collins and Jørgen Carling

Routledge
Taylor & Francis Group
LONDON AND NEW YORK

First published 2020
by Routledge
2 Park Square, Milton Park, Abingdon, Oxon, OX14 4RN

and by Routledge
52 Vanderbilt Avenue, New York, NY 10017

Routledge is an imprint of the Taylor & Francis Group, an informa business

British Library Cataloguing in Publication Data
A catalogue record for this book is available from the British Library

ISBN 13: 978-0-367-23695-3

Typeset in Minion Pro
by RefineCatch Limited, Bungay, Suffolk

Publisher's Note
The publisher accepts responsibility for any inconsistencies that may have arisen during the conversion of this book from journal articles to book chapters, namely the inclusion of journal terminology.

Contents

Citation Information

The chapters in this book were originally published in the *Journal of Ethnic and Migration Studies*, volume 44, issue 6 (May 2018). When citing this material, please use the original page numbering for each article, as follows:

Introduction
Aspiration, desire and drivers of migration
Jørgen Carling and Francis Collins
Journal of Ethnic and Migration Studies, volume 44, issue 6 (May 2018), pp. 909–926

Chapter 1
Push-pull plus: reconsidering the drivers of migration
Nicholas Van Hear, Oliver Bakewell and Katy Long
Journal of Ethnic and Migration Studies, volume 44, issue 6 (May 2018), pp. 927–944

Chapter 2
Revisiting aspiration and ability in international migration
Jørgen Carling and Kerilyn Schewel
Journal of Ethnic and Migration Studies, volume 44, issue 6 (May 2018), pp. 945–963

Chapter 3
Desire as a theory for migration studies: temporality, assemblage and becoming in the narratives of migrants
Francis L. Collins
Journal of Ethnic and Migration Studies, volume 44, issue 6 (May 2018), pp. 964–980

Chapter 4
Forced to leave? The discursive and analytical significance of describing migration as forced and voluntary
Marta Bivand Erdal and Ceri Oeppen
Journal of Ethnic and Migration Studies, volume 44, issue 6 (May 2018), pp. 981–998

Chapter 5
Shifting migration aspirations in second modernity
Elisabeth Scheibelhofer
Journal of Ethnic and Migration Studies, volume 44, issue 6 (May 2018), pp. 999–1014

Chapter 6

Desiring 'foreign talent': lack and Lacan in anti-immigrant sentiments in Singapore
Peidong Yang
Journal of Ethnic and Migration Studies, volume 44, issue 6 (May 2018), pp. 1015–1031

Chapter 7

Navigating aspirations and expectations: adolescents' considerations of outmigration from rural eastern Germany
Frank Meyer
Journal of Ethnic and Migration Studies, volume 44, issue 6 (May 2018), pp. 1032–1049

For any permission-related enquiries please visit:
http://www.tandfonline.com/page/help/permissions

Notes on Contributors

Oliver Bakewell is a Senior Lecturer in Migration Studies at the Global Development Institute at the University of Manchester, UK.

Jørgen Carling is a Research Professor at the Peace Research Institute Oslo, Norway.

Francis L. Collins is Professor of Geography in the National Institute of Demographic and Economic Analysis at the University of Waikato, New Zealand.

Marta Bivand Erdal is Research Professor in Migration Studies at the Peace Research Institute Oslo, Norway.

Katy Long is an Independent Consultant based in San Francisco, USA, and Oxford, UK.

Frank Meyer is a Researcher at the Leibniz Institute for Regional Geography, Germany.

Ceri Oeppen is a Global Fellow at the Peace Research Institute Oslo, Norway, and a Lecturer in Human Geography in the Department of Geography at the University of Sussex, UK.

Elisabeth Scheibelhofer is an Associate Professor in the Department of Sociology at the University of Vienna, Austria.

Kerilyn Schewel is a Doctoral Candidate in Sociology in the Faculty of Social and Behavioural Sciences at the University of Amsterdam, the Netherlands.

Nicholas Van Hear is a Senior Researcher and Deputy Director at the Centre on Migration, Policy and Society (COMPAS) at the University of Oxford, UK.

Peidong Yang is an Assistant Professor at the National Institute of Education at Nanyang Technological University, Singapore.

INTRODUCTION

Aspiration, desire and drivers of migration

Jørgen Carling and Francis Collins

ABSTRACT
Introducing a special journal issue by the same title, this article provides a foundation for seven other articles with a theoretical mission to better understand the forces and frictions through which migration comes about and is experienced. The collection seeks to contribute to migration theory by considering crosscutting themes related to the concepts of *aspiration*, *desire* and *drivers of migration*. This introductory article locates the three concepts within the development of migration scholarship. First, we show how a reappraisal of theory is grounded in influential developments in migration scholarship, such as the transnational turn, feminist approaches and, more recently, a growing theoretical interest in emotions and temporalities. Second, we examine the ways in which 'aspiration' and 'desire' have figured in migration theory. Sometimes treated as synonyms, the terms both belong to a broader semantic field of potentiality, yet connect with different theoretical approaches. Third, we address the rise of 'drivers of migration' as an analytical concept, noting how it seems to be replacing 'causes' and 'determinants' in the literature.

Introduction

Imagined, desired, resisted, experienced, managed, and represented, migration is a multifaceted reality. The various ways of engaging with migration intersect with traditional concerns of migration theory – why people migrate, where they choose to go and how migration flows wax or wane. Scholarly engagements with migration also address perennial social-scientific themes, such as the interplay between agency and structure and the merits of models based on rational choice. The real-world dynamics of migration encompass all these facets with substantial complexity and immediacy in terms of their effects in people's lives. But the study of migration too often remains fragmented and compartmentalised in predictable ways: between quantitative and qualitative research, different geographical contexts, forms or types of migration and theoretical influences. In this special issue and introduction, we seek to contribute to understanding migration by taking a step back and considering crosscutting themes through analysing the concepts of aspiration, desire and drivers of migration.

This article introduces a special journal issue by the same title. In addition to this one, it brings together seven articles, each with a theoretical mission to understand the forces and frictions through which migration comes about and is experienced. In lieu of conventional synopses, we provide an overview of the articles in Table 1 and weave references to each article into our discussion of this special issue's overarching themes.

The articles were written against the backdrop of momentous developments in international migration dynamics and discourses. They include what has been called the 'long summer of migration' in 2015 when over one million people sought refuge in Europe, the United Nations Summit for Refugees and Migrants in 2016 and prominent debates about immigration in the campaigns that led to the Brexit vote in the United Kingdom and the election of Donald Trump as president of the United States.

The notion that migration is an inexorable reality of the twenty-first century has fuelled these developments. It is particularly evident in the resurgence of populism and nationalist anxiety in Europe and North America and the reinvigorated focus on borders and exclusion that is manifesting in its wake. Images of lines of migrants trudging vast distances, border walls designed to halt flows of newcomers, ships filled to capacity crossing dangerous waters and bodies of those who died seeking safe passage portray migration in a way that suggests people are impelled to move and that only the most drastic state actions will alter that. Similarly, political rhetoric around managed economic migration continues to

Table 1. Overview of articles in the special issue.

Author(s)	Title	Empirical foundations or illustrations	Theoretical thrust
Nicholas Van Hear, Oliver Bakewell and Katy Long	Push–pull plus: reconsidering the drivers of migration	Afghan migration to Iran and Pakistan; Somali migration to southern Africa	Generating a framework labelled 'push–pull plus' that is founded on the distinction between four types of drivers of migration
Jørgen Carling and Kerilyn Schewel	Revisiting aspiration and ability in international migration	Diverse case studies: global country-level data	Examining extensions and implications of the aspiration/ ability model of migration and identifying 'two-step' approaches' as an analytical class in migration theory
Francis Collins	Desire as a theory for migration studies: temporality, assemblage and becoming in the narratives of migrants	Migration from South East Asia to South Korea	Exploiting the analytical potential of 'desire' to examine the temporalities, assemblages and transformative potential of migration experience
Marta Bivand Erdal and Ceri Oeppen	Forced to leave? The discursive and analytical significance of describing migration as forced and voluntary	Afghan and Pakistani migration to Europe	Unsettling the forced–voluntary dichotomy through analysing stages of the migration process: leaving, journeying, arriving, settling and returning
Elisabeth Scheibelhofer	Shifting migration aspirations in second modernity	Austrian migrants in the United States	Using the concept of 'second modernity' to contextualise the changing meaning and content of aspirations within migratory projects
Peidong Yang	Desiring 'foreign talent': lack and Lacan in anti-immigrant sentiments in Singapore	High-skilled immigration to Singapore, especially from China	Drawing on the notion of desire in Lacanian psychoanalysis to examine immigration policy and discourse
Frank Meyer	Navigating aspirations and expectations: adolescents' considerations of outmigration from rural eastern Germany	Outmigration of adolescents from rural eastern Germany	Locating adolescents' migratory decision-making between a contested field of expectations and personal attempts of becoming

propose that regardless of whether migrants are entrepreneurs, workers or students, more or less skilled or affluent, they will identify and assess which locations will provide the greatest benefit for them and their families. *Homo economicus* haunts pronouncements about migration policy, whether in discussing opening borders and attracting desirable migrants or reducing and discouraging the arrival of people. The notion that individualised rational action underpins migration choices has become unquestionable.

Critical migration scholars know very well that such imagery and ideology reveal little of migration's complexity and the manner in which it is embedded in social relations, imaginations of the world, economic settings and opportunities and political controls. Yet, scholars have also collectively struggled to condense these more complex accounts in a way that might alter popular and political conceptions of why and how migration occurs. In some instances, the unquestioning uptake of economic rationality and forced nature of migration have perpetuated the theoretical underpinnings of common misunderstandings. In the space of economic migration, for example, de Haas (2011, 20) suggests that while it is unrealistic to assume that 'people are free from constraints, enjoy full access to information, and make migration decisions with the aim of maximizing their utility', these ideas have not been fundamentally challenged in migration studies. There is a great risk here, not only in reproducing stereotypes of migrants as individual and collective subjects, but also in bolstering repressive approaches to policing movement. As the contributors to the collection 'New Keywords: Migration and Borders' put it, 'migration knowledge' can 'often result in unexamined discourses, architectures, and practices that in turn render knowledge of migration as an object of governmentality' (Casas-Cortes et al. 2015, 63). Migration scholarship cannot, in other words, only be seen as a scientific endeavour, but must rather critically engage with its own place in the politics of mobility.

This special issue aims to break new ground in the conceptualisation and examination of the motive forces that generate and impede migration. Its collective view is that while the shortcomings of orthodox theories of migration have been identified for several decades (Adam 1984; Goss and Lindquist 1995; Halfacree and Boyle 1993; Silvey 2004), we have not established alternative conceptualisations that might advance accounts of migration beyond a reliance only on economic rationality and completely involuntary displacement. Migration theory needs to account for the multiplex componentry of migration, the way it is situated in imaginative geographies, emotional valences, social relations and obligations and politics and power relations, as well as in economic imperatives and the brute realities of displacement. The seven articles in this special issue do exactly that. They take established and underutilised theoretical perspectives and conceptual vocabulary and propose alternative ways of framing migration that speak to a wide variety of movements and their implications.

Our core concepts – aspiration, desire and drivers of migration – do not comprise an equally weighted triad. Aspiration and desire are synonyms in common parlance, and they are, matters of individual cognition and emotion. Drivers of migration, by contrast, is an analytical category that reflects particular understandings of how the world works. Yet, the friction between the three concepts arises from their connectedness: they all relate to how migration is initiated, experienced and represented. Later in this article, we examine the three concepts in greater detail, structuring the discussion by starting with aspiration and desire, relating them to the broader semantic field to which they both belong.

Subsequently, we turn to the notion of drivers. First, however, we account for the key theoretical developments upon which we build.

Foundations for a reappraisal of migration theory

Clearly, migration scholarship has advanced significantly since the heyday of gravity models and migration laws. Students and scholars are now confronted with an array of theoretical lenses through which to view various aspects of migratory processes and understand the politics generated in the mobility and encounter that migration brings. While it has been rare for scholars to offer new theoretical perspectives on what generates and sustains migration, important developments in its study over the last three decades offer a foundation for our own intervention in this special issue. They include the focus on transnationalism; feminist critiques and analyses of gender in migration; emotions and migration; the timing of migration; and efforts to explore the infrastructures that support migration processes. Each development has made it possible for scholars to expand the different features of migration that we include in our analysis and to examine the implications of migration beyond what they mean for individual migrants and the societies they leave from and arrive in.

Perhaps the most notable intervention into migration scholarship over the last three decades has been the proposition that we need to examine the transnational dimensions of moving in the world. Established in the 1990s by anthropologists exploring ethnic community formation and politics in the United States (Basch, Glick Schiller, and Szanton Blanc 1994; Rouse 1991), transnationalism has become a marker of all kinds of cross-border initiatives that are involved in migratory and other social, cultural and economic processes (Collins 2009). As a theoretical optic, a transnational approach has allowed analysis of migration to get beyond looking at migrants within either 'sending' or 'receiving' nation states as distinct geographical entities. Moreover, the idea that migration can be understood as a single linear movement from origin to destination is disrupted within transnationalism. This requires scholars to acknowledge the different ways migrants are embedded in transnational social fields (Levitt and Glick Schiller 2004), move through transnational channels (Findlay and Li 1998) and utilise transnationally stretched resources for political, social and economic life (Smith 2001). The transnational approach is fundamental to reconfiguring our understanding of the drivers of migration because it emphasises how processes of migration, incorporation into new contexts and the establishment and maintenance of connections to homeland and other locales occur simultaneously and mutually inform each other. All of the articles in this special issue can be seen in this light. They address the generation and sustenance of migration as something that is distributed across borders, in transnational social and economic linkages (Carling and Schewel 2018; Collins 2018; Erdal and Oeppen 2018; Van Hear, Bakewell, and Long 2018) or within migration's imaginative dimensions as they are constituted across borders (Meyer 2018; Scheibelhofer 2018; Yang 2018). In perspective, the figure of the migrant as an autonomous agent located in one place is disrupted by an emphasis on migrants as situated in social fields that cross borders and play a role in enabling and shaping migration processes and outcomes.

The 1990s also brought the feminist critique of long-standing emphasis on men as primary agents in migration, a greater focus on the gendered dimensions of migration and discussion of how migration is entangled in myriad social, cultural and emotionally laden power relations (Pratt and Yeoh 2003; Silvey 2004; Silvey 2006). The contributions of feminist approaches to migration studies have been wide-ranging (see Espín and Dottolo 2015; Kofman and Raghuram 2015; Oishi 2005), though of most significance for our discussion is the attention given to subjectivity and identity. Critically, unlike much earlier work in migration studies, feminist scholars have highlighted the constructedness of identities and subjectivities in migration as well as their on-going transformation. Hence, the migrant cannot be understood as only a calculating autonomous self, but rather 'constituted through a range of intersecting, sometimes competing, forces and processes, and as playing agentic roles in these processes' (Silvey 2004, 499). Such a perspective surfaces in the reconsideration of migration as an on-going process of subjective becoming (Collins 2018), in how the aspirations of migration are situated in relation to social norms and expectations (Carling and Schewel 2018) and in the manner that migration must be negotiated vis-à-vis gendered roles of care and obligation (Scheibelhofer 2018). Methodologically, too, feminist interventions have been pivotal in establishing the value of migrants' stories about themselves (Lawson 2000). This material has broadened our understanding of migration so as to acknowledge the less determinate features of moving and its embeddedness in power relations and politics (see Collins 2018; Meyer 2018; Scheibelhofer 2018).

Rethinking the drivers of migration to foreground notions of aspiration and desire requires relinquishing the primacy of economic rationality that has long held an almost sacred place in theories of migration. It means recognising that even economic narratives of movement are socially constructed and can only be read in relation to the subjectivities of migrants, their states of feeling and the circulation of affect within and across borders. Accordingly, we expand here on important interventions in examining the emotional componentry of migration. Scholarship on emotions in human mobility provides insight into how emotions are involved in people's plans to migrate, their interactions with people met through the migratory process, attachments to homelands and a sense of belonging in new environments (Boccagni and Baldassar 2015; Svašek 2010). As Tazreiter (2015, 100) notes, emotion in migration may relate to 'bodily experience – pleasure or pain resulting from a tangible interaction' or be 'about a thought, a memory, a feeling in response to an image, a text, and a symbol'. Both expressions of emotion are dealt with in this special issue. Some article authors situate migration in relation to particular feelings about the places they are in (Collins 2018; Meyer 2018); others refer to the imaginative dimension of migration and either explicitly (Yang 2018) or implicitly (Carling and Schewel 2018) draw attention to the emotional valences that run through his. Moreover, we argue that drawing attention to emotions is critical to humanising migration, thus allowing our scholarship to blur boundaries between different types of migration (Erdal and Oeppen 2018) and to see the subjectivity and identity of migrants as always in formation rather than predetermined by place of origin and mode of arrival.

A fourth development offering insight into rethinking the drivers of migration involves recent efforts by scholars to take time more seriously as a constitutive feature of migration (Collins and Shubin 2015; Cwerner 2001; Griffiths, Rogers, and Anderson 2013; McCormack and Schwanen 2011; Robertson 2014; Shubin 2015). In orthodox accounts of migration, time is often interpreted as linear and relatively compartmentalised, able to be broken up into durations of pre-migration, migration and then either settlement or return. The result has been an emphasis on what are perceived to be 'normal' temporal practices and, within a focus on the drivers of migration, an ability to codify standardised patterns of *when* migration occurs. One consequence is the presumption that individual migrants have complete agency over their migration decisions and can foresee future trajectories and assemble their present migration strategies accordingly. Such a view operates through excluding uncertain and surprising experiences of time that scholars monitoring individual narratives of migration regularly observe. It also bolsters a view that migrant 'decision-making' occurs at a singular moment in time, or at least within a relatively defined period before departure that involves the gathering and assessment of available information in an objective fashion. The authors in this special issue collectively present migration in a way that is much more temporally distributed: aspiration as socially situated but also future-oriented (Carling and Schewel 2018); the on-going-ness of migratory processes (Erdal and Oeppen 2018); opening and blockages that can start but also end migratory pathways (Collins 2018); and even the more structural account of mediating drivers as part of maintaining and shaping migratory flows (Van Hear, Bakewell, and Long 2018).

Lastly, we draw on renewed focus on the migration industry that has emerged through increasing emphasis on processes of intermediation and the connections and infrastructures that generate and enable migration (Hindman and Oppenheim 2014; Lindquist, Xiang, and Yeoh 2012; Xiang 2007, 2012; Xiang and Lindquist 2014). This body of work, particularly that which focuses on migration agents and brokers, helps illustrate how migration is entangled in the actions of mediating actors who not only make mobilities happen, but also seek to actively shape its contours and outcomes. Like earlier studies of transnationalism that lay down a conceptual foundation for this scholarship, a focus on the infrastructures of migration demonstrates that analysis of migration must rather address 'the systematically interlinked technologies, institutions, and actors that facilitate and condition mobility' (Xiang and Lindquist 2014, 124). Such infrastructures do not operate independently, as Van Hear, Bakewell, and Long (2018) demonstrate, but rather can 'cluster in complexes' that have effects exceeding the sum of their separate components. Indeed, if we include the gamut of infrastructures that Xiang and Lindquist (2014) identify – commercial, regulatory, technological, humanitarian, social – then we can conceive of the wide-scale economic, social and political drivers of migration as well as how they get articulated in individual bodies' will and capacity to migrate.

Each of these theoretical and methodological developments in migration studies has been crucial to displacing the view of migrants as autonomous, male, rational calculating subjects. They have also demonstrated the entanglement of migration in broader social and political processes as well as its implications for migrants' identities and subjectivities and the lived experiences of the places they traverse and reside in. Yet, despite such advancements, these approaches have not, even when taken together, established an alternative agenda for understanding the motive forces involved in migration. Recent emphasis on the infrastructures of migration has come closest to doing this, but it has done so principally by decentring the migrant in analyses and instead emphasising the role of mediating actors. This is an extraordinary contribution, though it fails to answer how we can explore the forces of migration for migrants or prospective migrants themselves. It is to this question that we now turn, further unpacking our own priority to aspiration, desire and drivers of migration.

Aspiration and desire

'Aspiration' and 'desire' are common terms in migration scholarship, although neither has been the subject of much explicit theorising and too often both are accepted as shorthand for 'what migrants want'. While they have some semantic overlapping, they also open up distinct conceptual possibilities for migration theory. But exploring these distinctions requires an initial reflection on how the two words have been applied to migration. If we consider migration as a question of human subjects' actual or potential mobility, then aspiration and desire are, in simple terms, relevant to three types of relations:

- A subject's relation to migration possibilities
- A subject's relation to potential transformations in the context of migration
- An other's relation to mobile or potentially mobile subjects.

The last point's 'other' could take various forms, including a state, as in Yang's (2018) analysis of Singapore's desire for foreign talent. The defining element of this relation is its converse of the first two points: those who migrate can also be objects of desire or aspiration. This special issue's articles demonstrate how the three types of relation intersect and blur. As Collins (2018) shows, desire's use as a label for individual preference can also be more fundamentally replaced by alternative ontologies that emphasise the processual character of mobility and its intersections with imagination and subjective transformation. Despite these complexities, the notion of three types of relation can help structure reflection on aspiration, desire and migration.

A subject's relation to migration possibilities is often conceptualised as 'migration aspirations'. In fact, this is probably the most established term for describing the conviction that leaving would be better than staying (Alpes 2014; Carling 2002; Castles, de Haas, and Miller 2014; Creighton 2013; Crivello 2015; de Haas 2010). Other terms, including migration 'desires', 'wishes' and 'preferences', are used less consistently and in nearly synonymous ways, suggesting that they may be subsumed under 'migration aspirations' as a generic term (cf. Carling and Schewel 2018). The term thus leads a dual existence: as an umbrella category and, at times, as a more specific manifestation of thoughts and feelings about potential mobility.

Carling and Schewel (2018) extensively discuss the generic version of migration aspirations as a constitutive element of what they call two-step approaches to analysing migration – that is, the disaggregation of migration processes into the formation and realisation of migration aspirations. They also examine the theoretical implications of differently phrased survey questions about migration aspirations. If we leave this generic usage aside and consider 'aspiration' in its specific form, how do the nuances of this concept help us understand the appeal of migration? Unlike alternative terms, such as 'intention', 'plan' and 'wish', 'aspiration' marks an intersection of personal, collective and normative dimensions. As Ray (2006, 209) puts it, aspirations are the 'social grounding of individual desire'. But whereas Ray sees desire as an inherently individualistic contrast to the social, Collins (2018) explicitly foregrounds desire 'as a social force'. Inspired by the work of Deleuze and Guttari (1983), he argues that a subject's interest in migration only exists within a particular social context and is only possible because of desires invested in that social formation.

The social grounding of aspiration and desire

One aspect of the social grounding of aspiration and desire is that individual attitudes towards migration cannot be amicably divorced from those that are manifest in the social context. An aspiration to migrate reflects the transformative potential of migration and implies that this imagined transformation is not only viewed positively by the prospective migrant, but is also institutionally embedded. Though analytical vocabularies differ, this observation is well established in analyses of so-called cultures of migration (Horváth 2008; Timmerman, Hemmerechts, and Marie-Lou De Clerck 2014).

The notion of migration aspirations reflects not only socially sanctioned behaviour, but also social mechanisms of diffusion: people may observe the migratory achievements of their peers, come to see migration as a realistic prospect and develop migration aspirations (Kandel and Massey 2002). In this way, migration becomes part of what Ray (2006) refers to as the 'aspirations window' of individuals. This logic of emulative aspirations can be reinforced, or even overshadowed, by the cultural virtue of being someone who aspires. Two contrasting studies of aspirations in another sphere – education – illustrate this point. Frye (2012) shows how, among teenage girls in Malawi, expressions of educational aspirations serve primarily as assertions of identity. The girls seem to embrace an aspiration-centred cultural model that connects them from a 'mundane reality to a transcendent potentiality' (Frye 2012, 1599). This cultural model is actively promoted by donors and policymakers, and resonates with neoliberal educational policies that are also pursued in the global North. In a study among working-class teenage boys in South London, Stahl (2014) shows how the 'aspiration agenda' clashed with the boys' valuation of egalitarianism and ordinariness and took the form of an 'affront' rather than a resource. Though their outcomes are opposite, the two studies demonstrate the value of examining individual assertions and experiences in the context of aspirational norms.

Educational aspirations feature in policy discourses as something to be bolstered. Migration aspirations, by contrast, have been politicised in greatly disparate and differentiated ways. In the 1980s and 1990s, the dominant mood in countries of origin shifted from condemnation to celebration of emigrants, and the migrant-as-role-model became an officially sanctioned driver of migration aspirations. This shift was epitomised by Philippine President Corazon Aquino's famed and controversial address to Filipina domestic workers in Hong Kong, in which she referred to them as the new 'heroes' of the Philippine economy (Carling 2005; Chang 2016). While the message was delivered to people who had already migrated, it disseminated the idea that becoming a migrant means being a hero. This focus on the heroes of migration also stipulates 'a desire realizable only outside of the nation, yet recognizable only within its borders' (Rafael 1997, 271), a relation that generates a sense of lack in national and local life by comparison to the ineffable possibilities of foreignness. This resonates with Yang's (2018) contrasting Lacanian take on the Singaporean state's desire for 'foreign talent', expressed as a sense of lack when it comes to the role of young people, particularly in Singapore's aspirations for global success. The bolstering of aspirations and desire must thus be viewed not only in terms of their focus, but also their implications for other people, places and possible futures.

Another version of mobility celebration has evolved in higher education and research. Institutions and authorities encourage and endorse international academic mobility as intrinsically virtuous. Some have described the efforts as mobility fetishism (Robertson 2010; Sidhu et al. 2016). Even if mobile academics are motivated by concrete, individual gains from mobility, as Leung (2013) and (Bauder, Hannan, and Lujan 2016) have shown, the normative policy context matters: aspiring to be internationally mobile as an academic is generally considered virtuous.

For academics in the global South, however, aspirations for international mobility are often met with brain drain concerns. This distinction illustrates how the virtuousness of migration aspirations depends on the who, the where and the how of hypothetical mobility. Meyer (2018) describes how young adults in rural eastern Germany are encouraged to develop their human capital through mobility, but implored to return and exploit this capital 'at home'. Aspiration and desire can, in other words, be applied simultaneously to young people's prospects for transformation through outmigration and their home region's efforts to retain them.

As Meyer shows, authorities in depopulating regions can seek to subdue young people's migration aspirations by invoking local patriotism but, ultimately, may prove powerless. In international migration governance, by contrast, states have a range of tools – from visas and fences to fines and detention – for curbing unwanted migration. Still, 'aspirations management' is becoming an increasingly important part of international migration governance. Countries that face unauthorised migration inflows are investing heavily in campaigns that essentially aim to quash migration aspirations (Schans and Optekamp 2016). The most well known, perhaps, are Australia's so-called Overseas Public Information Campaigns, which target potential asylum seekers, aiming to portray 'home' as safe and financially stable while rendering irregular migration to Australia as dangerous and futile (Watkins 2017).

Such campaigns specifically set out to discourage irregular migration; they address aspirations to migrate without attending to aspirations more broadly. But it is pertinent to both migration management and migration theory to ask what it is that people aspire to when they aspire to migrate. Perhaps the concept of aspirations is more relevant to those ultimate objectives? Bakewell once argued that 'people do not *aspire* to migrate; they aspire to *something* which migration might help them achieve'.[1] This claim reflects the distinction between migration as a means to an end and migration as an end in its own right (Carling 2014). If we follow Bakewell's assertion and consider migration as something instrumental – a means to an end – then the nature of the underlying aspirations is pivotal to migration theory. This also brings the focus on aspiration slightly closer to post-structural conceptualisations of desire that emphasise the way that specific expressions of desire, such as an interest in or will to migrate, are necessarily social determinations of more free-floating desires for individual becoming (Holland 1999). The significant relation to study, then, is not between subjects and migration possibilities, but rather between subjects and their potential transformation through migration.

The distinction between aspiration and desire *for migration* versus migration and desires pursued *through migration* does not preclude an integrated analysis of both. As Carling and Talleraas (2016) show, 'life aspirations' and 'migration aspirations' can play distinct roles in a coherent framework of connections between root causes and migration outcomes. And as in-depth ethnographic research can show, it is striking how these two aspects of aspiration or desire are inseparably woven together. Sooudi (2014, 2–3) makes this explicit in her study of Japanese in New York, whereby she examines 'migration and the narrative and representational practices surrounding it as forms of aspirational self-making'. The notion of aspirational self-making resonates with Scheibelhofer's (2018) examination of the changing meaning and content of aspirations within migratory projects. Scheibelhofer points to insights that may be gleaned from researching 'the opportunities migrants have to realise their personal potential by trying out life elsewhere'.

Addressing desire also demands attention for dimensions of migration that can be overlooked when aspiration is taken to refer to plans, ideas, strategies and goals. Indeed, desire indexes not only these cognitive dimensions, but also foregrounds embodied, affective and material components of becoming and its relation to migration possibilities and enactments (Papadopoulos and Tsianos 2007). If migration takes place in relation to imaginative geographies of the world, then it also works through affective responses to the possibilities of different places, the stories of others and the opportunities and constraints that people face in their lives (Hindman and Oppenheim 2014). Desire is expressed in the actions people take in these circumstances. Yet, that does not mean that the outcomes of migration are predictable, either for migrants or for nation states seeking to manage flows to maximise economic or other outcomes. Collins (2018) addresses exactly this concern by developing a theoretical account of desire that foregrounds the processual and contingent character of migration, the way it can be both enabled and blocked in encounters individuals have and the uncertain transformations in subjectivity that emerge through becoming a migrant.

The semantic field of potentiality in migration

Aspiration and desire are part of a semantic field which relates the present or actual with the future or potential. Migration has been coupled with a range of terms within this field, including 'hope', 'risk' and 'waiting'. We identified 15 such words, listed in Table 2. This list is hardly exhaustive, but the terms provide the contours of a thematic sphere in migration research that is not bound together by a unified approach or theoretical foundation. Each term on the list merits a full conceptual discussion, which is, in many cases, provided by the selected references. What is feasible here is to reflect of the field, as a whole, and the elements that differentiate the concepts.

Table 2. Selected terms applied to analysis of potentiality in migration.

Term	Selected references
Aspiration	Carling and Schewel (2018), Meyer (2018), Scheibelhofer (2018)
Desire	Collins (2018), Hindman and Oppenheim (2014), Papadopoulos and Tsianos (2007)
Dream	Cairns et al. (2017)
Expectation	Benson and O'Reilly (2009), De Jong (2000), Meyer (2018)
Hope	Kleist (2016), Kleist and Thorsen (2016), Mar (2005)
Imaginaries	Fortier (2012), Salazar (2014)
Imagining	Koikkalainen and Kyle (2016), Thompson (2016), Vigh (2009)
Intention	De Jong et al. (1986)
Limbo	Brun and Fabos (2015), Richter (2016)
Prospects	Czaika (2015)
Risk	Hernandez-Carretero and Carling (2012), Williams and Baláž (2012)
Stuckness	Khan (2013), Stock (2012)
Uncertainty	Horst and Grabska (2015), Williams and Baláž (2012)
Waiting	Conlon (2011), Kwon (2015), Turner (2015)
Yearning	Bal (2014), Burman (2010)

Nearly all 15 words are used widely and often casually, without particular theoretical intentions. At the same time, they give pause, inviting us to consider the nuances and implications of their meaning and the consequent implications for applying them to the study of migration. A case in point, Kleist (2016) recently explored the analytical potential of 'hope', as we did for 'aspiration' and 'desire'. Since all 15 terms reflect some form of relation between the present or actual and the future or potential, they can be related to the temporalities of migration. The temporal turn is, as we noted, one of the developments that holds potential for new directions in migration theory.

While the temporal is a unifying element in this semantic field, the emotional rather breaks it up. The 15 terms differ greatly in emotional potency and hue. These differences underlie interactions between different aspects of potentiality. For instance, Hernández-Carretero (2016) shows how migration uncertainties differ through the mediating effect of hope. Her informants embrace the hope-filled uncertainty of emigration, but resent the hopeless uncertainties of return. The terms also differ in the way they represent temporalities and potentialities as something embodied. Desire stands out in this respect, speaking to the material and imaginative generation of migration at the level of the body. Finally, Table 2's terms diverge in their representations of agency and constraint. At one extreme, 'stuckness' implies an externally imposed inability to realise potentials; at the other, 'intention' foregrounds individual capacity to act, even when outcomes are uncertain. Within this diverse semantic field of potentiality, aspiration and desire appear to be adjoining. However, the preceding discussion has demonstrated the value of exploring nuances in meaning, connotation and theoretical implication.

Drivers of migration

Going from aspiration and desire to drivers of migration implies a shift in perspective. While the first two terms require identifying with actors, the latter reflects analysis by an outside observer. Such analyses are a long-held feature of migration scholarship and theorising, present as far back as Ravenstein's (1885) laws and foregrounded in Lee's (1966) model of migration. As migration issues have risen on policy agendas, academics have also faced demand for knowledge about the factors that shape migration flows and, by extension, might be influenced by policy measures.

While the search for explanatory factors is long-standing, there has been a shift in dominant vocabularies. In particular, 'drivers' of migration has quite recently gained prominence alongside 'determinants' and 'causes'. Figure 1 illustrates this development through tracking citations of the words in publications from 1990 to 2016. Since the annual number of social-scientific publications on migration has grown more than tenfold during this period, the graph shows the relative incidence of the three key terms. Since the 1990s, 'determinants' has become less commonly used, 'causes' occurs with more or less constant frequency and 'drivers' has rapidly become a dominant theoretical concept after debuting in the early 2000s. Van Hear, Bakewell, and Long (2018) are, to our knowledge, the first to provide a comprehensive discussion of 'drivers of migration' as a theoretical concept.

The emergence of 'drivers' in the migration literature has been boosted by the growing interest in environmental influences on migration, especially in light of climate change

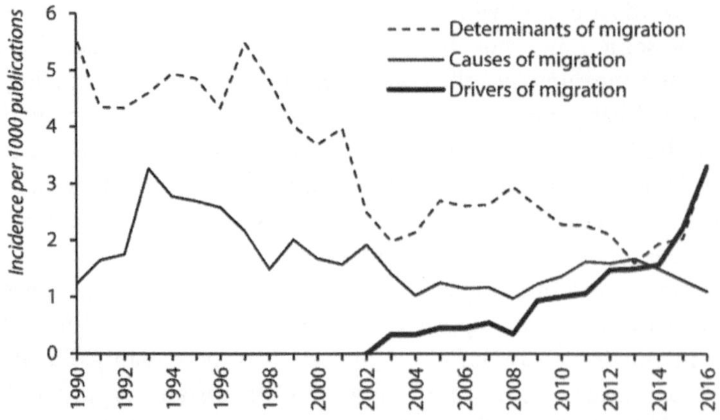

Figure 1. Frequency of selected analytical terms in academic publications on migration. Source: Scopus.
Notes: Numbers refer to publications that use the respective term in their title, abstract or keywords. The denominator is the total number of publications that refer to migration. All numbers are restricted to publications in the social sciences. Graphs are based on sliding averages.

(Black et al. 2011; Etzold et al. 2014; Raleigh 2011). It has become obvious that environmental change could plausibly shape migration in significant ways. But given the complex interactions with socioeconomic diversity, it seemed overly crude to claim that climate change is a determinant of migration. The concept of drivers provided an analytical alternative. In the introduction to a seminal special issue on environmental change and migration, Black et al. (2011) proposed five drivers of migration: economic, political, demographic, social and environmental. This framework, they wrote, 'seeks to focus attention away from the idea that environmental change directly causes migration, towards an understanding of the broader drivers of migration, and how these are susceptible in different and inter-linked ways to environmental change' (Black et al. 2011, S10).

The effects of environmental change highlight more general points about the difficulty of assigning causal status to particular influences on migration. The vocabulary of drivers might therefore also have been bolstered by a more general anxiety about claims to causality in migration research. Compared to 'determinants' and 'causes' of migration, 'drivers' carries less intimidating ontological commitments.

While 'causes' of migration appear to be losing ground in academic publications, it is significant that the particular notion of 'root causes' is being revived in policy circles. In response to the migration and refugee crisis of 2015, European governments, in particular, stressed the need to address migration challenges by 'tackling the root causes', and sought to direct international development cooperation accordingly. However, the merits of such a strategy are highly questionable (Carling and Talleraas 2016; Clemens 2014). This is partly because of the mediating role of aspirations, which tend to rise with socioeconomic development. The shift from 'causes' to 'drivers' allows for analyses that are more attuned to the complex dynamics that shape migration.

Where Black et al. (2011) proposed a pentagon of thematically classified drivers, Van Hear, Bakewell, and Long (2018) raise the level of abstraction and differentiate instead between predisposing, proximate, precipitating and mediating drivers. They courageously label the proposed framework 'push–pull plus' in recognition of the analytical contributions made by migration theorists a half-century ago. This tribute contrasts with the dominant trend in the migration literature, which is rather to invoke push–pull only as a crude counterpart that implicitly props up the author's own analytical sophistication.

Forging connections and looking forward

The juxtaposition of three key concepts in this special issue raises the question of how they are connected. In particular, do aspirations and desire represent drivers of migration? Van Hear, Bakewell, and Long (2018) take this question head-on, arguing that while others see aspirations and desire playing such a role, the term 'driver' should 'be reserved for the more external material forces that influence mobility'. In this view, drivers cannot alone explain migration; rather, they facilitate or constrain individual agency. Several other articles in this special issue also relate aspirations or desire to a structure-agency framework, at least implicitly. But, as we have highlighted here, theoretically sound analyses of aspiration or desire situate expressions of these concepts in wider structures or social formations, rather taking them as reflections of atomistic and autonomous examples of individual preference.

Individually, the articles in this special issue demonstrate different ways scholars of migration can approach ideas of aspiration, desire and drivers of migration to address a range of empirical questions. For example, what drivers operate in labour, asylum, educational, settler, irregular and other kinds of migration? How are they combined and what effects do they have? What sorts of aspirations and desires are expressed in these movements, and how does a focus on desire and aspiration help us explore the future in migration and migrant lives? How are different actors – families, states, migrants, intermediaries – involved in the circulation of aspiration and desire and the instigation and mediation of migration? What are the cultural circuits involved in shaping migration and crafting imaginaries of migrants as desirable or undesirable subjects?

Through their focus on aspiration, desire and drivers of migration, the articles in this special issue together make several important contributions to advancing scholarly understandings of migration. First, the articles demonstrate the conceptual promise of re-engaging drivers of migration in ways that neither reify individual decision-making nor totally displace the individual migrant in favour of social networks or transnational communities. Second, the articles build on long-standing criticisms of binaries in migration by teasing apart distinctions between internal and international migration, migrants and non-migrants and the linear timing of decision-movement-outcome. Third, by recognising the openness of aspiration and desire in migration, the special issue also responds to and builds on the social sciences' renewed interest in, generally speaking, the future.

Note

1. Oliver Bakewell's contribution to discussions at the explorative workshop 'Aspirations and Capabilities in Migration Processes', co-organised by the International Migration Institute (IMI) and the Peace Research Institute Oslo (PRIO), Oxford, 10–11 January 2013.

Disclosure statement

No potential conflict of interest was reported by the authors.

ORCID

Jørgen Carling http://orcid.org/0000-0001-5520-3444
Francis Collins http://orcid.org/0000-0001-9453-4465

References

Adam, H. 1984. "Rational Choice in Ethnic Mobilization: A Critique." *International Migration Review* 18 (2): 377–381.

Alpes, M. J. 2014. "Imagining a Future in 'Bush': Migration Aspirations at Times of Crisis in Anglophone Cameroon." *Identities* 21 (3): 259–274.

Bal, E. 2014. "Yearning for Faraway Places: The Construction of Migration Desires Among Young and Educated Bangladeshis in Dhaka." *Identities* 21 (3): 275–289.

Basch, L., N. Glick Schiller, and C. Szanton Blanc. 1994. *Nations Unbound: Transnational Projects, Postcolonial Predicaments and Deterritorialized Nation-States*. Amsterdam: Gordon and Breach.

Bauder, H., C.-A. Hannan, and O. Lujan. 2016. "International Experience in the Academic Field: Knowledge Production, Symbolic Capital, and Mobility Fetishism." *Population, Space and Place* 23 (6): e2040.

Benson, M., and K. O'Reilly (eds.). 2009. *Lifestyle Migration: Expectations, Aspirations and Experiences*. Abingdon.

Black, R., W. N. Adger, N. W. Arnell, S. Dercon, A. Geddes, and D. Thomas. 2011. "The Effect of Environmental Change on Human Migration." *Global Environmental Change*, 21 (Supplement 1): S3–S11.

Boccagni, P., and L. Baldassar. 2015. "Emotions on the Move: Mapping the Emergent Field of Emotion and Migration." *Emotion, Space and Society* 16: 73–80.

Brun, C., and A. Fabos. 2015. "Making Homes in Limbo? A Conceptual Framework." *Refuge: Canada's Journal on Refugees* 31 (1): 5–17.

Burman, J. 2010. *Transnational Yearnings. Tourism, Migration and the Diasporic City*. Vancouver: UBC Press.

Cairns, D., V. Cuzzocrea, D. Briggs, and L. Veloso. 2017. *The Consequences of Mobility*. Cham: Palgrave Macmillan.

Carling, J. 2002. "Migration in the age of Involuntary Immobility: Theoretical Reflections and Cape Verdean Experiences." *Journal of Ethnic and Migration Studies* 28 (1): 5–42.

Carling, J. 2005. *Gender Dimensions of International Migration*. Global Migration Perspectives, 35. Geneva: Global Commission on International Migration.

Carling, J. 2014. "The Role of Aspirations in Migration." Paper presented at *Determinants of International Migration*, International Migration Institute, University of Oxford, Oxford, 23–25 September.

Carling, J., and K. Schewel. (2018) "Revisiting Aspiration and Ability in International Migration." *Journal of Ethnic and Migration Studies* 44 (6): 945–963. doi:10.1080/1369183X.2017.1384146.

Carling, J. and C. Talleraas. 2016. *Root Causes and Drivers of Migration*. PRIO Paper. Oslo: Peace Research Institute Oslo.

Casas-Cortes, M., S. Cobarrubias, N. De Genova, G. Garelli, G. Grappi, C. Heller, S. Hess, et al. 2015. "New Keywords: Migration and Borders." *Cultural Studies* 29 (1): 55–87.

Castles, S., H. de Haas, and M. J. Miller. 2014. *The Age of Migration*. 3rd ed. Basingstoke: Palgrave Macmillan.

Chang, G. 2016. *Disposable Domestics: Immigrant Women Workers in the Global Economy*. Chicago: Haymarket Books.

Clemens, M. 2014. *Does Development Reduce Migration?* Working Paper, 359. Washington, DC: Center for Global Development.

Collins, F. L. 2009. "Transnationalism Unbound: Detailing New Subjects, Registers and Spatialities of Cross-border Lives." *Geography Compass* 3 (1): 434–458.

Collins, F. L., and S. Shubin. 2015. "Migrant Times Beyond the Life Course: The Temporalities of Foreign English Teachers in South Korea." *Geoforum; Journal of Physical, Human, and Regional Geosciences* 62: 96–104.

Collins, F. L. (2018) "Desire as a Theory for Migration Studies: Temporality, Assemblage and Becoming in the Narratives of Migrants." *Journal of Ethnic and Migration Studies* 44 (6): 964–980. doi:10.1080/1369183X.2017.1384147.

Conlon, D. 2011. "Waiting. Feminist Perspectives on the Spacings/Timings of Migrant (Im)mobility." *Gender, Place and Culture* 18 (3): 353–360.

Creighton, M. J. 2013. "The Role of Aspirations in Domestic and International Migration." *Social Science Journal* 50 (1): 79–88.

Crivello, G. 2015. "'There's No Future Here': The Time and Place of Children's Migration Aspirations in Peru." *Geoforum; Journal of Physical, Human, and Regional Geosciences* 62: 38–46.

Cwerner, S. B. 2001. "The Times of Migration." *Journal of Ethnic and Migration Studies* 27 (1): 7–36.

Czaika, M. 2015. "Migration and Economic Prospects." *Journal of Ethnic and Migration Studies* 41 (1): 58–82.

de Haas, H. 2010. "The Internal Dynamics of Migration Processes. A Theoretical Inquiry." *Journal of Ethnic and Migration Studies* 36 (10): 1587–1617.

de Haas, H. 2011. *The Determinants of International Migration. Conceptualizing Policy, Origin and Destination Effects*. DEMIG Project Paper, 2. Oxford: International Migration Institute.

De Jong, G. F. 2000. "Expectations, Gender, and Norms in Migration Decision-making." *Population Studies* 54 (3): 307–319.

De Jong, G. F., B. D. Root, R. W. Gardner, J. T. Fawcett, and R. G. Abad. 1986. "Migration Intentions and Behavior: Decision-making in a Rural Philippine Province." *Population and Environment* 8 (1–2): 41–62.

Deleuze, G., and F. Guttari. 1983. *Anti-Oedipus: Capitalism and Schizophrenia*. Minneapolis: University of Minnesota Press.

Erdal, M. B., and C. Oeppen. (2018) "Forced to Leave? The Discursive and Analytical Significance of Describing Migration as Forced and Voluntary." *Journal of Ethnic and Migration Studies* 44 (6): 981–998. doi:10.1080/1369183X.2017.1384149.

Espín, O.M., and A. L. Dottolo, eds. 2015. *Gendered Journeys: Women, Migration and Feminist Psychology*. Houndmills: Palgrave.

Etzold, B., A. U. Ahmed, S. R. Hassan, and S. Neelormi. 2014. "Clouds Gather in the Sky, but No Rain Falls. Vulnerability to Rainfall Variability and Food Insecurity in Northern Bangladesh and its Effects on Migration." *Climate and Development* 6 (1): 18–27.

Findlay, A. M., and F. L. N. Li. 1998. "A Migration Channels Approach to the Study of Professionals Moving to and from Hong Kong." *International Migration Review* 32 (3): 682–703.

Fortier, A.-M. 2012. "The Migration Imaginary and the Politics of Personhood." In *Migrations: Interdisciplinary Perspectives*, edited by M. Messer, R. Schroeder, and R. Wodak, 31–41. Vienna: Springer Vienna.

Frye, M. 2012. "Bright Futures in Malawi's New Dawn: Educational Aspirations as Assertions of Identity." *American Journal of Sociology* 117 (6): 1565–1624.

Goss, J., and B. Lindquist. 1995. "Conceptualizing International Labour Migration: A Structuration Perspective." *International Migration Review* 29 (2): 317–351.

Griffiths, M., A. Rogers, and B. Anderson. 2013. *Migration, Time and Temporalities: Review and Prospect*. COMPAS Research Resources Paper. Oxford: Centre on Migration, Policy and Society.

Halfacree, K. H., and P. J. Boyle. 1993. "The Challenge Facing Migration Research: The Case for a Biographical Approach." *Progress in Human Geography*, 17 (3): 333–348.

Hernandez-Carretero, M., and J. Carling. 2012. "Beyond 'Kamikaze Migrants': Risk Taking in West African Boat Migration to Europe." *Human Organization* 71 (4): 407–416.

Hernández-Carretero, M. 2016. "Hope and Uncertainty in Senegalese Migration to Spain: Taking Chances on Emigration but not upon Return." In *Hope and Uncertainty in Contemporary African Migration*, edited by N. Kleist and D. Thorsen, 1–20. New York: Routledge.

Hindman, H., and R. Oppenheim. 2014. "Lines of Labor and Desire: 'Korean Quality' in Contemporary Kathmandu." *Anthropological Quarterly* 87 (2): 465–495.

Holland, E. W. 1999. *Deleuze and Guattari's Anti-Oedipus*. New York: Routledge.

Horst, C., and K. Grabska. 2015. "Introduction: Flight and Exile – Uncertainty in the Context of Conflict-induced Displacement." *Social Analysis* 59 (1): 1–18.

Horváth, I. 2008. "The Culture of Migration of Rural Romanian Youth." *Journal of Ethnic and Migration Studies* 34 (5): 771–786.

Kandel, W., and D. S. Massey. 2002. "The Culture of Mexican Migration: A Theoretical and Empirical Analysis." *Social Forces* 80 (3): 981–1004.

Khan, N. 2013. "A Moving Heart: Querying a Singular Problem of 'Immobility' in Afghan Migration to the UK." *Medical Anthropology* 32 (6): 518–534.

Kleist, N. 2016. "Introduction: Studying Hope and Uncertainty in African Migration." In *Hope and Uncertainty in Contemporary African Migration*, edited by N. Kleist and D. Thorsen, 1–20. New York: Routledge.

Kleist, N., and D. Thorsen, eds. 2016. *Hope and Uncertainty in Contemporary African Migration*. New York: Routledge.

Kofman, E., and P. Raghuram. 2015. *Gendered Migrations and Global Social Reproduction*. Basingstoke: Palgrave.

Koikkalainen, S., and D. Kyle. 2016. "Imagining Mobility: The Prospective Cognition Question in Migration Research." *Journal of Ethnic and Migration Studies* 42 (5): 759–776.

Kwon, J. H. 2015. "The Work of Waiting: Love and Money in Korean Chinese Transnational Migration." *Cultural Anthropology* 30 (3): 477–500.

Lawson, V. A. 2000. "Arguments Within Geographies of Movement: The Theoretical Potential of Migrants' Stories." *Progress in Human Geography* 24 (2): 173–189.

Lee, E. S. 1966. "A Theory of Migration." *Demography* 3 (1): 47–57.

Leung, M. W. H. 2013. "'Read Ten Thousand Books, Walk Ten Thousand Miles': Geographical Mobility and Capital Accumulation among Chinese Scholars." *Transactions of the Institute of British Geographers* 38 (2): 311–324.

Levitt, P., and N. Glick Schiller. 2004. "Conceptualizing Simultaneity: A Transnational Social Field Perspective on Society." *International Migration Review* 38 (3): 1002–1039.

Lindquist, J., B. Xiang, and B. S. A. Yeoh. 2012. "Introduction: Opening the Black Box of Migration: Brokers, the Organization of Transnational Mobility and the Changing Political Economy in Asia." *Pacific Affairs* 85 (1): 7–19.

Mar, P. 2005. "Unsettling Potentialities: Topographies of Hope in Transnational Migration." *Journal of Intercultural Studies* 26 (4): 361–378.

McCormack, D. P., and T. Schwanen. 2011. "Guest Editorial: The Space – Times of Decision Making." *Environment and Planning A* 43 (12): 2801–2818.

Meyer, F. (2018) "Navigating Aspirations and Expectations: Adolescents' Considerations of Outmigration From Rural Eastern Germany." *Journal of Ethnic and Migration Studies* 44 (6): 1032–1049. doi:10.1080/1369183X.2017.1384163.

Oishi, N. 2005. *Women in Motion: Globalization, State Policies, and Labor Migration in Asia*. Stanford: Stanford University Press.

Papadopoulos, D., and V. Tsianos. 2007. "The Autonomy of Migration: The Animals of Undocumented Mobility." In *Deleuzian Encounters. Studies in Contemporary Social Issues*, edited by A. Hickey-Moody and P. Malins, 223–235. Basingstoke: Palgrave Macmillan.

Pratt, G., and B. Yeoh. 2003. "Transnational (Counter) Topographies." *Gender, Place & Culture*, 10 (2): 159–166.

Rafael, V. L. 1997. "Your Grief Is Our Gossip": Overseas Filipinos and Other Spectral Presences." *Public Culture* 9 (2): 267–291.

Raleigh, C. 2011. "The Search for Safety: The Effects of Conflict, Poverty and Ecological Influences on Migration in the Developing World." *Global Environmental Change – Human and Policy Dimensions* 21: S82–S93.

Ravenstein, E. G. 1885. "The Laws of Migration." *Journal of the Statistical Society of London*, 48 (2): 167–235.

Ray, D. 2006. "Aspirations, Poverty, and Economic Change." In *Aspirations, Poverty, and Economic Change*, edited by A. V. Banerjee, R. Bénabou, and D. Mookherjee, 409–421. Oxford: Oxford University Press.

Richter, L. 2016. "On the Edge of Existence: Malian Migrants in the Maghreb." *Culture Unbound: Journal of Current Cultural Research* 8 (1): 74–87.

Robertson, S. L. 2010. "Critical Response to Special Section: International Academic Mobility." *Discourse: Studies in the Cultural Politics of Education* 31 (5): 641–647.

Robertson, S. 2014. *The Temporalities of International Migration: Implications for Ethnographic Research*. ICS Occasional Paper Series, 5 (1). Sydney: Institute for Culture and Society.

Rouse, R. 1991. "Mexican Migration and the Social Space of Postmodernism." *Diaspora* 1 (1): 8–23.

Salazar, N. B. 2014. "Migrating Imaginaries of a Better Life ... Until Paradise Finds You." In *Understanding Lifestyle Migration*, edited by M. Benson and N. Osbaldiston, 119–138. Houndmills: Palgrave Macmillan.

Schans, D. and C. Optekamp. 2016. *Raising Awareness, Changing Behavior? Combatting Irregular Migration Through Information Campaigns*. Cahier, 2016-11. The Hague: Wetenschappelijk Onderzoek- en Documentatiecentrum (WODC), Ministerie van Veiligheid en Justitie.

Scheibelhofer, E. (2018) "Shifting Migration Aspirations in Second Modernity." *Journal of Ethnic and Migration Studies* 44 (6): 999–1014. doi:10.1080/1369183X.2017.1384151.

Shubin, S. 2015. "Migration Timespaces: A Heideggerian Approach to Understanding the Mobile Being of Eastern Europeans in Scotland." *Transactions of the Institute of British Geographers* 40 (3): 350–361.

Sidhu, R., F. Collins, N. Lewis, and B. Yeoh. 2016. "Governmental Assemblages of Internationalising Universities: Mediating Circulation and Containment in East Asia." *Environment and Planning A* 48 (8): 1493–1513.

Silvey, R. 2004. "Power, Difference and Mobility: Feminist Advances in Migration Studies." *Progress in Human Geography* 28 (4): 490–506.

Silvey, R. 2006. "Geographies of Gender and Migration: Spatializing Social Difference." *International Migration Review* 40 (1): 64–81.

Smith, M. P. 2001. *Transnational Urbanism. Locating Globalization*. Malden: Blackwell.

Sooudi, O. K. 2014. *Japanese New York: Self-reinvention and Migrant Artists on the World Stage*. Honolulu: University of Hawai'i Press.

Stahl, G. 2014. "The Affront of the Aspiration Agenda: White Working-class Male Narratives of 'Ordinariness' in Neoliberal Times." *Masculinities & Social Change* 3 (2): 88–118.

Stock, I. 2012. *Transit to Nowhere: How Sub-Saharan African Migrants in Morocco Confront Life in Forced Immobility*. Nottingham: School of Sociology and Social Policy, University of Nottingham.

Svašek, M. 2010. "On the Move: Emotions and Human Mobility." *Journal of Ethnic and Migration Studies* 36 (6): 865–880.

Tazreiter, C. 2015. "Lifeboat Politics in the Pacific: Affect and the Ripples and Shimmers of a Migrant Saturated Future." *Emotion, Space and Society* 16: 99–107.

Thompson, M. 2016. "Migration Decision-making: A Geographical Imaginations Approach." *Area* 49 (1): 77–84.

Timmerman, C., K. Hemmerechts, and H. Marie-Lou De Clerck. 2014. "The Relevance of a 'Culture of Migration' in Understanding Migration Aspirations in Contemporary Turkey." *Turkish Studies* 15 (3): 496–518.

Turner, S. 2015. "'We Wait for Miracles': Ideas of Hope and Future Among Clandestine Burundian Refugees in Nairobi." In *Ethnographies of Uncertainty in Africa*, edited by E. Cooper and D. Pratten, 173–191. Houndmills: Palgrave Macmillan.

Van Hear, N., O. Bakewell, and K. Long. (2018) "Push-pull Plus: Reconsidering the Drivers of Migration." *Journal of Ethnic and Migration Studies* 44 (6): 927–944. doi:10.1080/1369183X.2017.1384135.

Vigh, H. 2009. "Wayward Migration: On Imagined Futures and Technological Voids." *Ethnos* 74 (1): 91–109.

Watkins, J. 2017. "Australia's Irregular Migration Information Campaigns: Border Externalization, Spatial Imaginaries, and Extraterritorial Subjugation." *Territory, Politics, Governance* 5 (3): 282–303.

Williams, A. M., and V. Baláž. 2012. "Migration, Risk, and Uncertainty: Theoretical Perspectives." *Population Space and Place* 18 (2): 167–180.

Xiang, B. 2007. *Global 'Body Shopping': An Indian Labor System in the Information Technology Industry*. Princeton: Princeton University Press.

Xiang, B. 2012. "Predatory Princes and Princely Peddlers: The State and International Labour Migration Intermediaries in China." *Pacific Affairs* 85 (1): 47–68.

Xiang, B., and J. Lindquist. 2014. "Migration Infrastructure." *International Migration Review* 48: S122–S148.

Yang, P. (2018) "Desiring 'Foreign Talent': Lack and Lacan in Anti-immigrant Sentiments in Singapore." *Jounal of Ethnic and Migration Studies* 44 (6): 1015–1031. doi:10.1080/1369183X.2017.1384157.

Push-pull plus: reconsidering the drivers of migration

Nicholas Van Hear, Oliver Bakewell and Katy Long

ABSTRACT

Drivers can be understood as forces leading to the inception of migration and the perpetuation of movement. This article considers key drivers of migration and explores different ways that they may be configured. We modify existing explanations of migration to generate a framework which we call *push-pull plus*. To understand migration flows better, analysts could usefully distinguish between predisposing, proximate, precipitating and mediating drivers. Combinations of such drivers shape the conditions, circumstances and environment within which people choose to move or stay put, or have that decision thrust upon them. In any one migration flow, several driver complexes may interconnect to shape the eventual direction and nature of movement. The challenge is to establish when and why some drivers are more important than others, which combinations are more potent than others, and which are more susceptible to change through external intervention. Drawing on Afghan and Somali movements featuring 'mixed migration', the article concludes that proximate and mediating drivers, rather than those in the structural and precipitating spheres, appear to offer greater potential for intervention. To be effective, though, migration policy should be understood not simply as a stand-alone lever, but within the wider political economy.

Introduction

Why do people migrate? And how do they choose where to go? These questions are not only of interest to social scientists, but also to policy-makers seeking to direct, increase or decrease immigration and emigration (Carling and Collins 2018). This article builds on existing frameworks for understanding migration – notably, the 'push-pull' model – to develop a more nuanced account of the fluid and shifting *driver complexes* that shape migration. We present an analytical framework that teases apart the different mechanisms through which any particular factor might serve to influence people's migration decisions and migration processes. We call these factors, often functioning in combination, *drivers*. We observe how they operate differently across contexts, interacting with each other to shape the ever-changing structural space in which people make their mobility decisions.

Over the last two decades, scholarly consensus has established that structural forces lead to both the *inception* of migration and the *perpetuation* of movement (Massey et al. 1998). Taken together, these structural forces can be understood as the drivers of migration – the factors that get migration going and keep it going once begun. This article sets out to identify migration's key drivers and explore how they may be configured. It points out ways to assess their different significance, or weight, and to investigate their relationship with development.

We see drivers as structural elements that enable and constrain the exercise of agency by social actors. While some may describe aspirations and desires as driving people's migrations (Benson and O'Reilly 2009), we propose the term driver be reserved for the more external material forces that influence mobility, such as political climate or the existence of transport infrastructure. Though drawing attention to the structural quality of drivers, we are not using the term in a determinist sense, as if they are factors that propel people on set paths. Instead, we argue that drivers work by making certain decisions, routes or destinations more likely and bringing them within the orbit of people's capabilities.

While acknowledging the critiques of analysts who view push–pull models as too simplistic and determinist (Skeldon 1990; de Haas 2011), we still find some merit in the simple notion of push–pull, with its intuitive and empirically grounded idea that structural forces shape migration processes. By offering a more nuanced understanding of how these forces work, however, this article provides a more solid conceptual base for analysing them. In short, we are making a case for what might be called 'push-pull plus'. Our objective is to offer a conceptual framework as a starting point for analysing complex migration flows that continually confound expectations.

To achieve this, we start the next section with a brief discussion of the literature on the drivers of migration and how they are incorporated in different theoretical models. The subsequent section sets out our framework for analysing the drivers and introduces the concept of driver complexes, whereby drivers interact and shape migration patterns. We then ground the discussion by applying this framework to complex migration streams – those of Afghans and Somalis – that feature both 'forced' and 'voluntary' migration. Our decision to focus on two developing and conflict-ridden regions as our empirical examples reflects our own research interests. However, it also addresses policy-makers' specific concern with shaping, managing and controlling migration from these regions and the fact that structural factors driving migration from them are often plainly in evidence. Nevertheless, our framework has global application: for instance, it could as easily be used to examine the structural factors shaping migration between high-income countries as those in the 'global south' that we highlight.

Push–Pull Redux

Explaining migration's inception and perpetuation has conventionally focussed on disparities in conditions between place of origin and place of destination. Push–pull models in some of the classical literature suggested that migrants were pushed by low incomes in their countries or regions and pulled by better prospects in more affluent areas (Lee 1966; Harris and Todaro 1970). Critics of this approach argued that longstanding inequities deriving from centuries of poor countries being exploited by rich ones drove migration, which was perpetuated by the structures of labour markets in richer countries (Castles and Kosack 1973; Sassen 1988). Others have suggested that push–pull models amount to little more than lists of factors 'which lack a framework to bring them together in an explanatory system' (Skeldon 1990, 125). The static character of such models is another shortcoming. In presenting migration as a single action rather than a process, push–pull in its original incarnation failed to account for changing motivations, altered circumstances or modified decisions en route (de Haas 2011).

Other explanations for migration's inception and perpetuation have been sought at the micro-level, such as in household decision-making, or the meso-level, such as in social networks. Some have seen migration as a household strategy motivated by the need to spread risk, rather than an individual matter (Stark 1991). Others have underlined the importance of chains, networks and culture in keeping migration going once it is established by pioneers (Boyd 1989). Such approaches provide valuable nuance and highlight the relevance of individual and group agency. However, they risk understating the extent to which migration is also shaped by other structural dimensions.

Poverty was at first held as a key structural driver of out-migration. However, since the early 1990s, there has been recognition that the poorest rarely can migrate since resources are needed to do so, especially for international migration (Tapinos 1990). It is, therefore, typically not the 'poorest of the poor' who migrate (UNDP 2009). While there may be a strong relationship between migration, poverty and its alleviation, poverty in itself may not be a driver of migration (Van Hear and Sørensen 2003). This acknowledgement has led to much debate about the relationship between migration and development, in particular whether development can reduce the pressures that drive migration or can in fact stimulate more migration by giving people the resources to move (for reviews of the debate on migration and development, see de Haan 1999; Spaan, van Naerssen, and Hillmann 2005; Skeldon 2008; Faist 2008; de Haas 2010). Others have argued that analysis should focus on inequality and uneven development, rather than poverty, as the major driver of South–North migration (e.g. Castles 2004).

While our focus is on the structural forces shaping people's migration behaviour, we do not come from a structuralist position that only seeks explanation in forces that operate beyond the reach of the individual migrant or other social actors. Instead, we understand decisions to migrate – or to not migrate – and the emergence of wider patterns of migration as being the outcome of an interplay between these social structures and agency.

Notions of structure and agency are the subject of lively on-going debates in migration studies (Goss and Lindquist 1995; Bailey 2001; Morawska 2001; Bakewell 2010; King 2012). The term agency is often simply used to refer to an individual's freedom of choice, as it is exercised in the face of macro-level social structures that serve to both enable and constrain their action. However, this tends to reduce the discussion to one level of analysis: the micro versus the macro – say, the plucky individual working with or against the larger impersonal forces they encounter. This individualistic account of agency tends to obscure how individuals' ability to act depends on the social milieu in which their action is performed. The nineteenth-century migration of Irish smallholders to the US during the Great Famine, for instance, demonstrated not just the exercise of free choice, but also the structural framing of US migration policy, UK agrarian policy and transatlantic shipping routes, among other drivers.

Thus, we take agency to be not only about individuals' power to act in and of themselves, but also to have a more relational quality. As Sewell (1992, 20) puts it: 'To be an agent means to be capable of exerting some degrees of control over the social relations in which one is enmeshed, which in turn implies the ability to transform those social relations to some degree.' In this sense, agency is concerned with people's capabilities to take their aspirations and transform them into changed positions in the social – and geographical – world.

Yet, agency is still enabled and constrained by structural conditions that lie beyond the scope of any one individual's social relations. This is not to say that structural conditions simply arise from the outside world since they may encompass an individual's attributes given or fixed at the time of the decision to act. Such attributes include gender, race, age and level of education. Moreover, the repertoire of possible and, indeed, desirable behaviours is structured by choices and consequences of past decisions and behaviour, which may play a critical role in enabling and constraining action. However, we do not think of these as drivers, but rather as internal or ascribed characteristics. For analytical purposes in this article, the term drivers is reserved to describe the array of factors that may make up the external structural elements shaping the decision space for those considering migration. Drivers thus shape the broader context within which aspirations and desires to migrate are formed and in which people make their migration decisions – whether to move or not. To be sure, those decisions and actions can ultimately help shape structures – or put another way, agency and structure play into one another – but our purpose in this article is to separate for analytical purposes the structural character of drivers from migrant agency, aspirations and desires.

In developing this notion of drivers, our concern is to achieve a more nuanced understanding of how such aspirations and desires arise, how individuals make their decisions and how broader migration patterns emerge, which then help create structural conditions for subsequent migration (Bakewell et al. 2016). As we show in this article, drivers comprise elements in the chain of causation – from root causes to immediate triggers – that compel people to finally set off on their journeys or alternatively to stay put. We therefore echo the distinction by Carling and Talleraas (2016, 6) between root causes as 'the social and political conditions that induce departures' and drivers as 'a more inclusive term that also encompasses the mechanisms that eventually produce migration outcomes'. We acknowledge that our definition of drivers is broad, but by laying out the mechanisms by which different drivers actually influence migration processes, we present them as the more comprehensive twenty-first-century descendants of their push–pull forebears.

Identifying drivers

This section looks at ways in which drivers may be identified and then specifies a framework for understanding them, both singly and in interlocking complexes. Crucial questions include how, where and when drivers operate to shape migration. As we elaborate, they may operate at different *scales* and *levels* of social structure. They may operate in different *locations*, at places of origin, transit and destination. They may influence migration over different *timeframes* – as Massey et al. (1998, 42) observe, 'the conditions that initiate international movement may be quite different from those that perpetuate it across time and space'. Accounts of migration's inception and perpetuation need to address these different dimensions, which we pick up later in the article.

Mindful of our discussion so far, we explore the relationship between drivers of migration that may be deeply embedded in the economic, social, political, cultural and environmental context and more immediate drivers that intrude on people's lives to impel movement. There has been a longstanding debate on such dynamics. Drawing on the work of Giddens, Richmond (1994) described factors that enable and constrain migration of proactive and reactive kinds, identifying what he called predisposing factors, structural constraints, precipitating events and enabling circumstances. In a modification of this approach, Van Hear (1998) suggested that predisposing, proximate, precipitating and intervening factors shaped what he termed 'migration orders'.

We take these ideas as a point of departure for developing our conceptual framework. We aim to emphasise how the role of a particular factor – whether located in economics, politics, security, geography or another sphere – may change over time or affect individuals and communities differently. This means that rather than seeing particular factors as having fixed roles, we view them as having a range of functions which drive migration processes. Put simply, we see *factors* as conditions that may shape migration and *drivers* as activated factors. We now elaborate what we see as *predisposing, proximate, precipitating* and *mediating drivers.*

Predisposing drivers contribute to the creation of a context in which migration is more likely. Such drivers become manifest in structural disparities between migrants' place of origin and place of destination, both being shaped by the global macro-political economy. These drivers may include the unequal outcomes of broad processes such as globalisation, environmental change, urbanisation and demographic transformation. *Economic disparities* between territories of origin and destination comprise differences in earnings, livelihoods and living standards shaped by the unfolding global political economy and its inequities. *Political disparities* are affected by the relative prevalence of conflict, persecution and other dimensions of human rights and human security, often associated with nation-building, disintegration or reconstitution in origin regions. *Environmental disparities* between sending and receiving territories include the presence or absence of resources, the relative fertility of the soil, water availability and the extent of forest cover. *Geographical factors* – not least, proximity to borders and/or a desired destination – may also act as predisposing drivers. Some of these components are quantifiable, such as differentials concerning income per capita, per capita expenditure on health and education, number of health workers per capita and relative level of school enrolments.

Proximate drivers have a more direct bearing on migration and are derived from the aforementioned deep-seated structural features. In *countries and regions of origin*, they include manifestations such as economic or business cycle downturns; a turn for the worse in the security or human rights environments generated by repression or a power struggle; large-scale development projects that involve displacement and marked environmental degeneration, including the effects of climate change. In *places of destination*, they include manifestations such as economic upturn or wider societal improvement, yielding new employment opportunities, business development, the pursuit of trade and new educational opportunities. Some predisposing drivers may also act as proximate drivers. For example, any of the economic, political and environmental disparities – or taken collectively, disparities in human security – may become proximate drivers as they become more acute.

Precipitating drivers actually trigger departure, as individuals and households take decisions to move or stay put. Precipitating factors are usually tied to an identifiable *event* or events. They may occur in the economic sphere, such as a financial crisis, a drastic rise in unemployment, a factory closure, a collapse in farm prices, the imposition of punitive taxation or the disintegration of health, education or other welfare services. Or they may be located in the political/security sphere, involving persecution, disputed citizenship, the escalation of conflict, massacre, outbreak of war and invasion. Natural or environmental disasters such as earthquakes, hurricanes and floods may also precipitate the movements of populations. On the pull side, the opening up of employment opportunities, a liberalised environment for small businesses and the temporary relaxation of immigration controls and family reunion regulations are the kind of developments that may precipitate migration. Again, a strong relationship exists with proximate drivers, but unlike the previous two sets of drivers, precipitating drivers are often observable, identifiable events or developments. Although they usually occur in places of origin, they may come about in places of destination too.

Mediating drivers enable, facilitate, constrain, accelerate or consolidate migration, and may diminish migration too. Those that *facilitate* migration include the presence and quality of transport, communications, information and resources needed for the journey and transit period. Drivers that *constrain* migration include the absence of such infrastructure and the lack of information and resources needed to move. The migration regime, which embraces the efforts of national and international organisations to manage migration, has a mediating function, although there is debate about just how much influence the panoply of policies governing emigration, immigration and border crossing has (Castles 2004; Czaika and De Haas 2013). Policies and practices in other spheres – such as trade, education, agriculture, rural development, welfare and housing – are also likely to be drivers enabling or constraining migration. Migrant networks encompassing source, transit and destination countries, as well as the burgeoning smuggling industry, may also play an important mediating role (Bakewell et al. 2016). A related factor is the 'culture of migration' that can emerge among people and communities who become habituated to mobility (Cohen and Jónsson 2011). This constellation of mediating drivers has usefully been conceived of as 'migration infrastructure' (Xiang and Lindquist 2014), which has major bearing on the production of 'would-be migrants' – those who aspire to migrate but do not necessarily do so (Xiang 2014; Carling 2014). Such mediating drivers may be rather diffuse compared to those performing other functions that we have so far discussed. Still, through enabling and constraining movement (both in aspiration and actuality), they can play a decisive role in determining migration's volumes, forms and directions. If the decision to move is determined by precipitating drivers, the desire to move, the decisions about how and when to leave, which household members should go, and where to, are shaped by these mediating drivers.

Together, the various drivers of migration create the structural conditions within which people make decisions about whether to move or stay put. To reiterate, a structural account cannot alone explain migration. Rather, the particular manifestations of migration are shaped by decisions and actions of the people and communities affected: how they exercise their *agency* to 'process social experience and to devise ways of coping with life, even under the most extreme forms of coercion' (Long 2001, 16). The extent to which they exert agency reflects their individual and collective capabilities (Sen 1999) and how much room for manoeuvre there is to exercise them in a specific encounter (Long 2001). Such capabilities are shaped by people's gender, generation, class and ethnicity, among other social cleavages, all of which are crucial in moulding the aspirations and desires considered in this special issue. The influence of other actors and agents, such as national and local government officials, businesses, international agencies, civil society organisations and various kinds of brokers, also needs to be worked into the analysis. As already noted, the relationship between the agency of social actors and the structural conditions in which they operate is the subject of long-standing debate (Bakewell 2010). To develop a comprehensive understanding of migration processes, we recognise the importance of acknowledging the agency of the many actors involved. For this article, however, we continue to focus on the realm of drivers – which we have specified as arising outside the individual or household – rather than attempt to incorporate a full account of agency.

Refining the framework: dimensions of drivers

Having established a framework incorporating different orders of drivers, we now refine our understanding of them by looking at some of their *dimensions* and how they may be configured in *driver complexes*.

We may think of a driver as emerging from or being associated with a particular *domain* of the social world, such as culture, geography, politics, economics, history, environment or demography. However, this gets us only so far in analysis: distinguishing between a historical, political or geographic driver does not tell us much about what the driver does or how it operates. We rather aim to tease out dimensions that characterise drivers of migration and tell us something about how they work. Besides serving their *function* in the migration process – be they predisposing, proximate, precipitating or mediating drivers – the dimensions comprise *locality*, *scale*, *duration*, *selectivity* and *tractability*.

Locality

Some drivers might be associated more strongly with the place of origin, such as demographic or environmental pressures. Others are centred on the area of destination, such as immigration policies. Still others may help shape the journey, such as geographical proximity. We also need to consider those drivers which operate transnationally or translocally, such as transnational labour markets, which might involve recruitment by agents in the place of origin to meet labour demands in destination countries.

Scale

Two kinds of scale are considered here. Drivers operate at different *spatial* scales, from the local, national and regional to the global. A famine may force people living in a whole region to consider moving. By contrast, a large factory's closing or opening may change migration patterns from or to a specific town. Drivers may also operate at different *social* scales, from the individual, household or family to the community and wider society.

Selectivity

We may also need to explore the extent of drivers' coverage of a range of social groups. A driver may have differing impacts on various social cleavages, according to gender, generation, class, language, ethnicity, religion and so forth. For example, the establishment of a new university may draw in new migrants from a wide geographical area for education, but we would expect the migrants involved to be mainly in one age group, young adults.

Duration

Drivers operate over different time frames. For example, an acute political crisis may force people to leave their homes very quickly and take refuge elsewhere, as has been the case for many fleeing the Syrian crisis. Conversely, a chronic crisis, such as the political and economic turmoil in Zimbabwe in recent years, may result in an on-going exodus of people over a long period. It is important to note that here we are concerned with the timeframe of the driver, not of the migration. A short-term driver, such as violent conflict, may result in long-term or permanent migration and, likewise, a long-term driver may cause periodic movements back and forth rather than long-term migration.

Tractability

Here we try to distinguish between drivers that operate on the surface of society, which may be liable to change readily with contextual shifts, and those that are more deeply embedded and intractable. For example, the driver can be seen as deeply culturally embedded if spending time away from one's community is seen as an essential step towards adulthood. Consider, for example, Mandela's (1994, 31) claims about the South African labour migration system in the 1930s: 'In those days, working in the mines was almost as much of a rite of passage as circumcision school … ' Other drivers – for example, in the economic sphere – may be less embedded and more responsive to changes in policies, such as visa requirements or employment restrictions, which make migration more expensive and less rewarding.

Understanding driver complexes

Having characterised drivers in terms of their *functions* and having explored some of the *dimensions* along which they operate, we now turn to how drivers may combine to form different *complexes* or *configurations* which shape migration processes.

As we have indicated, particular migration drivers may predispose a population to move. However, they do not work in isolation to precipitate people's movement or to shape it once underway. Instead, migration drivers work in combination – in *driver complexes* – to shape the specific form and structure of population movements. As we show in our case studies, drivers can cluster to operate as more than the sum of the single drivers that constitute them. Consider this example of driver complex that can generate migration: a country of destination has growing labour market opportunities while a country of origin is in recession (both national situations reflect proximate economic drivers); the countries have a language in common (a cultural predisposing driver); and there is the presence of migration brokers and recruitment agencies (infrastructural mediating and precipitating drivers). Similar driver complexes may develop in very different settings. The type of cultural–economic driver complex can be associated with the Afghan and Somali migrations we analyse here as well as with the movement of highly skilled workers from the UK to the US or Australia. Moreover, in any one migration flow, several driver complexes may themselves interconnect in shaping the eventual direction and nature of a group's movement.

In the next section, we consider the migration flows of Afghans to Iran and Pakistan and Somalis to southern Africa. For each case, we identify three sets of driver complexes, each operating at the place of origin, on the journey and in the destination area. We selected these two flows because they have rich, especially complex histories, connecting political insecurity, economic inequalities and cultural and social expectations. Both cases include 'forced' and 'economic' migrants, and both have been subject to direct policy interventions intended to influence their movements' direction and duration. So while neither the Afghan case nor the Somali case can be held as 'typical' migration flows, they provide highly useful illustrations of the interconnectedness of migration drivers, in terms of function and dimension.

Afghan migration to Iran and Pakistan

Driver complex one: outward migration and the political economy of conflict

Migration to Iran and Pakistan long predates the slow collapse of the Afghan state that followed the overthrow of the Afghan monarchy in 1973 (Monsutti 2006). After four decades of political insecurity, the Afghan out-migration complex has shifted. It has gone from being a fluid, continuous and multidirectional movement, motivated above all by cultural and economic interdependency in border regions (a predisposing driver), to being a set of longer term, often irregular movements shaped (the result of proximate and precipitate drivers) by conflict and insecurity.

The Afghan refugee population peaked in 1990 at 6.22 million, a number which at the time represented around 40% of the entire Afghan population. Despite huge repatriation efforts – seeing 4.8 million Afghans return with international assistance following the removal of the Taliban from power in 2002 – as of May 2016, there remained around 2.6 million registered Afghan refugees, 1.5 million of whom were residing in Pakistan and 950,000 of whom were residing in Iran (UNHCR 2016). There are also 1.2 million internally displaced Afghans, a figure forecast to rise. At the same time, rising demographic pressure – the population of Afghanistan tripled from 12 million in 1990 to 35 million in 2015 – has increased competition for scarce resources and compounded the difficulties encountered in attempting to stabilise the post-conflict economy.

Contemporary Afghan out-migration to Iran and Pakistan is thus driven both by the continuing failure of the Afghan state to foster a functioning and secure society and the existence of a large Afghan diaspora. The proximate cause of such migration is not the direct impact of conflict and militarisation, but continuing poor prospects for refugee reintegration, especially in urban areas (UNODC 2010), and broader economic stress.

Continuing Afghan labour migration to Iran and Pakistan was viewed as an almost inevitable reaction to endemic state fragility and chronic economic underdevelopment from decades of conflict and state militarisation. Pre-existing labour networks and cultural familiarity with migration as an effective livelihood strategy have thus been co-opted into current outflows caused by the lack of a functioning Afghan economy. Personal lived experience of displacement in Pakistan and Iran also means that these areas and regions may often be viewed as at least as plausible a home as Afghanistan for many returnees who were born in exile or left as children. The political economy of conflict therefore comes to function as a proximate, precipitating and increasingly (as the driver timeframe expands) predisposing driver of Afghan out-migration.

Driver complex two: inward migration and the political economy of opportunity

The inability of the Afghan state to provide security – the political economy of *conflict* – explains the out-migration of many of its citizens. Afghan migrants' reasons for *choosing* to move *towards* Iran and Pakistan, however, are closely tied to a political economy of opportunity. These drivers also operate across different multiple dimensions (scale, locality, timeframe) and functional levels (predisposing, proximate).

The most potent structural driver predisposing Afghans to move towards Iran and Pakistan is economic inequality. GDP per capita in the three countries shows the disparity: Afghanistan's is $634 US Dollars, in contrast to Pakistan's $1317 US Dollars and Iran's $5443 US Dollars (World Bank 2015). Furthermore, the Iranian and the Pakistani economies are structurally dependent on cheap migrant labour.

Additionally, certain economic activities – for example, driving a taxi in the town of Quetta, which lies in Pakistan just across the border with Afghanistan – have become the preserve of the Afghan migrant population. Specific contributions of some local skilled workers – notably, Turkmen carpet weavers in Pakistan's Khyber Pakhtunkhwa (formerly North West Frontier Province) – have also been recognised as making a valuable economic contribution to Pakistan.

Cultural ties and geographical proximity are additional predisposing drivers influencing the choice of Iran and Pakistan as destination countries. Close cultural ties reflect economic interdependencies between the Pashtun communities that straddle the Afghan–Pakistan border. Similar ties to Iran are seen among the Tajiks (Persian-speaking Afghans in Herat Province) and the Hazara (a Shiite minority residing in central and northern Afghanistan). These ethnic and cultural ties are mirrored in the profiles of the Afghan communities in Iran and Pakistan (ICG 2009).

It is important to note that perception of a political economy of opportunity in Pakistan and Iran is relative to Afghans' socio-economic status. The populations who continue travelling to Pakistan and Iran are not the poorest within Afghan society and have some access to capital. However, they should be broadly categorised as labourers rather than middle-class or elite Afghans. There is also a *global* Afghan diaspora, with significant resident populations in the US, Canada and the EU, often holding dual citizenship, as well as considerable numbers of elite Afghans resident in the UAE and other Gulf states (Jazayery 2002). The global diaspora magnifies the economic stratification within the regional diaspora and the ability of the wealthiest migrants to travel out towards greater opportunities in other political settings (Van Hear 2006, 2014). Socio-economic status can, therefore, be seen as a mediating driver, especially for establishing migration's volume and locality.

Driver complex three: the journey

In the past decade, international and state-driven policy responses, aimed at both facilitating refugee return and regulating Afghan migration, have made Afghan migrants' journeys to Iran and Pakistan overwhelmingly irregular, clandestine and risky.

Both the Iranian and Pakistani governments' insistence on linking refugee repatriation with permanent removal of Afghan populations from their territory has ignored the deep structural drivers of migration we have so far outlined. The situation has been exacerbated by increased restrictions on labour market access by Afghans (even those from registered refugee populations). The result is that irregular flows have come to replace earlier refugee movements. In Iran and Pakistan, the governments stay fixated on the idea of return, and have periodically set deadlines for the return of all Afghan refugees. At the time of writing (December 2016), Pakistan's government was saying that all registered Afghans would be expected to leave by March 2017, prompting a new surge in returns to Afghanistan (Parvaz 2016).

Irregular migration is also mediated by deep local drivers, culture and geography. Kin networks and tribal links facilitate the development of informal migrant networks and smuggling routes. The close proximity of cities such as Kabul and Peshawar makes planning journeys to Pakistan relatively simple. The route between Kabul and the Pakistani Torkham border, thanks to a new road built by the US, now takes just three and a half hours.

Some strategies to encourage refugee return have acknowledged the connection between labour migration and repatriation – for example, Iran's promotion of a labour-permit scheme, whereby registered Afghan refugees could qualify for a permit granting them rights to reside and work (renewable for up to three years) if they first took their families 'home' to Afghanistan (UNHCR 2008, 20). However, many observers see the Iranian government's actions as a covert means of boosting return rates by increasing bureaucratic obstacles to legal residency and opportunities for deportation.

The corridor from south-central Somalia to Southern Africa

Driver complex one: outward migration and the political economy of conflict

Out-migration from Somalia is a result of human insecurity culminating from endemic conflict and consequent inability to access secure livelihoods. This on-going conflict arises from the interaction of different political, economic and cultural factors within Somalia. A close relationship exists between the proximate drivers of Somali out-migration – conflict and insecurity – and the deeper predisposing impact of structural economic underdevelopment. Both local drivers have, in turn, been exacerbated by regional environmental stress, with the large wave of out-migration in 2011 and 2012 precipitated by the intersection of drought and insecurity causing famine.

South-central Somalia is the region to have suffered most from the effects of conflict and insecurity in recent years. Concentrating on the drivers operating here, we see that the majority of those on the move between 2009 and 2012 were compelled to flee by armed conflict between the Transitional Federal Government of Somalia (TFG) and Al-Shabaab, Hizbul Islam and other Islamist groups. We therefore observe that it is the absence of basic security which provokes flight. However, it should be noted that it may be a *lull* in fighting which actually, finally, triggers a population's movement, even though the migration's proximate causes are violence and insecurity (see Lindley 2011).

Somalis are often portrayed as nomadic wanderers, culturally predisposed to migrate, as perceived in the existence of a global Somali diaspora with deep historic roots. However, some of the south-central Somalia clans most affected by recent conflict and drought lack a history of seafaring 'adventure' and do not make up a significant proportion of the Somali diaspora. Groups including the Digil, the Rahanweyn and the non-Somali Juba and Wabi Shebelle Valley populations are not traditionally nomadic, but rather are sedentary agriculturists who since 1991, have found themselves especially vulnerable to attack by armed militia (Prunier 1996, 51). Nevertheless, for other south-central groups, such as the Ogaaden, close cultural affinities with Somali populations in Ethiopia and Kenya as well as a long history of cross-continental diaspora movements may have predisposed the cultural use of migration as a means of maximising opportunity.

Importantly, the impact of the 2009–2012 conflict was heavily influenced by proximate environmental stressors. Persistent rains from March 2010 caused flooding across southern and central Somalia by June, leading to widespread destruction of property, livestock and crops. At least 6000 additional household displacements were triggered by the floods, many moving into IDP camps. UNHCR reported a rise in the number of refugees arriving in Kenya. This single event is the manifestation of deeper environmental insecurities (drought in 2005 precipitated similar out-migration).

The migration drivers of south-central Somalia's out-migration can thus be conceptualised as a complex centring on conflict and ensuing human insecurity. In the Somali case, the lack of rule of law and basic physical security has devastating proximate economic consequences. The duration of the war and the absence of a functioning Somali state, however, means that these proximate causes of flight have, over time, become more deeply rooted predisposing drivers.

Driver complex two: inward migration and the political economy of opportunity

Incoming Somali migration to the Republic of South Africa (RSA) is due to a political economy of opportunity, reflecting structural inequalities between Somalia and RSA in terms of wealth and security. Since the end of apartheid in 1994, South Africa has established a relatively stable, democratic government under a constitution which guarantees a plethora of rights and freedoms to 'all people in our country', not just citizens or legal migrants (RSA Constitution 1996: Article 7). It is unlikely that these rights are themselves a predisposing factor explaining the choices of Somali refugees and migrants to move towards RSA, but rather it is the political economy of opportunity that they foster. Onward movement of Somali refugees from Kenya is driven not by a search to find freedom from persecution or violence, but above all by an interest in accessing the labour market and maximising economic opportunities. Importantly, South Africa (which does not recognise the Somali population as refugees on a prima facie basis) allows asylum seekers to work.

South Africa is the regional economic powerhouse, a middle-income country on a continent of low-income, often fragile states. It is integrated into the global capitalist economy and has excellent transport connections. These economic advantages have facilitated the growth of Somali trade links and explain the economic rationale behind Somali migration to the region. Also offering considerable business opportunities is the size of the South

African internal market – RSA's GDP per capita was $6483 US Dollars in 2014 (to compare, it was $1358 US Dollars in Kenya, East Africa's regional economic power). Somalia's GDP per capita in 2014 was $543 US Dollars (World Bank 2015).

Trade and entrepreneurship hold a high cultural value for Somali populations, thereby creating predisposing cultural drivers of migration. The extent of the Somali diaspora and its well-established trading networks, not only in RSA but more widely across Africa, in Europe and North America, help Somalis be recognised as effective and successful businesspeople. They are often seen as able to undercut local traders, adding a further proximate driver to the complex shaping in-migration from Somalia to RSA. However, Somali businesspeople have been particular targets of xenophobic attacks, arguably in part because of their success at capitalising on the economic opportunities offered in South Africa (Polzer 2010).

It is also relevant to assess how crucial RSA's structural dependence on foreign labour is in attracting Somali refugees and migrants. This predisposing driver is often cited in explaining intraregional migration from other southern African states, and it undoubtedly plays a key role in explaining RSA's relative openness to in-migration, in general. Yet, Somalis are broadly traders, shopkeepers and businesspeople, rather than labourers. While more research is needed to properly map Somali occupations within RSA, the overall structure of the South African economy – as a capitalist market economy governed by a democratic state – is more important in Somalis' assessment of RSA as a potential migration destination.

In sum, the political and economic freedoms afforded by post-apartheid South Africa match the cultural values and resources of Somali out-migrants. Somali culture places a higher value on trade and economic opportunity than aid-dependent subsistence. South Africa's constitutional provisions allowing asylum seekers to work offer this possibility, which is denied to those refugees who remain in East Africa. A large diaspora presence has existed in South Africa since 1994. This facilitates economic trade networks and the perpetuation of cultural values that encourage migration to South Africa, but impede social integration, which comes in contrast to other African migration flows to RSA.

Driver complex three: the journey

A second collection of drivers combine to shape the nature of Somali journeys to southern Africa, especially the RSA. These interrelated mediating drivers can be categorised in terms of logistics, culture, economics and policy. Logistics, in this sense, can be considered the practical dimensions of planning a journey – for example, migration routes offered by smuggling networks, modes of transport available and access to food or shelter.

Given the large role of conflict and human insecurity in driving Somali out-migration, many Somalis, especially from south-central Somalia, first cross the border with Kenya to arrive as refugees at Dadaab camp. However, the Kenyan state insists on Somali refugees' encampment, thereby heavily curtailing Somali freedom of movement and preventing refugees' legal access to labour markets. Since the 2013 Westgate Mall attack in Nairobi, Kenya has hardened its stance towards Somalis and repeatedly sought to shut down Dadaab camp and return all refugees to Somalia, citing security concerns over terrorism. The government has announced plans to close Dadaab entirely by May 2017 (Al Jazeera 2016).

Somalis' onward journeys towards southern Africa are thus heavily influenced by the intersection of predisposing cultural values and practices. While they stress entrepreneurship, utility of migration for trade and the value of business, Kenyan government policies intended to restrict such movement limit economic opportunity and encourage return.

Labelling all Somalis as 'refugees' has also influenced the operation of migration drivers. Practices have developed in which refugee camps are used as pitstops on journeys southwards, with Somalis identifying the camps as points for accessing international aid to help sustain their continued movement. Up to 80% of Somalis who arrive in RSA pass through a single refugee camp, Dzaleka, in Malawi (IOM 2009; Long and Crisp 2010). In this sense, international policy – considering all Somalis refugees and a specific understanding of what 'refugee' and 'international protection' involve – combines with logistical needs to shape Somali journeys to RSA. This, in turn, creates a mediating driver complex.

Though very little is known about the mechanics of Somali smuggling, it is clear that a sizeable economy is based on people smuggling from the Horn of Africa towards southern Africa, generating around 40 million US Dollars per annum (IOM 2009). Predisposing drivers include the strength of the Somali kin and clan networks, as well as the presence of a large diaspora in Nairobi and RSA who can fund smuggling and provide information to new arrivals.

Perhaps the most important of all driver complexes mediating the Somali journey to RSA, however, is the interaction between cultural expectations, logistical capacity and a migrant's economic class and status. It is well recognised that economic status bears a direct relation to the distance travelled by those moving (Van Hear 2006, 2014). Those who are able to move to southern Africa are likely to have access to significant resources (or at least significant credit), not least because of the high fees demanded by the smuggling economy. Access to resources also plays a notable role in determining the mode of transport used – the 5% of Somalis who arrived in South Africa by air are likely to be those with the greatest access to funds to pay for air tickets and ensure they hold the documents necessary to pass through airport immigration screening (IOM 2009).

Conclusion

Both the Afghan and the Somali cases discussed, and further summarised in Table 1, underline the complex interactions that drive migration. We suggest that these and other cases can be productively analysed using our driver complex framework, notably its key notion of the clustering of particular drivers into complexes which are more than the sum of their parts. In both cases, deep-rooted cultural understandings and practices of migration reflect longstanding structural economic inequalities between places of origin and places of destination. In both cases, conflict and insecurity have made outmigration more likely, adding proximate drivers to the predisposing ones. And in both cases, international policy efforts intended to mediate migration by containing it have had the consequence not of stopping migration, but rather changing it into an irregular clandestine activity.

Table 1 provides a comparison of the two case studies. They are not intended to be exhaustive, but only to test the applicability and usefulness of our analytical framework in understanding how migration is shaped by driver complexes featuring different dimensions of locality, scale, selectivity, duration and tractability.

Table 1. Comparison of Afghan and Somali case studies.

Driver complex	Afghan Migration to Pakistan and Iran	South-central Somali migration to southern Africa
Outward migration	Political economy of conflict Migration culturally embedded as livelihood strategy, earlier refugee waves (predisposing) Long-running conflict and continuing insecurity (proximate > predisposing) Economic, demographic and environmental stress (proximate > precipitating)	Political economy of conflict Migration culturally embedded as livelihood strategy (predisposing) Long-running conflict and continuing insecurity (proximate > predisposing) Economic, demographic and environmental stress (proximate > precipitating)
Inward migration	**Political economy of opportunity** Marked income inequality (2× GDP/capita Pakistan, 9× Iran) (predisposing) Structural dependence on cheap labour (predisposing) Cultural ties (including strong Afghan control of some sectors of labour market) (proximate > predisposing) Geographic proximity (precipitating) Socio-economic status (mediating)	**Political economy of opportunity** Marked income inequality (3× GDP/capita Kenya, 13× RSA) (predisposing) RSA protection of capitalist market economy (predisposing > proximate) Cultural value of trade and entrepreneurship, diaspora networks (proximate > predisposing) Kenyan hostility and policies of encampment/ return (proximate > precipitating) Socio-economic status (mediating)
The journey	Socio-economic status (mediating) Infrastructure and presence of roads/taxis networks (mediating) Smuggling networks (proximate > predisposing) Iranian and Pakistani refugee and migration policy (mediating) Smuggling networks (proximate > predisposing)	Socio-economic status (mediating) Kenyan hostility and policies of encampment/ return (mediating) Diaspora presence and strength of clan ties (predisposing) Smuggling networks (proximate > predisposing) International refugee and migration policy (mediating)

The case studies highlight two additional crucial points. First, in the absence of appropriate and successful mediation, proximate drivers of migration – such as conflict and environmental stress – may harden into predisposing drivers. In both the Afghan and the Somali cases, a failure to mitigate the political economies of insecurity and conflict driving out-migration over the past several decades can be read as having turned a proximate driver, conflict, into a predisposing one: endemic state dysfunction. More generally, this sedimentation or transmuting of one kind of driver into another to some degree addresses the static nature of the push–pull model that we have taken as our point of departure.

Second, in-migration – that is, the choice of destination – is heavily influenced by socio-economic status: in effect, inequality (Van Hear 2014). This can be most easily quantified as economic inequality – for instance, between Iran and Afghanistan, or RSA and Kenya/ Somalia. However, it is perhaps better understood as inequality of *opportunity*.

All this suggests that those interested in mediating or managing migration from such regions, and others, should focus efforts on initiatives that redress the imbalances. Still, these structural features tend to be deeply embedded and to change only slowly. Indeed, donor governments, international organisations and origin countries are unlikely to be able to influence the deeply embedded structural predisposing factors that drive migration. Their capacity to influence precipitating drivers very much is also limited, since they largely comprise events that are difficult to predict. This leaves the proximate drivers and mediating factors as the likely spheres for the most potential to exercise influence. However, as this article has argued, it is not simply a matter of influencing particular drivers. After all, they may combine to form configurations which have aggregate effects different from the particular drivers they combine, making whole different from the sum of the parts. This underlines the now often made point that to influence migration, we need a comprehensive approach. And that includes not just migration policies, but policy levers that have a wider reach – such as those covering trade, fiscal matters, welfare and security – and account for the unintended effects of policies on migration over time (de Haas 2011).

Finally, much depends on the goals of intervention – whether the purpose is to prevent or control migration, reduce migration pressure, enable people to choose to move or not or engage with migration flows in order to reduce poverty and optimise development. Our drivers of migration framework, with its push–pull plus provenance, cannot answer all these questions alone. As noted above, a fuller account would need to take account of agency, and, in particular, the migration aspirations and desires which are addressed in other contributions in this special issue. In considering drivers separately from these for analytical purposes, our aim in this paper is to offer 'push-pull plus' as an analytical tool to help recognise the limits on migration control and management through single-issue policy initiatives when deep-rooted political and economic structural inequalities remain in place. The wider hope is that this framework enhances our understanding of the changing structural configurations in which people's aspirations and desires to move or stay put are shaped and reshaped.

Acknowledgements

A previous version of this article was written as a working paper for the Migrating out of Poverty Research Programme Consortium based at the University of Sussex and funded by the UK Department for International Development.

Disclosure statement

No potential conflict of interest was reported by the authors.

References

Al Jazeera. 2016. "Kenya Delays Dadaab Refugee Camp Closure by Six Months." November 16, 2016 [online]. http://www.aljazeera.com/news/2016/11/kenya-delays-dadaab-refugee-camp-closure-months-161116130647820.html

Bailey, A. 2001. "Turning Transnational: Notes on the Theorisation of International Migration." *International Journal of Population Geography* 7 (6): 413–428.

Bakewell, O. 2010. "Some Reflections on Structure and Agency in Migration Theory." *Journal of Ethnic and Migration Studies* 36 (10): 1689–1708.

Bakewell, Oliver, Godfried Engbersen, Maria Lucinda Fonseca, and Cindy Horst, eds. 2016. *Beyond Networks: Feedback in International Migration*. Basingstoke: Palgrave.

Benson, M., and K. O'Reilly. 2009. "Migration and the Search for a Better Way of Life: A Critical Exploration of Lifestyle Migration." *The Sociological Review* 57 (4): 608–625.

Boyd, M. 1989. "Family and Personal Networks in International Migration: Recent Developments and New Agendas." *International Migration Review* 23 (3): 638–670.

Carling, J. 2014. "The Role of Aspirations in Migration." Paper presented at the conference Determinants of International Migration, International Migration Institute, University of Oxford, Oxford, September 23–25.

Carling, Jørgen, and Francis L. Collins. 2018. "Aspiration, Desire and Drivers of Migration." *Journal of Ethnic and Migration Studies* 44 (6): 909–926. doi:10.1080/1369183X.2017.1384134.
Carling, Jørgen, and Cathrine Talleraas. 2016. Root Causes and Drivers of Migration: Implications for Humanitarian Efforts and Development Cooperation." *PRIO Paper*. Oslo: Peace Research Institute Oslo.
Castles, S. 2004. "Why Migration Policies Fail." *Ethnic and Racial Studies* 27 (2): 205–227.
Castles, S., and G. Kosack. 1973. *Immigrant Workers and Class Structure in Western Europe*. London: Oxford University Press.
Cohen, R., and G. Jónsson. 2011. "Introduction: Connecting Culture and Migration." In *Migration and Culture*, edited by R. Cohen, and G. Jónsson, xiii–xxxii. Cheltenham: Edward Elgar.
Czaika, M., and H. De Haas. 2013. "The Effectiveness of Immigration Policies." *Population and Development Review* 39 (3): 487–450.
de Haan, A. 1999. "Livelihoods and Poverty: The Role of Migration – A Critical Review of the Migration Literature." *Journal Of Development Studies* 36 (2): 1–47.
de Haas, H. 2010. "Migration and Development: A Theoretical Perspective." *International Migration Review* 44 (1): 227–264.
de Haas, H. 2011. *The Determinants of International Migration: Conceptualizing Policy, Origin and Destination Effects*. Oxford: International Migration Institute. IMI Working Paper No. 32.
Faist, T. 2008. "Migrants as Transnational Development Agents: An Inquiry into the Newest Round of the Migration-Development Nexus." *Population, Space and Place* 14 (1): 21–42.
Goss, Jon, and Bruce Lindquist. 1995. "Conceptualizing International Labor Migration: A Structuration Perspective." *International Migration Review* 29 (2): 317–351.
Harris, J., and M. Todaro. 1970. "Migration, Unemployment and Development: A Two-sector Analysis." *American Economic Review* 60 (1): 126–142.
ICG (International Crisis Group). 2009. *Afghanistan, What Now for Refugees?* [online] October. www.crisisgroup.org/home/index.cfm?id=6290\&CFID=13882722\&CFTOKEN=11480080
IOM (International Organization for Migration). 2009. In Pursuit of the Southern Dream: Victims of Necessity, Assessment of the Irregular Movement of Men from East Africa and the Horn to South Africa [online]. June. http://publications.iom.int/bookstore/index.php?main-page=product-info&productsid=507
Jazayery, L. 2002. "The Migration-Development Nexus: Afghanistan Case Study." *International Migration* 40 (5): 231–254.
King, Russell. 2012. "Theories and Typologies of Migration: An Overview and a Primer." Vol. 3/12. *Willy Brandt Series of Working Papers in International Migration and Ethnic Relations*. Malmö: Malmö Institute for Studies of Migration, Diversity and Welfare (MIM) Malmö University.
Lee, E. 1966. "A Theory of Migration." *Demography* 3 (1): 47–57.
Lindley, A. 2011. "Between a Protracted and a Crisis Situation: Policy Responses to Somali Refugees in Kenya." *Refugee Survey Quarterly* 30 (4): 14–49.
Long, N. 2001. *Development Sociology: Actor Perspectives*. London: Routledge.
Long, K., and J. Crisp. 2010. *A Long and Winding Road: Mixed Migratory Movements to Southern Africa from the East, Horn and Great Lakes Region of Africa*, Background paper for Regional Conference on Refugee Protection and International Migration, Tanzania, September 6–7.
Mandela, N. 1994. *Long Walk to Freedom*. London: Abacus.
Massey, D. S., J. Arango, G. Hugo, A. Kouaouci, A. Pellegrino, J. E., and Taylor 1998. *Worlds in Motion: Understanding International Migration at the End of the Millennium*. Oxford: Clarendon Press.
Monsutti, A. 2006. *Afghan Transitional Networks: Looking Beyond Repatriation*. Kabul: AREU. [online]. www.areu.org.af/index.php?option=com-docman\&Itemid=\&task=doc-download\&gid=432
Morawska, Ewa. 2001. "Structuring Migration: The Case of Polish Income-seeking Travelers to the West." *Theory and Society* 30 (1): 47–80.
Parvaz, D. 2016. "A Hard Winter: Afghan Refugees Return from Pakistan." *Al Jazeera*, November 24. http://www.aljazeera.com/indepth/features/2016/11/hard-winter-afghan-refugees-return-pakistan-161123070304234.html

Polzer, T. 2010. *'Xenophobia': Violence against Foreign Nationals and other 'Outsiders' in Contemporary South Africa* [online] June. www.migration.org.za/report/polzer-t-2010-xenophobia-violence-against-foreign-nationals-and-other-outsiders-contemporary

Prunier, G. 1996. "Somalia: Civil War, Intervention and Withdrawal (1990–1995)." *Refugee Survey Quarterly* 15 (1): 35–85.

Richmond, A. 1994. *Global Apartheid: Refugees, Racism and the New World Order*. New York: OUP.

Sassen, S. 1988. *The Mobility of Labor and Capital: A Study in International Investment and Labor Flow*. Cambridge: CUP.

Sen, A. K. 1999. *Development as Freedom*. Oxford: Oxford University Press.

Sewell, W. H. 1992. "A Theory of Structure: Duality, Agency and Transformation." *American Journal of Sociology* 98 (1): 1–29.

Skeldon, R. 1990. *Population Mobility in Developing Countries: A Reinterpretation*. London: Belhaven.

Skeldon, R. 2008. "International Migration as a Tool in Development Policy: A Passing Phase?" *Population and Development Review* 34 (1): 1–18.

Spaan, E., T. van Naerssen, and F. Hillmann. 2005. "Shifts in the European Discourses on Migration and Development." *Asian and Pacific Migration Journal* 14 (1–2): 35–69.

Stark, O. 1991. *The Migration of Labor*. Oxford: Blackwell.

Tapinos, G. P. 1990. *Development Assistance Strategies and Emigration Pressure in Europe and Africa*. Washington, DC: Commission for the Study of International Migration and Co-operative Economic Development.

UNDP. 2009. *Human Development Report. Overcoming Barriers: Human Mobility and Development*. New York: UNDP.

UNHCR. 2008. *Discussion Paper: 'Towards a Comprehensive Solution for Displacement from Afghanistan'* [online] July 2003.Accessed August 6, 2011. www.unhcr.org/refworld/docid/3f1be2224.html

UNHCR. 2016. *Pakistan Factsheet*, May. http://reporting.unhcr.org/sites/default/files/UNHCR%20Pakistan%20Factsheet%20-%20MAY16.pdf

UNODC (United Nations Office on Drugs and Crime). 2010. *Corruption in Afghanistan: Bribery as Reported by the Victims* [online]. www.unodc.org/documents/data-and-analysis/Afghanistan/Afghanistan-corruption-survey2010-Eng.pdf

Van Hear, N. 1998. *New Diasporas: The Mass Exodus, Dispersal and Regrouping of Migrant Communities*. London: UCL Press.

Van Hear, N. 2006. ""I Went as Far as My Money Would Take Me": Conflict, Forced Migration and Class." In *Forced Migration and Global Processes: A View from Forced Migration Studies*, edited by F. Crepeau, 125–158. Lanham, MA: Lexington/Rowman and Littlefield.

Van Hear, N. 2014. "Reconsidering Migration and Class." *International Migration Review* 48: S100–S121. Special Issue: International Migration in the 21st Century: Advancing the Frontier of Scholarship and Knowledge.

Van Hear, N., and N. N. Sørensen. 2003. *The Migration-Development Nexus*. Geneva: International Organisation for Migration.

World Bank. 2015. GDP Per Capita: Current US $. http://data.worldbank.org/indicator/NY.GDP.PCAP.CD?page=5

Xiang, Biao. 2014. "The Would-be Migrant: Post-socialist Primitive Accumulation, Potential Transnational Mobility, and the Displacement of the Present in Northeast China." *TRaNS: Trans -Regional and -National Studies of Southeast Asia* 2: 183–199.

Xiang, Biao, and J. Lindquist. 2014. "Migration Infrastructure." *International Migration Review* 48: S122–S148.

OPEN ACCESS

Revisiting aspiration and ability in international migration

Jørgen Carling and Kerilyn Schewel

ABSTRACT

It is a refreshingly simple thought that migration is the combined result of two factors: the aspiration to migrate and the ability to migrate. Without having to resort to overly structural or individualistic explanations, this analytical distinction helps disentangle complex questions around why some people migrate but others do not. Still, aspiration and ability raise their own thorny theoretical and methodological questions. To begin with, what does it mean to have migration aspirations? How can such concepts be objects of empirical research? And is it meaningful to say that individuals possess the ability to migrate if their preference is to stay? The aspiration/ability model was originally proposed in this journal and has since been diversely applied and adapted. In this article, we look back at more than a decade of research to examine a series of theoretical and empirical developments related to the aspiration/ability model and its extensions. We identify *two-step approaches* as a class of analytical frameworks that share the basic logic of the aspiration/ability model. Covering expansive theoretical, methodological and empirical ground, we seek to lay a foundation for new research on global migration in its diverse forms.

Introduction

Under what conditions do people decide to move? That has been the key question in migration theory, with the assumption being that if people so decide, they move. But such a model seems untenable in a world where prospective migrants face overwhelming obstacles in the form of legal hurdles, exorbitant costs or dangerous journeys. Actual migration requires more than a positive assessment of its costs and benefits. Many migration desires remain unfulfilled, but nevertheless have consequences for individuals and communities.

The conceptual pair of aspiration and ability was introduced in this very journal by Carling (2002) to explain the prevalence of what he termed 'involuntary immobility' – the aspiration to migrate but the inability to do so – among people in Cape Verde. This analytical framework has resonated with the work of other migration researchers who have taken issue with sweeping accounts of mobility and focused on what Vigh (2009, 93) has called 'the restricted character of social and global mobility' (e.g. Alpes 2012; Burrell 2012; Gaibazzi 2014; Jónsson 2008; Paul 2011). Beyond highlighting the frustrations of restricted mobility, the distinction between wishing to migrate and being able to do so has inspired more general analyses of migration processes (de Haas 2010; Docquier, Peri, and Ruyssen 2014). In this article, we revisit the potential of the aspiration/ability model (Carling 2002) and its offshoots in migration theory. The model was presented as a general framework, appropriate 'for analysing migration within most contexts' (Carling 2002, 8). Here we address diverse aspects of the model's applicability and limitations. We look back on more than a decade of research to examine areas of progress and of continuing challenge. We start by relating the aspiration/ability model to a broader set of approaches to migration theory. In 10 sections we then examine methodological, empirical and theoretical developments in the study of migration aspiration, migration ability and interaction between the two.

Our objective is neither to endorse a preservation of the aspiration/ability model in its original form nor to promote a particular revision of it. Instead, we use the model as a starting point for consolidating diverse strands of research that disaggregate migration dynamics along similar lines. The next section accounts for this common feature, which we refer to as a two-step approach.

Before proceeding, we briefly review the original model and its constituent elements (Figure 1). In this model, a migration 'aspiration' is defined simply as a conviction that migration is preferable to non-migration; it can vary in degree and in the balance between choice and coercion. The fluid boundary of migration aspirations is represented by a dashed line in the figure. Among those who aspire to migrate, some have the ability to do so, manifest in their actual, observable migration. Those who do not migrate fall into two categories: *involuntary non-migrants*, who have aspirations to migrate but lack the ability, and *voluntary non-migrants*, who stay because of a belief that non-migration is preferable to migration.

Each of the two decisive factors – aspiration and ability – is determined simultaneously from above and below. The aspiration to migrate emerges within a particular macro-level *emigration environment*, encompassing the social, economic and political context in which particular social constructions of migration exist. *Individual characteristics* interact with this environment to determine patterns of who wishes to leave and who wishes to stay.

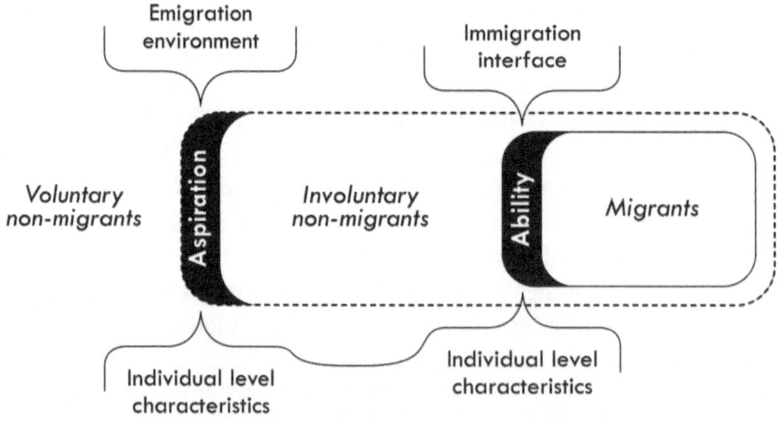

Figure 1. The aspiration/ability model. Reproduced from Carling (2002).

In a similar vein, the ability to migrate is conditioned by the macro-level context of obstacles and opportunities, referred to in the model as the *immigration interface*. The interface comprises a range of possible modes of migrating, either in compliance with or defiance of the various migration regulations, such as legal labour migration, family reunification, asylum migration and visa overstaying. Each mode is associated with a different set of barriers and requirements, reflected in person-to-person variation in the ability to migrate.

Taking a two-step approach

The aspiration/ability model centres on the break-up of migration into two separate steps: the evaluation of migration as a potential course of action and the realisation of actual mobility or immobility at a given moment. Looking at the past decade's diverse migration research, we can identify such a two-step approach as a broad class of analytical frameworks. Many studies do not use the vocabulary of aspiration and ability, nor do they form a cross-referenced body of literature. Still, the underlying logic is distinct.

Two-step approaches are united by their attention to thoughts and feelings that precede migration outcomes. These psychological elements have been variously described as migration aspirations, desires, wishes, intentions or needs (Alpes 2014; Bal and Willems 2014; Black and Collyer 2014; Cai et al. 2014; Carling and Collins 2018; Czaika and Vothknecht 2014; De Jong, Richter, and Isarabhakdi 1996). There are substantive nuances between some of these terms, which we consider in the following section. But for the fundamental logic of the theoretical model, our preferred term migration 'aspirations' is interchangeable with migration 'wishes' or 'desires'.

Two-step approaches share the premise that migration aspirations may or may not result in actual mobility. Variation in migration across time or between groups can be attributed to differences in aspiration, ability or both. And when there is no observable variation, there might be differences in aspiration and ability that cancel each other out. As an example, consider the international migration rates from urban and rural areas in Mexico. Compared to urban dwellers, rural residents are *more* likely to *want* to migrate but *less* likely to *realise* these desires if they have them (Creighton 2013). If we try to explain rural–urban differences on the basis of observed outcomes alone, we are muddling the two underlying processes.

Various renditions of two-step approaches have been applied in disparate areas of the migration research landscape. The notion of two steps is most explicit in quantitative studies that employ data on both aspirations and behaviour. A number of such studies have addressed residential mobility in high-income countries (e.g. Coulter 2013; de Groot et al. 2011). In the realm of international migration, Docquier and his economist colleagues (2014) recently combined country-level survey data on migration desires with estimates of net migration flows to model what they refer to as 'the determinants of potential and actual migration'. Their two-step framework of migration draws from labour market economics, with the analogy of people entering a pool of jobseekers first and finding employment opportunities second. In the context of humanitarian crises, geographers Black and Collyer (2014) use the metaphor of being 'trapped' to describe populations who are in need of escaping danger but are unable to do so. Across various disciplines and areas of application, two-step approaches not only help explain migration patterns, but also yield insights into the absence of migration: immobility could result from a preference to stay or an inability to fulfil migration desires.

Measuring migration aspirations

Two-step approaches hinge on identifying migration aspirations, which are inherently elusive. Many researchers have sought to do so through surveys, but how can survey questions properly determine whether or not people wish to migrate? The various survey instruments reflect methodological challenges and raise theoretical questions about what exactly it is we are trying to measure.

Survey questions enquiring into the possibility of migrating to another country take seven main forms, as laid out in Table 1. The diversity of forms lies not only in wording variation; the questions differ fundamentally. The first type of question, which directly addresses migration aspirations or desires, indexes a general evaluation of whether or not migrating would be better than staying. Its core concept is 'pure' preference, disregarding any possible constraints on carrying through. The pertinent question in the Gallup World Poll (GWP) begins with 'Ideally, if you had the opportunity… ', which is the notion captured by our use of the word 'aspiration': a wish, desire or preference to migrate.

Table 1. A typology of survey questions on migration aspirations and related concepts.

Theoretical concept	Selected survey questions
1. Aspiration, desire or preference to migrate	'Ideally, if you had the opportunity, would you like to move permanently to another country, or would you prefer to continue living in this country?' (OECD 2015); 'Ideally, if you had the opportunity, would you like to go abroad to live or work some time during the next five years, or would you prefer staying in [this country]?' (Carling 2013); 'Would you like to someday live in the United States?' (Becerra et al. 2010); 'Would you like to move from your current location to a different place at some point in the next 10 years?' (Young Lives 2013)
2. Intentions or plans to migrate	'Do you intend to migrate abroad?' (van Dalen, Groenewold, and Schoorl 2005); 'Are you planning to move to [preferred destination country] in the next 12 months, or not?' (Gallup 2008); 'Will you try to go to [preferred destination country] within the next five years?' (Carling 2013)
3. Preparations for emigration	'Have you done any preparation for this move (for example, applied for residency or visa, purchased the ticket, etc.)?' 'During the past five years, have you obtained a visa for going to Europe? Have you applied for one during the past five years?' (Ersanilli, Carling, and de Haas 2011)
4. Consideration of migration	'Have you and your family seriously considered moving to another country?' (Wood et al. 2010); 'Are you thinking about looking for work abroad after finishing your studies?' (Kureková 2014); 'Have you thought about moving in the future, outside the locality/community where you currently live?' (Creighton 2013)
5. Conditional willingness to migrate	'If someone were to give you the necessary papers for going to live or work in Europe, what would you do? Would you stay here or go to Europe?' (Carling 2013); 'If you could improve your work or living conditions, how willing or unwilling would you be to move outside your country?' (Drinkwater 2002)
6. Necessity of migration	'Do you think you will have to migrate to the United States?' (Becerra et al. 2010); 'I feel that I'm going to have to migrate to the U.S. when I graduate in order to find a job to support myself or my family' (Becerra 2012)
7. Likelihood of migration	'How likely do you think it is that you will live elsewhere in the future?' (Bjarnason and Thorlindsson 2006); 'Do you expect to be living in this city in two years?' (Madhavan and Landau 2011); 'In the next 12 months, are you likely or unlikely to move away from the city or area where you live?' (Dustmann and Okatenko 2014)

Notes: References are primarily to publications that present results based on each question. Dustmann and Okatenko (2014) and OECD (2015) use data from the GWP. Carling (2013) and Ersanilli, Carling, and de Haas (2011) are publications from the EUMAGINE project.

The second type of question addresses *intentions or plans*, endeavouring to narrow the gap between preferences and behaviour. Some surveys first ask about preferences and then follow with queries about intentions and plans (Carling 2013; OECD 2015). The third type of question goes even further towards the realisation of migration and asks about *preparations*, such as obtaining a passport or applying for a visa. These three question types thus form a continuum of concreteness, generally correlated with a sharp decline in prevalence. For instance, the GWP found that 32% of respondents in sub-Saharan Africa had a desire to emigrate, 4% planned to do so within the next year and 1% were making relevant preparations (OECD 2015).

The fourth type of question examines whether or not people have *considered* migration at all. Like the questions about preparations, this type enquires about empirical facts. All six other types address preferences and assessments that have no 'true' answer and could change in either direction from one day to the next.

The fifth type of question presents respondents with a hypothetical scenario. When the EUMAGINE project asked whether respondents would migrate to Europe if they were given the necessary papers, many who did not express a preference for migration nevertheless answered the question affirmatively (Carling et al. 2013). This seems counterintuitive, but makes sense in societies where migration is a scarce yet coveted opportunity.

The sixth type of question addresses respondents' perceived *necessity* to migrate. It is an uncommon approach, which implicitly assumes that people migrate because they have to and not because they want to. In their version of a two-step analysis of migration in humanitarian crises, Black and Collyer (2014) also referred to mobility needs rather than desires, although without considering implications for survey questions.

The final type of question enquires about the *likelihood* of migration and differs from all the others in two ways. First, it takes a bird's-eye view on the respondent's future. Second, it collapses the entire two-step approach by asking about an outcome that will depend on both aspiration and ability.

The questions vary not only with respect to theoretical concept (aspiration, intention, likelihood, etc.), but also in terms of how the action itself is described. Some refer to 'migrating', but others to 'moving' or 'living elsewhere'. The choice of words may bias a response, for example, when 'migration' has particular, culturally specific connotations. EUMAGINE avoided using 'migration' in questions and referred instead to 'living or working abroad'.

We see three challenges arising from attempts to capture migration aspirations using survey methodology. The first is the conceptual vagueness surrounding the object of evaluation, which we return to later in this article. Earlier migration research more explicitly tried to disentangle the relationship between concepts – such as intentions, expectations, social norms and residential satisfaction – and their influence on migration behaviour. These efforts could be observed particularly through the elaboration of decision-making models that treated each as distinct determinants of migration preferences (De Jong 2000; De Jong et al. 1983; Fawcett 1985 ; Gardner et al. 1985). However, today's migration scholars have generally not picked up where their predecessors left off.

A second challenge, common to much survey research, lies in trying to capture complex phenomenon through posing simple questions. For good reasons, most of the examples in Table 1 are yes/no questions. Yet, migration aspirations can be understood as a continuum, in which only people at or near the extremes – with firmly established convictions to leave or to stay – give predictable answers. A large segment in the middle gives answers that heavily depend on the context and the formulation of the question (Carling 2014). An apparent solution would be to use Likert scales, which differentiate between strengths of attitudes. But such scales introduce new problems, especially in cross-cultural settings. A better approach is to include a series of questions that together elicit descriptions of different strengths and dimensions of migration aspirations.

The third challenge is perhaps the trickiest: capturing the potentially transient nature of aspirations. A few panel studies have examined changes over time (Coulter 2013), and Gallup has published select time series from the GWP. But in most cases, surveys are one-off data collection exercises. This constraint can be loosened by including questions about past considerations of migration and about hypothetical responses to migration opportunities (cf. Table 1).

Mapping migration aspirations

Surveys with questions about migration aspirations have produced extensive empirical data. Where Carling (2002) made the informed guess that migration aspirations and involuntary immobility were widespread, we are now in a position to assemble quantitative estimates. The GWP is unique in its near-global coverage and consistent methodology. Although its data have not contributed much to understanding the dynamics of migration aspirations since very few scholars have been granted access to the microdata, the published aggregate data can be mined for analytical insights.

Figure 2 maps the global prevalence of migration aspirations based on responses to the GWP question 'Ideally, if you had the opportunity, would you like to move permanently to another country, or would you prefer to continue living in this country?' The proportion of positive responses reaches its highest levels in Sierra Leone (56%), Liberia (54%), Haiti (52%) and the Dominican Republic (52%). Questions about migration *intentions* and

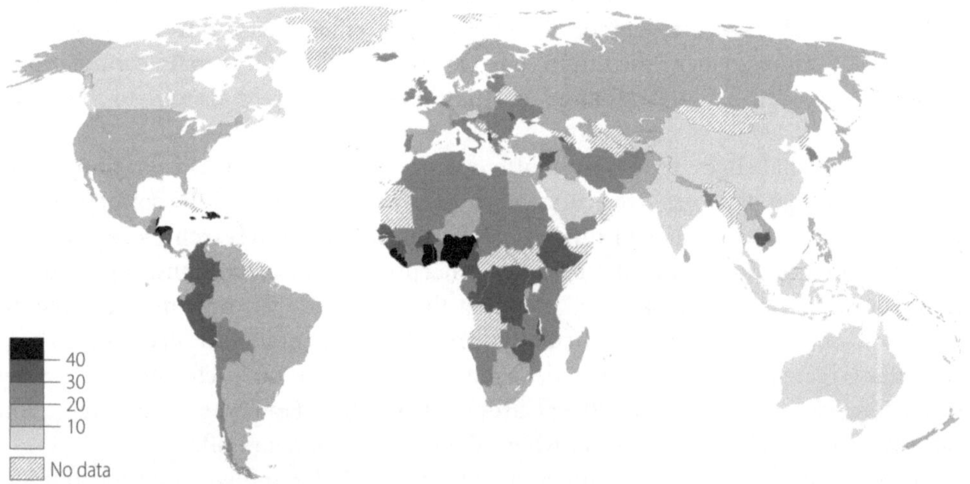

Figure 2. Migration aspirations illustrated by the proportion of GWP respondents who would prefer to move permanently to another country. Based on data reported in OECD (2015) for the period 2007–2013. For exact question, see Table 1.

preparations produce very different levels and other country rankings though preserve the same overall picture of regional differences: migration aspirations are particularly high in West and Central Africa, Central America and the Caribbean. They also tend to be higher in small countries.

Beyond geographical differences, a key point of interest is the global prevalence of migration aspirations. The GWP estimated that 14% of the world's adult population around 2010 aspired to migrate, which is much higher than the proportion of actual migrants, about 4% (OECD 2015). Such statistics support the argument that we live in an 'age of involuntary immobility' rather than an 'age of migration' (cf. Carling 2002). But, we must ask, are the people who respond affirmatively to the GWP question truly involuntarily immobile?

The GWP question has two shortcomings. First, responses to the counterfactual 'Ideally, if you had the opportunity ... ' are exceedingly hard to interpret. We do not know what distinguishes the 'ideal' situation from respondents' actual circumstances. Differences in how people interpret the conditional framing of the question might overshadow differences in attitude towards migration. Second, the GWP underestimates migration aspirations by restricting the question to moving 'permanently'. A large share of migrants initially intend to return, though many indefinitely postpone their return and thus become permanent migrants. If respondents take the GWP question literally, the results exclude aspirations for circular or eventually return migration. Yet, this restriction would often make little sense. For instance, consider Syrian refugees in the Middle East, who may or may not prefer to go to Europe rather than remain in the region. The GWP question would single out those who want to settle permanently in Europe, while those who want leave but have a hope of one day returning would be collapsed with respondents who did not want to leave at all.

These challenges do not discredit the GWP data, though they underscore the need for differentiated analyses. Table 2 illustrates the effect of GWP's reference to permanent migration by comparing results with those of EUMAGINE. This survey included a question that resembles GWP's but refers to 'living and working abroad' with the implicit possibility of returning. While the GWP uses nationally representative samples, the EUMAGINE team selected four research areas within each country, deliberately representing a diversity of contexts. Figures in Table 2 show the range of estimates for the four localities.

Two points stand out. First, the *ordering* of the four countries with respect to migration aspirations is the same in both surveys (based on the comparable below-25 age groups and the median of the EUMAGINE data range). This suggests that there are relatively stable

Table 2. Comparative display of survey results about migration aspirations.

	GWP (2007–2013) 'Move permanently to another country'		EUMAGINE (2011) 'Go abroad to live or work some time during the next five years'	
	Age 15+	Age 15–24	Age 18–39	Age 18–24
Senegal	37	51	57–84	69–87
Morocco	29	45	48–66	57–71
Ukraine	21	37	40–54	41–61
Turkey	11	16	37–42	43–55

Source: OECD (2015) for GWP data; original data from the EUMAGINE survey.

cross-national differences in the prevalence of migration aspirations. Second, the figures from the EUMAGINE survey are *consistently higher* than those from the GWP. A likely explanation for this consistency is the different wording of the question.

EUMAGINE data uncover a caveat regarding country-level data: differences in migration aspiration can be greater between regions within a country than between countries. Analyses of the EUMAGINE data show that the effect of localities on migration aspirations remains large after controlling for socioeconomic characteristics (Carling, Ersanilli, and de Haas 2012). A more meaningful map of migration aspirations would thus be more fine-grained than the one here (Figure 2). It would reveal regions of high emigration desires in Brazil, China and India, for instance, which are obscured by national averages.

Contextualising migration aspirations

Survey questions about migration aspirations are meant to reveal variation that we can interpret, yet the comparability of the data is something that must be called into question. To illustrate, when we read the GWP results that desires to emigrate are higher in the United Kingdom (29%) than Afghanistan (21%), our conventional view on migration pressures is challenged. But the survey's follow-up questions then reveal important differences: the proportion of people making *preparations* for emigration is three times higher in Afghanistan than in the United Kingdom. We see, therefore, how multiple survey questions can add depth to cross-national comparisons and sociocultural environments can shape people's thoughts about migration in more subtle ways.

The context of migration aspirations includes social norms and expectations about migrating or staying, opportunities for migration and the more general structural forces facilitating or constraining particular migration trajectories. The environment not only affects the *level* of migration aspirations, but also their inherent *meaning*. Answers to survey questions reflect the interplay between question formulation and context-specific meanings. For instance, Mondain and Diagne (2013, 512) claim that in Senegal, migration is 'an almost obligatory rite of passage among young men'. A survey question on migration aspirations is likely to capture a desire that exists in that respondent's imagination before the question is posed. In the United Kingdom, by contrast, the high level of positive responses may reflect a non-committal, context-dependent evaluation more than a pre-existing life ambition. Yet, a young Brit who is actually preparing for migration may be making a more radical choice than a Senegalese guy who is following the 'near-obligatory' social blueprint.

Ethnographic studies have explored and theorised a variety of culturally specific thoughts and feelings about migration. Pajo (2008) emphasises the geographical rootedness of migration aspirations in detailing how Albanians in Greece see onward migration as a form of 'fulfilment' that is territorialised as the property of other countries. Mains (2011), in his research among Ethiopian youth, theoretically connects migration aspirations with experiential temporalities. His informants experienced unemployment as a problem of how time unfolds in Ethiopia, and saw migration as a way of re-entering linear processes of progress through time. The possibility of migration thus held the promise of a spatial fix to a temporal problem. Horst (2006) describes how intense resettlement desires among Somali refugees in Kenya were pathologised and interpreted as a form of spirit possession. In urban Côte d'Ivoire, Newell (2012) examined migration as a form of consumption, offering a novel approach to understanding how migration is evaluated and desired.

These four samples from the rich ethnographic literature on migration exemplify how concepts such as place, time, health and consumption can unpack emic understandings of migration aspirations and yield connections with unexpected bodies of theory. The focus in each case, however, has been on understanding the context-specific social dynamics, not on developing general theory.

Theorising migration aspirations

So what is actually captured when we speak about migration aspirations? What psychological processes are at work? And how are they socially conditioned? Within the migration literature, epistemological discussion about such issues is generally weak. But a potential for connecting with the broader psychological and social-science literature exists, as some migration scholars have shown with reference to capacity to aspire (Czaika and Vothknecht 2014), desire as a social force (Collins 2018), geographical imaginaries (Andrucki 2013), preference formation theory (Coulter, van Ham, and Feijten 2011), the Rubicon model (Kley 2011) and theory of planned behaviour (De Jong 2000).

Such frameworks cater to diverse epistemologies and theoretical interests. Discussing the merits of each is beyond the scope of this article, but they nonetheless highlight shared issues concerning *how* generic frameworks can be applied to the first step of what we have called two-step approaches to understanding migration. These issues can be illustrated through, for example, seeing migration aspirations as a form of attitude (Carling 2014). An attitude has been defined as 'a psychological tendency that is expressed by evaluating a particular entity with some degree of favour or disfavour' (Eagly and Chaiken 1993, 1). This definition is useful in the context of migration aspirations. 'Tendency' suggests balance between stability and volatility that resonates with what we know about migration aspirations; 'expressed' emphasises a communicative aspect. But the crucial point – which is common to the application of other conceptual frameworks – is the nature of the 'entity' being evaluated.

Here we see several possible conceptualisations, which intersect with each other. First, we can understand migration aspirations as a comparison of *places*. The value of living in a specific place depends on the characteristics of that place, modified by the individual's needs and preferences. This is the basic logic of push–pull models, connecting migration aspirations to concepts such as place utility, spatial preferences and geographical imaginaries. Potential destinations are an important part of the emigration environment, though they are present through the locally existing ideas and meanings attached to these places. This is true not only of specific locations elsewhere, but also of the more elusive deictic places such as 'here', 'there' and 'abroad'.

The second possible approach is to see migration aspirations as a comparison of culturally defined *projects*. People's notion of migration will often be based on a 'migration project', a socially constructed entity that embodies particular expectations. For instance, Lubkemann (2005) refers to an idealised 'emigrant script' and, as already noted, Mondain and Diagne (2013), like many others, have examined migration as a 'rite of passage'. In situations of conflict or repression, the classical trio of exit, voice and loyalty (Hirschman

1970) can be interpreted as three alternative projects – the first of which implies migration. When the importance of culturally defined projects is acknowledged, interpreting migration aspirations as the preference of one place over another seems a banal rendering of the processes at work. But the projects are nevertheless produced by the differentiated meanings attached to places.

A third possibility is to see the object of migration aspirations as a matter of personhood or identity. Migrating, then, is not ultimately about *where* you are, but *who* you are. Consequently, migration aspirations must be seen as aspirations to embody the figure of the migrant – or rather, the emigrant. This perspective connects the individual and the social in a more dynamic way than the prior two. It is also illuminating in calling attention to ambivalence; works of ethnography and fiction are replete with ambivalent accounts of emigrants as both admired and spurned (Carling 2008).

Cutting across the three types of aspirations is a distinction between migration's *instrumental* and *intrinsic* values (Carling 2012; de Haas 2014). We are used to thinking of migration as an instrumental undertaking: a means to an end, such as personal security, decent work or family co-residence. While such motives clearly matter, migration can be valued – and yearned for – in its own right. Theoretical approaches to migration aspirations must also recognise the pull of adventure, experience and independence.

Accommodating aspirations to stay

So far, we have followed the conventional approach of seeing migration aspirations as something that people either have or do not have. This line of thinking reflects society's sedentary bias and migration studies' corresponding mobility bias: sedentary life is the norm and migration is an aberration, demanding explanation. Although staying and leaving are not equal projects – migration generally requires greater effort and resources than staying – both can be an active choice, and under certain conditions, it may be the aspiration to stay that requires explanation. For example, in situations of oppression or occupation, some may decide to stay and resist while others flee. In rural or post-industrial communities threatened by depopulation, staying may represent a statement of commitment. In settings of a 'culture of migration' (cf. Kandel and Massey 2002), the volition to stay challenges social expectations and norms about the proper life trajectory. In settings with large-scale out-migration, *not* migrating may require the most agency and resources.

Aspirations behind staying remain little understood (Schewel 2015). Factors such as attachment to family or socioeconomic embeddedness are assumed, yet in themselves fail to clarify the 'different ways of staying put' and why, in similar contexts, we find both involuntary and voluntary immobility (Mata-Codesal 2015).

We identify two approaches for incorporating aspirations to stay into the study of migration. One is to inquire directly about staying preferences or, in survey questions on migration aspirations, to use deliberately balanced wording that presents migrating and staying as equivalent options (cf. Table 1). Another approach is to explore broader life aspirations of individuals and communities, and from this perspective, to analyse how the aspirations interact with perceived opportunities and constraints that give rise to the aspiration to migrate or to stay.

Examining migration ability

When people develop a wish to leave, the outcome depends on their capacity to convert this wish into reality, given context-specific obstacles and opportunities. This elusive confluence of factors is subsumed under the concept of 'ability' in the aspiration/ability model. Carling (2002) argued that the greatest barriers to migration are often restrictive immigration policies, particularly for those wishing to migrate from a poor country to a wealthier one. Immigration policies apply unevenly to different social groups or classes (Mata-Codesal 2015; Schiller and Salazar 2013; Van Hear 2014). They tend to facilitate movement of higher skilled people while simultaneously restricting it for low-skilled potential migrants. As legal channels for migration are blocked, the aspiration to migrate finds expression in alternative pathways (e.g. unauthorised migration) or involuntary immobility. Recognising this, we see how the ability to migrate is determined in relation to a particular *mode* of migration. The same person who cannot acquire a visa and fly legally to Europe may be able to garner enough resources to buy passage on a smuggler's boat. Depending on the mode of migration, different types of resources – financial, social or human capital – are required to be able to migrate (cf. Carling 2002).

There are essentially two ways to conceptualise migration ability: as *potential* or *revealed*. By potential ability, we mean a person's prospects of realising migration aspirations, regardless of whether the individual has such aspirations in the first place or prefers to stay. Revealed ability, by contrast, is the evident migration ability of someone who has actually migrated. By only discussing ability among people who *have* migration aspirations, the original aspiration/ability model sidestepped the distinction; it assumed that if aspiring migrants have not yet migrated, it is because they lack ability.

Empirical studies of migration ability are most straightforward when they focus on revealed ability. Several authors have taken quantitative two-step approaches and examined the transition from desired to observed migration. van Dalen and Henkens (2008) and Creighton (2013) made this connection at the level of individuals, while Docquier, Peri, and Ruyssen (2014) connected country-level migration aspirations from the GWP with national migration statistics.

Quantifying whether people would *potentially* be able to migrate is far more challenging. A multi-country data set, like the GWP one for migration aspirations, does not exist. What comes closest, perhaps, is the Henley & Partners (2015) Visa Restrictions Index which specifies the number of countries that holders of a given national passport can visit without a visa. Several governments also publish acceptance rates, by nationality, for visa applications. These statistics give an indication of differentiated migration ability. Another attempt to quantify migration restrictions worldwide is McKenzie's (2007) data set on passport costs. He found that in every 10th country, the cost of a passport exceeded 10% of annual per capita income.

Being able to visit another country on a short-term visa is not the same as being able to migrate. But short-term visits often play an important role in migration processes, such as when visitors overstay or make preparations for subsequent long-term migration. Visa restrictions have also had a statistical impact on migration flows (Czaika and de Haas 2016). Figure 3 thus uses data on visa requirements and acceptance rates to illustrate global differences in a key determinant of migration ability. The image is not quite the inverse of the distribution of migration aspirations (Figure 2). Although high-income

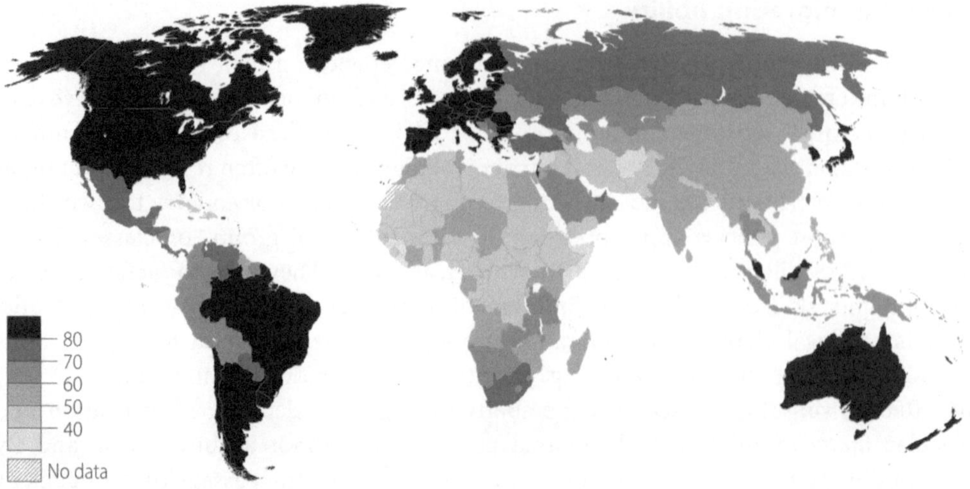

Figure 3. Migration ability illustrated through a travel freedom index. The index estimates the percentage of countries to which a citizen of each country would be able to travel. It is based on the assumption that half of the countries where a visa is required (Henley & Partners 2015) can be accessed with a likelihood equal to the average nationality-specific acceptance rate for visa applications to the Schengen Area (European Commission 2016) and the United States (US Department of State 2016), while the other half remains inaccessible. The rationale for the latter point is that the greatest barriers are often posed by the requirements for launching a complete application in the first place.

countries whose citizens enjoy a high degree of travel freedom do not have the least migration aspirations, travel freedom is minimal for citizens of African, Middle Eastern and Caribbean countries, where migration aspirations are most widespread.

Connecting with capabilities

The notion of ability resonates with an influential concept in the development literature: capability. The capabilities approach was first introduced by Sen as a people-centred approach to evaluating the ultimate aims of development. In his book *Development as Freedom*, Sen (1999) argues that the freedom to achieve well-being is a moral imperative, and this should be assessed in terms of people's capabilities to do and be what they have reason to value. de Haas (2003) applied capabilities as a conceptual refinement to the 'development' side of migration-development interactions. Certain capabilities were a precondition for large-scale labour migration, he argued, and migration could in turn further expand people's capabilities. de Haas (2014) later combined Carling's aspiration/ability model with the work of Sen into an 'expanded aspirations-capabilities framework' that encompasses two-way connections between migration and development.

Capability and ability are essentially synonyms, and they are often used interchangeably in migration research (Dimitriadi 2017; Jayasuriya 2014; Randell 2016). There are subtle theoretical differences, though, between the two terms and their associated theoretical approaches. The aspiration/ability model is a framework for explaining migration outcomes, and 'ability' is simply the component that denotes whether prospective migrants can turn their migration aspirations into actual migration. The expanded aspirations-capabilities framework, by contrast, conceives of migration processes as 'an intrinsic part of broader processes of social transformation' (de Haas 2014, 4). 'Capabilities', in the plural, scopes diverse aspects of well-being. The specific capability to migrate influences migration outcomes, which, in turn, may bolster people's capabilities in a broader sense through flows of financial, human and social capital.

The capabilities approach suggests that the *capability* to migrate is a valuable freedom in its own right, regardless of people's preferences for staying or leaving. Whereas the aspiration/ability model considers 'ability' to migrate only among people who aspire to migrate, the 'capability' to migrate is, by definition, equally relevant to all.

Identifying acquiescent immobility

The original aspiration/ability model accounted for three mobility categories (cf. Figure 1). Everyone who does not aspire to migrate is 'voluntarily immobile' regardless of whether an individual would have been able to migrate. In order to identify those who have neither the aspiration nor the ability to migrate, Schewel (2015) introduced a fourth mobility category: *acquiescent immobility*. The Latin verb from which the word 'acquiescent' derives means 'to remain at rest'.

Schewel (2015) introduced this mobility category to challenge dominant migration theories – in particular, neoclassical and push–pull models – that implicitly assume the aspiration to migrate is linearly correlated with poverty levels. Part of the assumption is that push factors are greatest for the poor and that migration's potential income gains are often substantial. Yet, this mobility category highlights that not all poor people desire to migrate. Furthermore, one could question whether immobility is *voluntary* for those who lack the ability to migrate in the same way it is for those with resources to migrate. The capabilities approach suggests this distinction is important. The emphasis on freedom means that acquiescent immobility is as problematic as involuntary immobility, even if it is not experienced as such by the people concerned.

Looking back at the two maps (Figure 2 and Figure 3), we see countries – China, India and Myanmar, to name a few – where international migration aspirations are rare and citizens face significant restrictions on international travel. Many people in these countries can thus be labelled acquiescently immobile: they would have a hard time migrating but, in any case, prefer to stay. Using EUMAGINE data, Schewel (2015) showed that almost one-third of young adults in Senegal who could not cover their own most basic needs did not want to, even under ideal circumstances, migrate abroad.

How do we understand this preference to stay? Under the category of acquiescent immobility we may find those who have never even imagined migrating – that is, migration does not meaningfully enter into their aspirational horizon or decision-making process. In such instances, an individual may lack the 'capacity to aspire' as well as the capability to move (Appadurai 2004; Czaika and Vothknecht 2014; de Haas 2014). From this perspective, it is unsurprising to find acquiescent immobility among the poorest of the poor. But we may also find those who despite having every economic incentive to migrate and an awareness of migration as a possible livelihood strategy, still prefer to stay in their home communities. In these cases, the influence of non-economic values and aspirations – such as the desire to stay with one's family or to exercise *voice* instead of *exit*, to use Hirschman's (1970) terms – demand attention (Schewel 2015).

Challenging the separation of aspiration and ability

Separating aspiration and ability is the foundational element of the aspiration/ability model, but the two also blur and interact (Carling 2002). In this final section, we raise crosscutting issues that concern their relationship.

First, the relationship between the two core elements involves the interaction of structure and agency. It is essential, however, to go beyond seeing aspiration as a form of agency and ability as a matter of structural constraints and opportunities. The interplay of structure and agency shapes *each* of the two steps. For instance, the nature of the agency involved in expressing a wish to stay depends on whether it is essentially a default option or a deliberate stance in a setting where 'everybody' wants to leave. And the nature of the environment is, of course, a product of other individuals' attitudes and actions. The very notion of leaving – as an option that individuals can have an opinion about – is socially constructed.

When we recognise the interplay of structure and agency in each step, the aspiration/ability approach can transcend the trap of extremes: either individualism or environmental determinism. The latter pitfall is avoided in part by appreciating aspirations to stay (Schewel 2015). Even in countries such as Liberia, Sierra Leone and Haiti, where half the population would like to leave, the other half wishes to remain. Understanding the role of agency in migration is also about understanding these wishes.

A second form of interaction between aspiration and ability concerns *adaptive preferences*. In the face of limited migration ability, individuals could react by subconsciously subduing their migration aspirations. Migration aspirations then become even more elusive, for both methodological and theoretical considerations. Within the capability approach, adaptive preferences are widely seen to undermine the value of subjective self-assessments. By extension, one could argue that asking people about migration aspirations is meaningless if they have internalised obstacles to mobility. In fact, a hard-line capabilities approach would pay little attention to migration aspirations altogether, since well-being would be seen to derive from the capability to migrate, regardless of whether it is a desired option. Unyieldingly focusing on capabilities could, in other words, undermine the explanatory power of two-step approaches to migration.

An alternative perspective could be that adaptive migration preferences represent a valuable psychological defence mechanism. If adaptive preferences shift people from a situation of involuntary immobility to one of acquiescent immobility, their subjective well-being might increase. Moreover, they might be more inclined to invest in local futures. Seeing adaptive preferences in such a positive light is pragmatic, but it is a decidedly non-radical position failing to challenge the global inequalities that fuel, shape and constrain migration aspirations in the first place.

The enigmas of adaptive preferences play out in the dynamics of family relationships. There has been a strong interest in families and households as units of analysis in migration research since the 1980s, though the nature of individual agency in family contexts remains a perplexing area for migration theory. Individual aspirations cannot always be disentangled from concerns for kin. And when such commitments discourage migration, it is not obvious whether the effect is about aspirations to stay, or rather, constraints on the ability to move.

Finally, the interaction between aspiration and ability becomes more complex over time. Migration theory has traditionally approached migration as a singular and fundamentally linear event. But in reality, many migrants have a range of potential destinations and pathways available to them at different stages of their journeys. A strand of recent research has engaged explicitly and theoretically with stepwise migration and trajectories. The work of Paul (2011), Wissink, Duvell, and van Eerdewijk (2013) and Schapendonk and Steel (2014) illustrate the potential for analysing aspiration and ability within such processual approaches.

Prospects for migration research

'Given the increasing complexity and diversity of migration and mobility processes ... ', writes King (2012, 147), 'all-encompassing theoretical generalisations will become more elusive, although I do not rule them out'. This observation addresses the core challenge for contemporary migration theory: dealing with diversity. There is an understandable tendency towards fragmentation and specialisation, whereby theoretical statements are restricted to certain types of migration contexts. But this approach is vulnerable to how we divvy up a priori the multifaceted and interconnected reality – for instance, in ways that reflect policy categories rather than social dynamics. Moreover, empirical diversity seems to preclude a universal theory of migration.

This analytical impasse calls for theory frames. Such analytical tools provide context and guidance for explaining or formulating hypotheses though stop short of making predictions (Rueschemeyer 2009). The aspiration/ability model is a theory frame for approaching an unknown and diverse migratory reality with migration 'aspiration' and 'ability' as universally meaningful concepts.

Migration aspirations can take a variety of forms, from lifestyle-driven preferences to urgencies to escape danger, with innumerable possibilities in between. The nature of each person's migration aspirations is an empirical matter. But migration aspirations can still be examined using concepts such as instrumentality, alternative strategies and steps towards realisation. Beyond migration aspirations, the differentiated constraints on migration ability appear evermore important for actual migration dynamics. A range of outcomes merits attention, including not just actual migration from origin to destination, but the inability to leave in the first place, entrapment in transit and deaths en route – all of which are produced by context-specific and multidimensional manifestations of migration ability.

The current migration regime also represents a political context for analyses. Will greater use of data on millions of prospective migrants in the Global South further provoke restrictivist tendencies? Perhaps. But such data and analyses offer better understandings of migration processes and, potentially, more successful policy engagement with the drivers of migration.

As the demand for compelling and advanced migration research grows, its theoretical foundation remains weak and fragmented. Early on in this article, we identified two-step approaches to understanding migration as a class of research that shares the basic premises of the aspiration/ability model. We then reviewed a range of applications and extensions with diverse theoretical, methodological and disciplinary orientations. In our opinion, these approaches are particularly potent for theorising migration in its contemporary forms and could underpin influential research in the years to come. The aspiration/ability model is not another competing theory to be chosen over others in an already fragmented field. Rather, this model and two-step approaches, more generally, hold the promise of striking a balance between unity and diversity in theoretical approaches to migration.

Acknowledgements

The authors are grateful for valuable comments from Francis L. Collins and Karina Hof. Kerilyn Schewel's research is supported by the MADE (Migration as Development) Consolidator Grant project, funded by the European Research Council under the European Community's Horizon 2020 Programme (H2020/2015-2020)/ERC Grant Agreement 648496.

Disclosure statement

No potential conflict of interest was reported by the authors.

ORCID

Jørgen Carling http://orcid.org/0000-0001-5520-3444

References

Alpes, M. J. 2012. "Bushfalling at All Cost: The Economy of Migratory Knowledge in Anglophone Cameroon." *African Diaspora* 5: 90–115.

Alpes, M. J. 2014. "Imagining a Future in 'Bush': Migration Aspirations at Times of Crisis in Anglophone Cameroon." *Identities* 21 (3): 259–274.

Andrucki, M. J. 2013. "'There's a Drumbeat in Africa': Embodying Imaginary Geographies of Transnational Whiteness in Contemporary South Africa." *Geoforum; Journal of Physical, Human, and Regional Geosciences* 49: 1–9.

Appadurai, A. 2004. "The Capacity to Aspire: Culture and the Terms of Recogniton." In *Culture and Public Action*, edited by V. Rao, and M. Walton, 59–84. Stanford: Stanford University Press.

Bal, E., and R. Willems. 2014. "Introduction: Aspiring Migrants, Local Crises and the Imagination of Futures 'Away From Home'." *Identities-Global Studies in Culture and Power* 21 (3): 249–258.

Becerra, D. 2012. "The Impact of Anti-immigration Policies and Perceived Discrimination in the United States on Migration Intentions among Mexican Adolescents." *International Migration* 50 (4): 20–32.

Becerra, D., M. Gurrola, C. Ayón, D. Androff, J. Krysik, K. Gerdes, L. Moya-Salas, and E. Segal. 2010. "Poverty and Other Factors Affecting Migration Intentions among Adolescents in Mexico." *Journal of Poverty* 14 (1): 1–16.

Bjarnason, T., and T. Thorlindsson. 2006. "Should I Stay or Should I Go? Migration Expectations Among Youth in Icelandic Fishing and Farming Communities." *Journal of Rural Studies* 22 (3): 290–300.

Black, R., and M. Collyer. 2014. "'Trapped' Populations: Limits on Mobility at Times of Crisis." In *Humanitarian Crises and Migration: Causes, Consequences and Responses*, edited by S. F. Martin, S. Weerasinghe, and A. Taylor, 287–305. Abingdon: Routledge.

Burrell, J. 2012. *Invisible Users: Youth in the Internet Cafes of Urban Ghana*. Cambridge, MA: MIT Press.

Cai, R., N. Esipova, M. Oppenheimer, and S. Feng. 2014. "International Migration Desires Related to Subjective Well-Being." *IZA Journal of Migration* 3 (8): 1–20.

Carling, J. 2002. "Migration in the age of Involuntary Immobility: Theoretical Reflections and Cape Verdean Experiences." *Journal of Ethnic and Migration Studies* 28 (1): 5–42.
Carling, J. 2008. "The Human Dynamics of Migrant Transnationalism." *Ethnic and Racial Studies* 31 (8): 1452–1477.
Carling, J. 2012. "Steps Towards a Theory of Migration Aspirations." Paper presented at aspirations and capabilities in migration processes, International Migration Institute, Oxford.
Carling, J. 2013. *Who Wants to Go to Europe? Results from a Large-Scale Survey on Migration Aspirations.* PRIO Policy Brief, 2013/4. Oslo: Peace Research Institute Oslo (PRIO).
Carling, J. 2014. "The Role of Aspirations in Migration." Paper presented at determinants of international migration, International Migration Institute, University of Oxford, Oxford, September 23–25.
Carling, J., and F. Collins. 2018. "Aspiration, Desire and Drivers of Migration." *Journal of Ethnic and Migration Studies* 44 (6): 909–926. doi:10.1080/1369183X.2017.1384134.
Carling, J., E. Ersanilli, and H. de Haas. 2012. "Men, Women and Migration Aspirations: A Comparative Analysis of Sixteen Areas of Origin." Paper presented at comparative and multi-sited approaches to international migration, Institut national d'études démographiques (INED), Paris, December 12–14.
Carling, J., P. D. Fall, M. Hernández-Carretero, M. Y. Sarr, and J. Wu. 2013. *Migration Aspirations in Senegal: Who Wants to Leave and Why Does It Matter?* European Policy Brief. Brussels: European Commission.
Collins, F. L. 2018. "Desire as a Theory for Migration Studies: Temporality, Assemblage and Becoming in the Narratives of Migrants." *Journal of Ethnic and Migration Studies* 44 (6): 964–980. doi:10.1080/1369183X.2017.1384147.
Coulter, R. 2013. "Wishful Thinking and the Abandonment of Moving Desires over the Life Course." *Environment and Planning A* 45 (8): 1944–1962.
Coulter, R., M. van Ham, and P. Feijten. 2011. "A Longitudinal Analysis of Moving Desires, Expectations and Actual Moving Behaviour." *Environment and Planning A* 43 (11): 2742–2760.
Creighton, M. J. 2013. "The Role of Aspirations in Domestic and International Migration." *Social Science Journal* 50 (1): 79–88.
Czaika, M., and H. de Haas. 2016. "The Effect of Visas on Migration Processes." *International Migration Review*. doi:10.1111/imre.12261.
Czaika, M., and M. Vothknecht. 2014. "Migration and Aspirations: Are Migrants Trapped on a Hedonic Treadmill?" *IZA Journal of Migration* 3 (1): 1.
de Groot, C., C. H. Mulder, M. Das, and D. Manting. 2011. "Life Events and the Gap Between Intention to Move and Actual Mobility." *Environment and Planning A* 43 (1): 48–66.
de Haas, H. 2003. "Migration and Development in Southern Morocco." PhD diss., Katholieke Universiteit Nijmegen, Nijmegen.
de Haas, H. 2010. "The Internal Dynamics of Migration Processes: A Theoretical Inquiry." *Journal of Ethnic and Migration Studies* 36 (10): 1587–1617.
de Haas, H. 2014. *Migration Theory: Quo Vadis?* Working Paper, 100. Oxford: International Migration Institute, University of Oxford.
De Jong, G. F. 2000. "Expectations, Gender, and Norms in Migration Decision-Making." *Population Studies* 54 (3): 307–319.
De Jong, G. F., R. G. Abad, F. Arnold, B. V. Cariño, J. T. Fawcett, and R. W. Gardner. 1983. "International and Internal Migration Decision-Making. A Value-Expectancy Based Analytical Framework of Intentions to Move from a Rural Philippine Province." *International Migration Review* 17 (3): 470–484.
De Jong, G. F., K. Richter, and P. Isarabhakdi. 1996. "Gender, Values, and Intentions to Move in Rural Thailand." *International Migration Review* 30 (3): 748–770.
Dimitriadi, A. 2017. "In Search of Asylum: Afghan Migrants in Greece." *European Journal of Migration and Law* 19 (1): 57–76.
Docquier, F., G. Peri, and I. Ruyssen. 2014. "The Cross-country Determinants of Potential and Actual Migration." *International Migration Review* 48 (s1): S37–S99.

Drinkwater, S. 2002. *Go West? Assessing the Willingness to Move from Central and Eastern European Countries*. Discussion Paper in Economics. Surrey: University of Surrey.
Dustmann, C., and A. Okatenko. 2014. "Out-migration, Wealth Constraints, and the Quality of Local Amenities." *Journal of Development Economics* 110: 52–63.
Eagly, A. H., and S. Chaiken. 1993. *The Psychology of Attitudes*. Fort Worth: Harcourt, Brace, Jovanovich.
Ersanilli, E., J. Carling, and H. de Haas. 2011. *Methodology for Quantitative Data Collection*. EUMAGINE Project Paper, 6A. Antwerp: University of Antwerp.
European Commission. 2016. *Statistics on Short-Stay Visas Issued by the Schengen States*. Brussels: DG Migration and Home Affairs.
Fawcett, J. T. 1985. "Migration Psychology: New Behavioral-Models." *Population and Environment* 8 (1–2): 5–14.
Gaibazzi, P. 2014. "Visa Problem: Certification, Kinship, and the Production of 'Ineligibility' in the Gambia." *Journal of the Royal Anthropological Institute* 20 (1): 38–55.
Gallup. 2008. *World Poll Questions*. Washington, DC: Gallup.
Gardner, R. W., G. F. De Jong, F. Arnold, and B. V. Cariño. 1985. "The Best-Laid Schemes: an Analysis of Discrepancies Between Migration Intentions and Behavior." *Population and Environment* 8 (1–2): 63–77.
Henley & Partners. 2015. *Visa Restrictions Index*. London: Henley & Partners.
Hirschman, A. O. 1970. *Exit, Voice, and Loyalty: Responses to Decline in Firms, Organizations, and States*. Cambridge, MA: Harvard University Press.
Horst, C. 2006. "Buufis Amongst Somalis in Dadaab: The Transnational and Historical Logics Behind Resettlement Dreams." *Journal of Refugee Studies* 19 (2): 143–157.
Jayasuriya, D. 2014. *Drivers of Irregular and Regular Migration from Sri Lanka: Evidence from a Large Scale Survey*. Irregular Migration Research Programme Occasional Paper Series, 09/2014. Canberra: Department of Immigration and Border Protection.
Jónsson, G. 2008. *Migration Aspirations and Immobility in a Malian Soninke Village*. Working Paper, 10. Oxford: International Migration Institute.
Kandel, W., and D. S. Massey. 2002. "The Culture of Mexican Migration: A Theoretical and Empirical Analysis." *Social Forces* 80 (3): 981–1004.
King, R. 2012. "Geography and Migration Studies: Retrospect and Prospect." *Population, Space and Place* 18 (2): 134–153.
Kley, S. 2011. "Explaining the Stages of Migration Within a Life-Course Framework." *European Sociological Review* 27 (4): 469–486.
Kureková, L. M. 2014. "*EU Accession and Youth Labour Mobility from Slovakia: Labour Market Perspective*." ECPR general conference, Glasgow, 3–6 September.
Lubkemann, S. C. 2005. "The Moral Economy of Nonreturn among Socially Diverted Labor Migrants from Portugal and Mozambique." In *Migration and Economy. Global and Local Dynamics*, edited by L. Trager, 257–287. Walnut Creek: Altamira Press.
Madhavan, S., and L. B. Landau. 2011. "Bridges to Nowhere: Hosts, Migrants, and the Chimera of Social Capital in Three African Cities." *Population and Development Review* 37 (3): 473–497.
Mains, D. 2011. *Hope Is Cut: Youth, Unemployment, and the Future in Urban Ethiopia*. Philadelphia: Temple University Press.
Mata-Codesal, D. 2015. "Ways of Staying Put in Ecuador: Social and Embodied Experiences of Mobility–Immobility Interactions." *Journal of Ethnic and Migration Studies* 41 (14): 2274–2290.
McKenzie, D. 2007. "Paper Walls Are Easier to Tear Down: Passport Costs and Legal Barriers to Emigration." *World Development* 35 (11): 2026–2039.
Mondain, N., and A. Diagne. 2013. "Discerning the Reality of 'Those Left Behind' in Contemporary Migration Processes in Sub-Saharan Africa: Some Theoretical Reflections in the Light of Data from Senegal." *Journal of Intercultural Studies* 34 (5): 503–516.
Newell, S. 2012. *The Modernity Bluff: Crime, Consumption, and Citizenship in Côte D'Ivoire*. Chicago: University of Chicago Press.
OECD. 2015. *Connecting with Emigrants: A Global Profile of Diasporas 2015*. Paris: OECD.

Pajo, E. 2008. *International Migration, Social Demotion, and Imagined Advancement: An Ethnography of Socioglobal Mobility*. New York: Springer.

Paul, A. M. 2011. "Stepwise International Migration: A Multistage Migration Pattern for the Aspiring Migrant." *American Journal of Sociology* 116 (6): 1842–1886.

Randell, H. 2016. "Structure and Agency in Development-Induced Forced Migration: The Case of Brazil's Belo Monte Dam." *Population and Environment* 37 (3): 265–287.

Rueschemeyer, D. 2009. *Usable Theory: Analytic Tools for Social and Political Research*. Princeton: Princeton University Press.

Schapendonk, J., and G. Steel. 2014. "Following Migrant Trajectories: The Im/mobility of Sub-Saharan Africans En route to the European Union." *Annals of the Association of American Geographers* 104 (2): 262–270.

Schewel, K. 2015. *Understanding the Aspiration to Stay: A Case Study of Young Adults in Senegal*. IMI Working Paper, 107-15. Oxford: International Migration Institute, University of Oxford.

Schiller, N. G., and N. B. Salazar. 2013. "Regimes of Mobility Across the Globe." *Journal of Ethnic and Migration Studies* 39 (2): 183–200.

Sen, A. 1999. *Development as Freedom*. Oxford: Oxford University Press.

US Department of State. 2016. *Nonimmigrant Visa Statistics*. Washington, DC: US Department of State.

van Dalen, H. P., G. Groenewold, and J. J. Schoorl. 2005. "Out of Africa: What Drives the Pressure to Emigrate?" *Journal of Population Economics* 18 (4): 741–778.

van Dalen, H. P., and K. Henkens. 2008. *Emigration Intentions: Mere Words or True Plans? Explaining International Migration Intentions and Behavior*. Tilburg: University of Tilburg.

Van Hear, N. 2014. "Reconsidering Migration and Class." *International Migration Review* 48 (s1): S100–S121.

Vigh, H. 2009. "Wayward Migration: On Imagined Futures and Technological Voids." *Ethnos* 74 (1): 91–109.

Wissink, M., F. Duvell, and A. van Eerdewijk. 2013. "Dynamic Migration Intentions and the Impact of Socio-institutional Environments: A Transit Migration Hub in Turkey." *Journal of Ethnic and Migration Studies* 39 (7): 1087–1105.

Wood, C. H., C. L. Gibson, L. Ribeiro, and P. Hamsho-Diaz. 2010. "Crime Victimization in Latin America and Intentions to Migrate to the United States." *International Migration Review* 44 (1): 3–24.

Young Lives. 2013. *Young Lives Round 4 Survey Child Questionnaire*. Oxford: University of Oxford.

Desire as a theory for migration studies: temporality, assemblage and becoming in the narratives of migrants

Francis L. Collins

ABSTRACT

This article explores the potential of desire as a conceptual vocabulary to enliven scholarly understandings of migrant mobilities. Desire and questions of human aspiration draw our attention to the generative potential of migration, not only the myriad forces that make migration possible but also the transformative possibilities for the subjects and spaces involved. By focusing on desire, then, it becomes possible to reconceptualise migration as an ongoing process of spatio-temporal differentiation rather than as a univalent and knowable phenomenon. The process of migration is in this respect also tied up with a concomitant process of becoming for migrants themselves, a transformation in subjectivity that also involves transformations for the places they move through and the people they move with. This article unpacks these conceptualisations of migration through three individual narratives of migration from Southeast Asia to South Korea. Through these narratives the article highlights three dimensions of migration that can be re-examined through the analytical emphasis on desire: the multiple *temporalities* of migrant lives and future potential; the *assemblage* of spatialities and relations articulated in migration; and the politics of migration that is generated through the enlisting of migrants by states and migrants' own desire for *becoming* through migration.

The migration problematic

Contemporary forms of migration are increasingly viewed through the lens of 'migration management'. As a regime for regulating borders and mobility, migration management makes claims about the shared benefits of migration and the need for rational planning and control of movement. In contrast to regimes of border exclusion, migration management advocates 'regulated openness' to 'balance the needs and interests of the sending, receiving and transit countries and the migrants themselves' (Ghosh 2007, 107). This utopic vision of regionally and globally integrated migration has come to manifest in diverse ways through national policy frameworks, regional agreements and the actions of international organisations (Geiger and Pécoud 2013). The political rationalities of migration management articulate most apparently through the vision of migration as either a solely economic behaviour or forced movement. Through this vision, states and organisations seek to assemble a transparent and regularised process for entry, work and departure or for the orderly control of individuals seeking asylum.

The figure of the migrant articulated within migration management has been significantly influenced by the principles and theories of migration studies (Garelli and Tazzioli 2013). Most importantly, migration management relies on an idea of the migrant as a utility-maximising individual who – when provided with full access to information and freed from constraints – can make migration decisions that will serve his or her own interests and for which he or she can be held responsible. Certainly, migration studies as a field has come a long way from advocating these principles explicitly, although in the absence of alternative conceptualisations, 'the utility-maximizing notion underlying decision-making has not been fundamentally challenged' (De Haas 2011, 20). As Hess (2010) formulates it, these knowledges about migration and migrants are a form of 'soft governance' that interact with and influence the ways that governments and populations respond to migration. They make it possible to imagine that 'regulated openness' will lead to orderly flows that will be mutually beneficial and where the politics of migration is business as usual.

In the absence of critical conceptualisations that focus on the generation of migration, there has remained an underpinning logic to much migration scholarship, mostly notably the claim that we know and can measure why people choose to migrate. This includes three key propositions. Firstly, there remains a presumption that migration is principally economic, that it results from unequal distribution of resources and migrants intentionally set out to address this for themselves, their families or their communities (Castles 2013). In addition to contributing to binaries around authorised and unauthorised migrations, this assumption relies on a problematic reading of intentionality and calculative rationality that constructs mobility and life as something to be individually predetermined and modulated. Accordingly, and secondly, much migration scholarship still reifies the individual migrant as a decision maker who chooses to migrate in a relatively autonomous or individualistic way (Kennan and Walker 2011). Consequently, migration decisions can be measured in terms of which destinations migrants prefer and codified according to migrant nationalities, types, statuses and other factors. Lastly, migration 'decision-making' is presumed to occur at a singular moment in time, or within a relatively short time horizon prior to departure, that involves the calculative assessment of available information in an objective and goal-oriented fashion (De Haas 2010). These foundational elements of migration studies have contributed to a situation where, as Nail (2015, 4) puts it, 'the migrant has been understood as a figure without its own history and social force'. Rather, the histories, presents and futures of the migrant have been scripted through the lens of the nation-state and citizen where stasis rather than movement is taken as the normal state of being (Casas-Cortes et al. 2015).

In the context of the present special issue on 'aspiration, desire and the drivers of migration' (Carling and Collins 2018), this article develops an alternative conceptual framing that focuses on the generation of migration, the social and temporal conditions that serve as a motive and sustaining force for movement. The approach developed here embraces rather than obscures the excesses and uncertainties of migrant mobilities, undisciplined movement across borders and the role of migration in constituting the places migrants move through. To do this, I foreground the conceptual vocabulary of *desire as a social force* that is developed through the social theory of Deleuze and Guattari (1983, 1986). Following Deleuze and Guattari, this article conceives of desire as the energies that draw different entities – human, non-human, symbolic – into relation with each other and in the process generates social forms and affects.

Using desire as a vocabulary for understanding migration means paying attention to how movement is instigated by a range of conscious and sub-conscious influences. Desire is expressed through the mobilities of migrants, the combinations of strategic planning, opportunism and fancies that manifest in movements to take individuals into other worlds, to achieve or avoid (un)desirable futures. A focus on desire, then, differs from other concepts in this special issue because it draws attention to the embodied and emotional generators of migration. By contrast, Carling and Schewel's (2018) account of aspiration and ability speaks to a two-stage process of mind-dependent thinking and body-dependent action; more prosaically 'intentions' and 'plans' index the arrangement of future actions that are assessed as carrying potential value. Unlike these vocabularies, a focus on desire draws attention to striving towards possibilities that are deemed good because we desire them, rather than vice versa. Migration is an ongoing process within which past, present and future are folded together in the emergence of migrant lives and subjectivities.

The next section of this article introduces the theoretical reading of desire and its potential to inform an alternative ontological position on the generation of migration. Migrant narratives are useful for exploring desire and the unpredictable dimensions of migration because they allow researchers and migrants themselves to piece together accounts of movement that cut across geographic and temporal settings. The narratives of three migrants are introduced, focusing on the ways in which they came to South Korea, their imaginings of migration and the actors involved in their mobility, their own involvement in remaking migratory routes and the framing of the future in present actions. The article concludes through a reflection on the insights generated through a reading of desire as a social force in migration – the multiple temporalities of migration, the relational spatialities or assemblages involved in migration and the necessarily transformative and excessive features of migrant subjectivity.

Desire as a theory for migration studies

> Migration [...] arises from the desire inherent in most men to 'better' themselves in material respects. (Ravenstein 1889, 286)

'Desire' is a commonly used word in migration studies. As Ravenstein's statement from 'The Laws of Migration' indicates, desire has been a reference point in migration scholarship since its earliest inception. Desire is also a common albeit undeveloped vocabulary within leading migration journals. Between 1990 and 2015, no less than 513 articles in the *Journal of Ethnic and Migration Studies* made reference to desire (24% of 2100 articles); in *International Migration* the figure was 689/1915 or 36% of all articles published; and in *International Migration Review* 10% or 285/2720 articles. There remain, however, very few examples of theoretical discussions of desire in migration that move beyond its use simply as a synonym for 'motive', 'reason' or 'want' (in relation to student migration, cf. Collins et al. 2014; in relation to international relations, cf. Doty 2003; in relation to consumption and migration, cf. Hindman and Oppenheim 2014). What is missing is a detailed elaboration of how desire can be developed to expand conceptions of migration and embrace a more multifaceted view of undisciplined mobility.

In developing desire as a conceptual vocabulary for migration, I draw on Deleuze and Guattari (1983, 31), who go so far as to suggest that 'there is only desire and the social, and nothing else'. For them, desire constitutes the human condition, the continual attempt to reaffirm our status as a becoming-subject (O'Shea 2002). This view contrasts substantially with the inert use of desire in most migration studies as a description for what migrants want. It also differs from the long history of philosophical work on desire including that of Plato, Hegel, Marx, Freud and Lacan, in which desire is treated as an effect of power and relations, often as something characterised by 'lack' and the striving for an impossible ideal (Goodchild 1996). Deleuze and Guattari depart from this tradition by positing that desire is the very force that animates the world – it is not an effect of power, but rather a force involved in the production and arrangement of social forms. From this perspective, existence is not determined through transcendence or by underlying collective interests, but rather by unconscious drives that emanate from particular 'assemblages', arrangements of bodies, things and ideas. Desire, then, acts to bring different bodies together in new and transformative formations. In this respect, desire is necessarily productive or affirmative in the sense that it creates conditions for particular actualisations as well as for generating new connections between subjects (Bignall 2008).

A focus on desire offers several avenues to extend analysis of migration to incorporate the multiple temporalities of mobility and its articulation across migrant bodies and social relations, through places of work and study, to urban, national, regional and global spaces. I focus on three conceptual issues where a focus on desire can advance current approaches to theorising migration: temporality, assemblage and becoming. Most importantly, a focus on desire makes it possible to move beyond the well-known fallacy that migration is only the result of a calculated rational choice at a singular point in time (Adam 1984). While it is possible to claim that an individual has an interest in migrating and through certain actions seeks to actualise this interest, for Deleuze and Guattari such interest only exists within a particular social context and is only possible because of desires invested in that social formation (Smith 2007). Accordingly, the temporality of what we call migrant decision-making cannot be understood as a singular now moment of the present – a fully rational and calculated choice – but rather in relation to articulations between future, past and present (Griffiths 2014; Shubin 2015). Migration, particularly that discussed in this article, is clearly coded in the norms of contemporary capitalism and the valorisation of economic, social and cultural powers that emanate through this assemblage. Of course, migration is articulated through other desires that emanate from variable, if not fully distinct, assemblages – a desire to embody different identities as a 'global subject' or 'cosmopolitan', feelings of filial piety and commitment to community and place, a yearning for travel, adventure and experience or to escape from social and institutional constraints (Collins et al. 2014). When we focus on desire as a social force in migration, each of these and other factors that instigate migration serve as expressions of desire, which is a more underlying force that cannot be reduced to rationales for action. The actualisation of migration articulates the complex interplay between these expressions of desire, between strategic planning and opportunism that manifest in movements to achieve or avoid certain kinds of futures. Migration in this respect is never singular in its temporality, but rather is an ongoing process where past, present and future are folded together in the emergence of migrant lives (McCormack and Schwanen 2011).

Further, a focus on desire in migration draws our attention to the manner in which the drivers of migration are part of dynamic social and material assemblages. The drive or impetus for migration does not emanate from a specific object (a certain amount of money, an overseas degree) or being (a successful migrant returnee), but rather is expressed in discursive productions of these things. Desire, then, is shaped by discourses that prescribe certain actions and proscribe others, or that code, overcode and decode objects, behaviours and opportunities as more or less desirable (Holland 2010). In migration these imaginaries are constructed not least by nation-states seeking to activate mobility to address labour shortages or demographic decline, to attract and capture foreign 'talent' or 'experts' or to capitalise on multicultural presence (Ong 2007). In addition to their role in disciplining and ordering migration flows, the mobility regimes of migration management are also caught up in enlisting migrants in the possibilities of migration. This occurs directly, through practices of state marketing such as on websites advertising migration opportunities along with the images and language used to make a particular destination attractive (Hindman and Oppenheim 2014). Just as often, migrants are enlisted in the possibilities for migration through a wider social assemblage of actors including brokers and other intermediaries (Xiang and Lindquist 2014), the cultural productions of places (Y. Kim 2013), networks of friends and family (McKay 2007), promotion in sending states (Collins et al. 2014) and cultural politics that valorise migration as development (Tyner 2013). This is not to suggest that migrant desires equate to these discourses, or that they can simply be 'recruited' for the purposes of the nation-state, employers or intermediaries, but rather to emphasise that desire is constituted by both complementary and contradictory flows that shape the form and processes of movement.

Lastly, a focus on desire emphasises the transformative dimension of migration, including its necessary practical and political implications. Deleuze and Guattari (2004, 225) insist that 'the analysis of desire, is immediately practical and political', it is 'the art of the new' and it 'actively participates in the drawing of the lines' between bodies, of creating and destroying assemblages. A focus on desire as a social force is necessarily affirmative in that it emphasises the processes of becoming that migration entails. Migration has long been understood as a transformative process, one in which migrants' place in the world, their ideas about themselves and possibilities for the future are reworked (Castles 2010). The tendency, however, has been to treat this as an effect of migration, rather than the very actualisation of this process. Likewise, for nation-states, migration is conceived as producing certain effects in society – more diversity, xenophobia, altered labour markets, ethnic enclaves – rather than recognising all of these objects and processes as interlinked from the outset (Doty 2003). This article posits migration as a process of desiring on the part of migrants that is already an expression of transformation, an actualisation of deterritorialising and reterritorialising processes both in individual subjects and the places they inhabit through migration. Despite the energy mobility regimes invest in crafting imaginaries and pathways – arrival, work, study, departure – scholarship suggests that there is substantial variation as migrants become irregular, subvert rules, transition between visas, depart early, demand rights or avoid support (Robertson 2013). There is then considerable unpredictability in migration – it creates new encounters between mobile and local subjects (Collins et al. 2014), raises questions about citizenship and politics (Doty 2003) and alters the expectations and subject positions that migrants inhabit (Hindman and Oppenheim 2014).

Narratives of migration

The focus on desire advocated here demands an approach that can draw attention to the ways that migration unfolds across multiple spatial and temporal horizons (Valentine and Sadgrove 2014). Migrant narratives generated through interviews are used as the vehicle to explore expressions of desire. Interviews do not reveal desire, but they do provide an opportunity to observe its effects in mobility and subjectivity. The use of narratives to explore expressions of desire has significant value because of the ways in which they centre on human experiences while also having scope to engender reflections on shifting forms and effects of subjectivity. This is particularly important for my purposes here, where I am focused on moving beyond normalised scripts of migration. Indeed, as Lawson (2000, 174) notes, stories 'can reveal the empirical disjuncture between expectations of migration [...] and the actual experiences of migrants'. They draw our attention to forms of agentive will, expressions of desire, as well as the social structures that these emerge within and exceed. At the same time, narratives such as those used here draw attention to how migration is situated not only in relation to present articulations of subjectivity, but also in co-existence with pasts that constitute migrant becoming and future possibilities that are desired but not yet accounted for (Shubin 2015).

The narratives presented in this article emerge from a project on the lives of temporary migrants in the Seoul Metropolitan Region of South Korea. The project included 40 interviews with individuals from Indonesia, the Philippines, Thailand and Vietnam. I rely on the narratives of three participants to draw out some of the ways in which desire emerges as a force in migratory processes, how it is enabled through connections, impeded through blockages and reworked through emergent migration assemblages. The narratives, hence, are not intended to be exemplars of the 'reasons' or 'patterns' of migrant mobility. Rather, they offer us a lens through which we might conceptualise the diversity of forces at work in making mobility possible, channelling migrants in particular directions and generating always unexpected transformations in individual and collective lives.

These interviews were undertaken between September and November 2011. The total participant sample included 35 men, 4 women and 1 transgender participant, a pattern that reflects the highly gendered character of labour migration in South Korea. The participants ranged from ages 22 to 45, and the length of time in South Korea ranged from 7 months to 15 years. Interviews were conducted by community researchers in the native language of each participant. The individuals whose narratives are presented below were selected because they provide nationality and gender diversity, demonstrate different temporal durations of migration and were part of a subset of more detailed interviews that offered significant depth and content on the processes of migration.

These three participants, identified here with the pseudonyms Tulus (male from Indonesia), Nonoy (male from the Philippines) and Thuy (female from Vietnam), migrated through different dimensions of the South Korean government's current approaches to migration management. Tulus and Nonoy entered through the Employment Permit System (EPS), a regime that was established in 2004 to manage flows of labour migrants from 15 countries in Asia. The EPS is a guest worker regime that seeks to manage the number, quality and tenure of migrant workers and, in doing so, address labour shortages, maintain minimum human rights and ensure departure once visas expire (M. J. Kim 2015). Through the EPS, migrants are recruited for five sectors: manufacturing, agriculture, construction, fisheries and services. Before departure and after arrival, migrants undergo job training, medical tests and orientation to South Korea. When Tulus and Nonoy migrated, they were granted visas that allowed them to work for a specified employer for three years, after which time they were expected to return home.

Not all migration occurs in such a regulated way. Thuy migrated through an intermediated marriage with a Korean man. Unlike Tulus and Nonoy, Thuy was not formally a labour migrant, although as her narrative suggests, she did conceive of her mobility in this way. Her narrative draws attention to less authorised pathways to becoming a labour migrant and the discrepancies between migrant types and drivers that can be revealed through an emphasis on expressions of desire. Equally, Nonoy and Tulus speak to quite different encounters with the EPS. Nonoy's mobility occurs through a relatively formal negotiation of regulation and timing of migration – he applied, was accepted, prepared, departed, took a job and followed all procedures. Tulus, by contrast, articulates blockages in his migration that are eventually resolved through an institution that fixes his application in an irregular fashion. These variations are not isolated to these individuals, but rather reflect the different ways that migrants negotiate the complex rules of mobility regimes, the work that is undertaken by other actors and the multiple ways that desire drives migrant mobility and transformation (Collins 2016).

Tulus: multiple temporalities

Tulus narrated a migration story of opportunities and impediments – and an always-evolving sense of what he wanted. The son of a teacher and a security guard, he has two brothers and three sisters and grew up in the Padang province of Sumatra. Tulus graduated from an academic senior high school. Afterwards, he sat university examinations several times, including after studying at a private academy in Jakarta, but failed to gain a place. Tulus followed his parents' advice and returned to Padang to enter a 'famous' private financial banking academy so that he could 'work as a public servant'. Tulus graduated in 1997 just as the monetary crisis hit Indonesia and effectively ended any possibility of employment for young new graduates. He carried on studying towards a bachelor's-level qualification without a clear sense of where it might lead, as he was biding time, waiting until an opportunity came along. That opportunity came in the first emergence of the prospect of migration.

> Well, after that I had a plan, to follow my relative's plan, [a relative] who was the same age like me [...], he had migrated to Japan after graduating. So, in 2000, I wished I could migrate to Japan, and somehow I took Japanese lessons.

Migration, in this context, speaks to connections between people – the social relations of family that circulate ideas about the possibility of migration and its potential.

> It seemed that it was really good to work abroad, sending money home, buying cameras; lots of friends in the '90s had been doing well. So I was motivated. Yes, I wanted to migrate to Japan too. [...] I joined the class that was really, the study, so promising, quickly, until I did well.

Desire generates all sorts of effects in Tulus' trajectory, compelling him to focus his energies on acquiring language competencies and skills and investing emotionally in what might be possible through migration such as acquiring consumer goods, sending remittances. Desire, in this context, is not simply about these material possibilities, however. Rather, desire manifests in terms of becoming otherwise, being drawn into another world that is expressed by these possibilities, becoming migrant. Desire moves Tulus; it is a force that directs his actions, but as his narrative reveals, movement is not in this instance something that the migration regime will permit.

> I applied [to go to Japan], but [was] refused. Do you know why? Because my high school graduation certificate was not acceptable. It ought to be accompanied by [a work training centre] statement of graduation. In [academic high school], you did not get it. Well, after that, I [asked] and they told me I had to undertake [further] study for three years.

We can conceive of these regulatory impediments as a 'blockage', 'a neutralization of experimental desire [...], like that desire blocked by the roof or the ceiling' (Deleuze and Guattari 1986, 4). Such a blockage is not the destruction of desire's force, but rather serves to redirect its movement. With his planned migration halted but his desire for different prospects in the world enlivened, Tulus pursued other opportunities. He moved to Batam island, a key node in the economic zone that incorporates Singapore, the Riau Islands in Indonesia and Johor province of Malaysia (Lindquist 2009). Batam is a major site of migration in Indonesia, one that offers possibilities for becoming part of global circulations but is also marked by considerable friction as many migrants fail to succeed.

> I went to Batam to join a friend who worked on the ship. A cruiser, a ship where people gamble. [...] I took the test at Batam View, I was guessing that I would pass the test with 70% scores, as I understood English a bit. [...] I had been awaiting for the result, but there was no call. You know what? There had been notorious cases caused by Indonesians when they were aboard. So the Chinese man assumed that all Indonesians were the same. I had been waiting about one year, and I was just stranded a year there.

With his mobility again halted by this new blockage, Tulus went to Tanjung Pinang in neighbouring Bintan and worked with a friend for three months in a printing business before his friend sent him home. Back in Padang, Tulus engaged in a range of overlapping activities: he worked for his sister in a water refilling business, collected, repaired and sold motorcycle parts and volunteered to help with earthquake recovery in Padang. Following his involvement in the recovery, a microfinance charity offered Tulus and his sister money for personal development – they undertook some courses in mobile phone repair but eventually started a catfish breeding business. While initially successful, the business collapsed after Tulus was cheated by a friend. This crisis coincided with the return of his cousin from Japan, and international migration loomed again.

> Everything was gone. After that, I intended to migrate to Korea. I would push my luck working in Korea. [...] I wanted to migrate to Korea. My cousin had just come back from Japan and wanted to migrate to Korea. I gained information about Korea from him. [...] Everyone I asked liked Korea. [...] I loved to talked about it, and it became exciting. Sharing information. I asked them: 'How was Korea? Did you find this, or this? How was the food?' They said everything was great in Korea. So I felt excited again.

South Korea emerges here at a moment of both crisis and opportunity as Tulus got relinked into the circuit of migration upon his cousin's return. The linkages between imagination and desire are particularly pronounced here, with South Korea emerging as a place known for food, culture and opportunity and, crucially, generative of 'excitement', of bodily energy for doing and being otherwise. As in his earlier experience, Tulus' desire to migrate is articulated through multiple connections, not least the requirements of the migration regime, here the EPS and its emphasis on skills and language. The path was challenging – Tulus failed the language test in 2008 and 2009, only passing finally in 2010 when he invested a significant sum of money in a 'special programme' which would 'guarantee' success.

In South Korea, Tulus worked in a cardboard collection and processing factory, work that he described as much harder and heavier than he had imagined. In a painful story of isolation and conflict, he recounted being the only Indonesian and speaking little Korean. Eventually, after constant requests he was provided a resignation letter and, at the time of his interview, was still looking for a new job. Tulus had no specific plans for the present or the future, but rather was again biding his time before the next opportunity, ready to anticipate what might come next. He said: 'It's better to be here anyway. If you want something, [it will] depend on how we manage it, negatively or positively. That depends on us.'

While these future trajectories point to the unfolding of new desires for action and potential mobility, I am concerned with the emergence of migration, its generation across multiple temporalities and the desire involved in making movement. What Tulus' account suggests is that we cannot limit our understanding of migration to singular moments and purely strategically oriented linear progression. Rather, Tulus' narrative reveals the multiple temporalities of migration (Cwerner 2001), the way it involves starts and stops, possibilities and prospects but also blockages and diversions. His migration is entangled in a whole array of expressions of desire, for livelihood, to support his family, to seek excitement and possibility, for being successful and, as he put it, 'risk' and 'speculation'. Critically, none of these trajectories is known in advance. Tulus is rather driven by desires for becoming otherwise, but he is also channelled along unexpected pathways to neighbouring towns, Jakarta, to Japan imaginatively but not corporeally, to Batam and Bintan, back to Padang and finally to South Korea. His arrival in South Korea is equally unknown, both in terms of what his life will be like and the kinds of possibilities that lie ahead. Even as he experiences limitation and difficulties in this new life, desire nonetheless drives his mobility and his will to remain in South Korea – it creates the conditions for doing things that are difficult and unpredictable; it generates, in other words, migration.

Nonoy: migration assemblage

Nonoy came from a family where migration was the norm. He grew up as the eldest of three children, born to a Spanish mother and a Filipino father, who lived across four different provincial areas of Luzon. His aunties raised him as his mother held jobs as a clerk, a teacher and a farm labourer while Nonoy's father was working in construction in Saudi Arabia. All of Nonoy's cousins have lived and worked abroad, and his younger sister is currently working abroad as a first-aid assistant in shipping.

Nonoy completed high school and holds a bachelor's degree in information systems. His aunties and parents had long encouraged independence – 'that was the rule in our household' – and Nonoy had been working and independently supporting himself both during and following university. After graduation, he planned to work for a while and then study nursing.

But then migration generally, and South Korea specifically, suddenly appeared on the horizon. Nonoy's cousin (whose siblings had all been to South Korea) proposed that they go see the recruiter. While Nonoy at the time had no migration intentions, he decided to go along as a favour. The recruiter they met had other ideas, immediately asking:

> 'Would you like to go to Taiwan? Because you're in already. All they look for in Taiwan is just the appearance, anyway. They want people who look tall, and then decent-looking, good-looking.' [...] So I said, 'Well!' But my cousin said the salaries were quite low. Then [the recruiter] said, 'What's booming now is Korea.'

This was 2004, and the EPS was being established as a new scheme for migrants. At the time, there was a minimum wage, backing came from the government and Korean popular culture flooded the Philippines. Desire lurks in such encounters not because individuals suddenly change their minds, but because desire is a force that draws subjects into wider social assemblages that generate possibilities once either unknown or shrouded; individuals themselves become part of a migration assemblage (Rubinov 2014).

A week later, Nonoy received a callback from the recruiter saying, 'You're in for the interview.' He had to make a difficult decision – he was due to pay tuition fees for nursing school that day and was also required to attend a medical examination, without which he could not go forward for migrant selection. He did the medical, though noted that study was 'the only thing on my mind'. It was his parents, who have their own histories of mobility, who added the extra motivation.

> I talked to my mom and dad. I said, 'Well. I might be going abroad. I would like to study again though.' I really wanted to study, and they knew it, that I wanted to study again. [...] They said, 'You don't know your luck – if you'd like to give it a try, since your papa went abroad in the past too.' [...] Then [Papa] said, 'Just try it and then lucks comes.' I passed the medical exam. So that's when I started training.

With one year until deployment, Nonoy started preparing, a process that engendered excitement and anxiety, feelings that we can understand as common results of desire. He met a Korean volunteer at university and started to learn the language, tried some Korean food – including a month of eating kimchi every day – and watched lots of dramas, films and videos to learn about Korea.

Nonoy's narrative is one of becoming part of a 'migration assemblage' – the social and material interactions that constitute migration as a process and set of practices (Rubinov 2014). This assemblage involves various actors and objects: recruiters, the intergovernmental agreement between South Korea and the Philippines, Nonoy's friends and family and the Korean volunteer as key facilitators; popular culture; objects like kimchi and other Korean foods; as well as Nonoy's own personal history and predilection for independence. These diverse components interact to generate migration. They articulate desire for movement as a necessary undertaking, one that takes Nonoy forward in the world, even if, as in Tulus' case, not in a direction he can fully grasp at this stage. The migration assemblage is one that stretches across territories, articulated through regulatory settings and border spaces, but nonetheless creating channels for mobility of different kinds.

In South Korea, Nonoy undertook the required training and was employed in Ulsan. In Ulsan, friends who had earlier migrated to South Korea helped Nonoy get oriented to his new setting and provided information about how to relating to employers and other people. Still, there was newness and conflicting feelings of pleasure, concern, excitement and anxiety.

> Korea is beautiful, but I said, 'This is the kind of beauty that's got something hidden behind it.' That's what I discovered, that Korea is beautiful, but there are things that you need to adjust to as a foreigner. [...] There's the feeling of excitement, [...] you're nervous, anxious, like what kind of attitude do these Koreans have, since all the Koreans I'd met at that point were very nice – but [the Korean volunteer] said, 'Not all Koreans are kind, they're rude.' [...] I'd only been at my company for a month, and I got to see all types of Korean attitudes.

Over his six years in South Korea, Nonoy became increasingly entangled in various migration assemblages. He stayed in Ulsan for two years until the factory closed and then moved to Cheonan for another two years before relocating to Suwon. Throughout this time he travelled frequently, visiting new places and equipped with only a map and a language book, meeting new people (often migrants) and learning about South Korea. These contacts shaped his mobilities in important ways, providing information about employers and conditions that he might find in different jobs. Nonoy also became involved in migrant organisations, initially in Ulsan, where he helped form a group to connect Filipino workers and Filipino wives of Korean men, and then in Cheonan, where he worked with a migrant community organisation. Eventually, as his profile grew, he was asked to take on a key role in a Filipino publication for migrant workers, which would have him shuttling from Seoul to Cheonan each week.

> I was an officer for a community there, an education community. The people who would visit were, people from the Philippine embassy, they said, 'Hey, you could be a writer for this publication in Seoul. [...] Just give it a try.'

Nonoy's mobility and practices can be understood as examples of the 'social and material interactions that constitute migrant assemblages' (Rubinov 2014, 186). His increasing involvement in these activities intensified his investment and role in migrant lives and networks in South Korea. It reflects how he was drawn into this world of opportunity not only for strategically imagined instrumental outcomes, but also as part of a wider process of becoming otherwise. Becoming part of these arrangements is about becoming increasingly central in the migration assemblage, about being one of the gears or cogs in the machine that makes migration possible; desire, in this context, can be understood as a person's 'fascination with these gears, his desire to make certain of these gears go into operation, to be himself one of these gears' (Deleuze and Guattari 1986, 56). Nonoy's narrative demonstrates that migration is relational, and that the desire that generates migration cannot be disentangled from the wider social and material assemblages that migrants become part of. Many migrants remain at the periphery of these arrangements, engaging in mobility that is generated through relations to various actors, materials, ideas and systems, but only taking a partial role as a gear in these assemblages. Others like Nonoy are driven by desires for not only migrating – a specific practice – but also becoming through that process, for being otherwise in ways that alter their own subjectivity and place in the world as well as the configurations of migration itself.

Thuy: becoming otherwise

Thuy grew up in a rural area north of Hanoi, Vietnam. Her parents were farmers and before coming to South Korea when she was 20, Thuy had not travelled outside their village. She described her family as 'poor' and described having limited opportunities. She completed secondary school, but could not afford further study and felt that she was not helpful on her parents' farm. The prospect of South Korea emerged in quite a different way than it did for Tulus, Nonoy and many other participants in this research. Through neighbours, Thuy's parents were introduced to a Korean man seeking a Vietnamese wife. During the interview she whispered:

> I decided to go to Korea to work to earn money. I came here because I wanted to work. In order to come here, I had to arrange a 'fake marriage'. [...] I was introduced by neighbours and people living around my home.

Initially, this 'fake marriage' brought Thuy to Busan, where she lived with her husband's family. The experience was difficult. A contrast to her aspirations for work and supporting her family in Vietnam, her new family envisaged her role as a wife and a future mother restricted to the household. The marriage lasted six months and was characterised by frequent arguments and domestic violence that eventually led Thuy to flee. She did not wish to travel back to Vietnam because she would not be permitted to return to South Korea. Without legal status outside the marriage, however, Thuy had to find a means to establish an undocumented way of living. She followed advice offered by other Vietnamese people and went to Gyeonggi Province in Seoul's outskirts, where she lived in an overcrowded apartment with other migrants.

> Eight people shared the apartment, so our lives were so complicated. At that time, I don't have a job so life is very tough and miserable. I lived for one year here just staying at home without working because I didn't dare collect my documents at that time and employers don't hire labourers without [their first having] legal documents. If I was lucky, they might hire me, but just for a few days. My earnings were so little that I had to borrow money from my friends.

Despite the stark differences in experience, Thuy's account was reminiscent of the social assemblage of migration that Nonoy described. She took advice from other Vietnamese people to escape her marriage and became part of a group of migrants who lived below the radar in Seoul's urban periphery (Collins 2016). The situation is more complex of course, with eight different women living together without status – a 'complicated' space where the hopes and aspirations of migration turn to 'misery'. Thuy's narrative also reminds us that migrant assemblages manifest both in transparent ways, such as the establishment of associations and publications, and below the radar, in situations where invisibility is a means for maintaining the possibilities of migration (Papadopoulos and Tsianos 2013).

What is desire, though, in this case? Surely in moments when life is 'miserable' staying does not appear as a desirable pursuit. 'Why do [people] fight *for* their servitude as stubbornly as though it were their salvation?' (Deleuze and Guattari 1983, 29). As Deleuze and Guattari (1983, 1986) remind us, desire should not be confused with choice or 'interest'; it needs to be understood as a wider investment in social formations. Thuy's investment in the prospects and possibilities of migration has drawn her into a wider social assemblage, which is not determined only by independent decisions about what might be calculated as best for her in a given situation. Desire is a force that makes it possible for individuals to do things in the world. Desire 'is not a question of a consciously willed personal decision' (Massumi 1992, 95), but rather of being taken elsewhere.

In the ensuing years, Thuy established a more secure but still marginal position for herself in South Korea. She eventually found a job in a car accessories factory, a very physically demanding role working from 8:30 in the morning until late in the evening. Thuy remained in this job for a year, during which time her family re-established contact with an aunt who had lived in South Korea for 11 years. This new connection made it possible for Thuy to have a more stable life even as she remained undocumented. Her aunt helped her to learn some Korean language, to find less demanding and exploitative work and to establish a sense of stability in life. At the time of her interview, Thuy had a quality-checking role at work, which she described as giving her increased autonomy on the job and fostering good relations with her employers and colleagues.

> I'm very satisfied. At the beginning, it was so difficult to learn from scratch that I wanted to give up sometimes. But now after three months, I've got used to it and find my job very interesting. Most of the people in the company – six colleagues including me, Filipino and Thai [colleagues] – are satisfied with this job. […] My boss is [also] very friendly. Sometimes he teases me when he meets me at work. I think other bosses must be different, but my boss is very easy-going.

Thuy also revealed a level of familiarity and comfort with living in her current neighbourhood, which may seem surprising for an undocumented migrant. She continued to learn Korean and talked about how she had established relationships with other foreigners in the area as well as elderly Korean neighbours. She also started to support a young Vietnamese woman who had left her marriage and began trying to establish a sustainable life without documents. Thuy herself is looking to the future.

> I want to live in Korea forever, but it is a pity that I have lived here for seven years without living with a family. I moved out to live, so I don't have legal documents. I am asking some people to help me to have Korean nationality so I can live here. I badly want to have nationality, but I don't know [if] my dream can come true or not. […] At first [my parents] were very worried about me, but now they feel better. I always tell them that I am fine here, live alone here very well, no bond or no difficulties. For the first time in Korea, it was really tough, but after seven years, I feel like I don't think I am Vietnamese anymore. Although my Korean is not so good, but I keep thinking that I am the same as other Korean people. I never think that I am a foreigner, a Vietnamese [person]. Now I think I am a Korean, I live in Korea so I am a Korean.

While caution is needed in assessing the possibilities for Thuy to be recognised as Korean, legally or socio-culturally, this assertion of an alternative future reveals a substantial transformation of subjectivity. Like other undocumented migrants, Thuy's insistence on remaining in South Korea despite her lack of status subverts the regulations of migration, both in the framework of the EPS, which limits migrants' time as workers, and in the marriage migration regime that links individual rights to a woman's role as wife and mother. Her articulation of desiring to become Korean, or to make a future in South Korea, was not shared by all participants in this research, but it does demonstrate the kinds of unforeseeable futures that emerge through migration. Indeed, the restrictions placed on migrants' rights or tenure in South Korea are designed to reduce the amount of experience that migrants might build up, to disrupt attempts to establish belonging and identification. Becoming undocumented subverts this because it exposes migrants to the risks and repression of irregular migrant life. This transformation also, however, allows individuals like Thuy to direct their own mobilities, to support the presence of others and to establish a new life and future. Desire makes things possible. It forces us towards futures that are not known in advance, entangles us in wider social assemblages and generates a new politics of becoming in the world through our own transformation.

Conclusion

The rationalities of migration management, such as those expressed in South Korean migration regimes, are based on the ideal of ordered and regulated flows. They presume that migrants will act in the manner of rational calculating subjects, making decisions from available information, assessing risks and planning for determinate futures within the constraints of regulation. The narratives presented here demonstrate the unpredictability and excess that is manifest in movement, even through highly regulated arrangements and despite the seemingly undesirable outcomes of migration. When read through the conceptual vocabulary of desire, it becomes possible to put aside more reductive visions of migration as always being a result of rational economic actions, which still haunt the field of migration studies today. This focus on desire is a particularly important tool for responding to the normatively charged optimism around migration and development and the idea that migration can be a 'win-win-win' scenario (De Haas 2010). A focus on desire demonstrates that migration is never so circumscribed, that it is rather caught up in forces that are entangled in migrant lives but are not theirs to fully control. The narratives presented here show that migrants can certainly direct their own mobilities in spite of regulation. However, it is also clear that this direction can only be revealed through careful attention to the ways in which desire emerges in a socially distributed, rather than simply atomistic way, and the manner in which desire is encouraged, enlisted, channelled or impeded in relation to migration regimes.

Three more specific points emerge from the notion of desire and its expression in these narratives. Firstly, the focus on migrant desires demonstrates the multiple temporalities and rhythms of migration – the ways in which the generation of migration is distributed across the pasts of migrants and their families and into their lives abroad. As Tulus, Nonoy and Thuy reveal, migration cannot be understood as generated in a singular moment of 'decision-making', but rather must be grasped across past–present–future. The prospect of migration emerges through family situations and orientations, encounters with images and imaginings of different places, the mobility of others, as well as the work of actors such as friends, agents and volunteers. As much as migration can be situated in relation to projective future-oriented aspirations, these stories also demonstrate how it hinges on opportunism and the time of grasping the moment. Migrants like Tulus, Nonoy and Thuy articulate a kind of 'anticipatory politics' (Simone 2010). They speak of taking chances when they arise, taking risks or speculating on opportunities in order to alter their position in the world or to achieve certain things for themselves or their families. Migration intersects, in other words, with drives for going elsewhere or being otherwise, for achieving or avoiding (un)desirable futures, that are often not the result of calculative rationality as it is so often conceived in migration research.

Secondly, migration involves relational spatialities, or what I have called 'migration assemblages'. As each participant has demonstrated, migration is entangled in relationships between multiple people, places and objects that come together to shape migration and its outcomes. Recognising the way desire works through these social formations is critical if we are to understand the ways in which migration regimes, such as those in South Korea, stretch across borders and into the lives of individuals in both sending and receiving nations. Yet, these assemblages cannot be understood simply as a static infrastructure. They must be examined in terms of the effects they have in migrant mobilities – the desires they generate or reconfigure, the possibilities they offer or impede. Desire also draws attention to the role of migrants as active constituents of these assemblages, actors who in different ways become the very gears in the machine that makes migration a desirable phenomenon in the world.

Lastly, these narratives and the focus on desire highlight the ways in which migration necessarily involves becoming as much as being. In their imaginaries, mobilities and everyday lives, migrants transcend mobility regimes and their attendant politics of truth. In their very being and becoming in the world, migrants both appropriate and rework the territorialising powers of migration regimes – they become the labouring bodies desired in these regimes as well as active human subjects whose presence can never be completely contained. They become key actors in organisations that alter the politics of migration, like Nonoy, or they subvert the workings of the migration regime by becoming undocumented, like Thuy, and insisting on their continuing presence and stability. In either case, such becoming, as this article has shown, is more than the result of calculative thought on the part of migrants or government. It demonstrates the way in which desire and the migration it generates is always about transformation of subjecthood, about becoming more than just a migrant.

Acknowledgements

This research would not have been possible without the contribution of four research assistants: Đô Diêu Khuê, Vorarerk Khunthongkum, Jeremiah Magoncia and Viko Zakhary. I would also like to thank Jørgen Carling and the anonymous reviewer for their commentary and guidance on the paper.

Disclosure statement

No potential conflict of interest was reported by the author.

Funding

This work was supported by the Korea Foundation [1022000-3992].

ORCID

Francis L. Collins http://orcid.org/0000-0001-9453-4465

References

Adam, Heribert. 1984. "Rational Choice in Ethnic Mobilization: A Critique." *International Migration Review* 18 (2): 377–381.

Bignall, Simone. 2008. "Deleuze and Foucault on Desire and Power." *Angelaki: Journal of Theoretical Humanities* 13 (1): 127–147.

Carling, J., and F. Collins. 2018. "Aspiration, Desire and Drivers of Migration." *Journal of Ethnic and Migration Studies* 44 (6): 909–926. doi:10.1080/1369183X.2017.1384134.

Carling, J., and K. Schewel. 2018. "Revisiting Aspiration and Ability in International Migration." *Journal of Ethnic and Migration Studies* 44 (6): 945–963. doi:10.1080/1369183X.2017.1384146.

Casas-Cortes, Maribel, Sebastian Cobarrubias, Nicholas De Genova, Glenda Garelli, Giorgio Grappi, Charles Heller, Sabine Hess, et al. 2015. "New Keywords: Migration and Borders." *Cultural Studies* 29 (1): 55–87.

Castles, Stephen. 2010. "Understanding Global Migration: A Social Transformation Perspective." *Journal of Ethnic and Migration Studies* 36 (10): 1565–1586.

Castles, Stephen. 2013. "The Forces Driving Global Migration." *Journal of Intercultural Studies* 34 (2): 122–140.

Collins, Francis L. 2016. "Migration, the Urban Periphery, and the Politics of Migrant Lives." *Antipode* 48 (5): 1167–1186.

Collins, Francis L., Ravinder Sidhu, Nicolas Lewis, and Brenda S. A. Yeoh. 2014. "Mobility and Desire: International Students and Asian Regionalism in Aspirational Singapore." *Discourse: Studies in the Cultural Politics of Education* 35 (5): 661–676.

Cwerner, Saulo B. 2001. "The Times of Migration." *Journal of Ethnic and Migration Studies* 27 (1): 7–36.

De Haas, Hein. 2010. "Migration and Development: A Theoretical Perspective." *International Migration Review* 44 (1): 227–264.

De Haas, Hein. 2011. *The Determinants of International Migration*. International Migration Institute Working Paper 32.

Deleuze, Gilles, and Felix Guattari. 1983. *Anti-Oedipus: Capitalism and Schizophrenia*. Minneapolis: University of Minnesota Press.

Deleuze, Gilles, and Felix Guattari. 1986. *Kafka: Toward a Minor Literature*. Minneapolis: University of Minnesota Press.

Deleuze, Gilles, and Felix Guattari. 2004. *A Thousand Plateaus*. London: Continuum.

Doty, Roxanne Lynn. 2003. *Anti-immigrantism in Western Democracies: Statecraft, Desire and the Politics of Exclusion*. London: Routledge.

Garelli, Glenda, and Martina Tazzioli. 2013. "Challenging the Discipline of Migration: Militant Research in Migration Studies, an Introduction." *Postcolonial Studies* 16 (3): 245–249.

Geiger, Martin, and Antoine Pécoud. 2013. *Disciplining the Transnational Mobility of People*. Houndmills: Palgrave Macmillan.

Ghosh, Bimal. 2007. "Managing Migration: Towards the Missing Regime?" In *Migration Without Borders: Essays on the Free Movement of People*, edited by Antoine Pécoud, 97–118. Oxford: Berghahn.

Goodchild, Philip. 1996. *Deleuze and Guattari: An Introduction to the Politics of Desire*. London: Sage.

Griffiths, Melanie B. 2014. "Out of Time: The Temporal Uncertainties of Refused Asylum Seekers and Immigration Detainees." *Journal of Ethnic and Migration Studies* 40 (12): 1991–2009.

Hess, Sabine. 2010. "'We are Facilitating States!' An Ethnographic Analysis of the ICMPD." In *The Politics of International Migration Management*, edited by Martin Geiger and Antoine Pécoud, 96–118. Houndmills: Palgrave Macmillan.

Hindman, Heather, and Robert Oppenheim. 2014. "Lines of Labor and Desire: 'Korean Quality' in Contemporary Kathmandu." *Anthropological Quarterly* 87 (2): 465–495.

Holland, Eugene. 2010. "Desire and Social Production." In *The Deleuze Dictionary*, edited by Adrian Parr, 67–69. Edinburgh: Edinburgh University Press.

Kennan, John, and James R. Walker. 2011. "The Effect of Expected Income on Individual Migration Decisions." *Econometrica* 79 (1): 211–251.

Kim, Youna. 2013. *Transnational Migration, Media and Identity of Asian Women: Diasporic Daughters*. London: Routledge.

Kim, Min Ji. 2015. *The Republic of Korea's Employment Permit System*. ILO International Migration Papers, No. 119.

Lawson, Victoria A. 2000. "Arguments Within Geographies of Movement: The Theoretical Potential of Migrants' Stories." *Progress in Human Geography* 24 (2): 173–189.

Lindquist, Johan A. 2009. *The Anxieties of Mobility: Migration and Tourism in the Indonesian Borderlands*. Honolulu: University of Hawaii Press.

Massumi, Brian. 1992. *A User's Guide to Capitalism and Schizophrenia: Deviations from Deleuze and Guattari*. Cambridge: MIT Press.
McCormack, Derek P., and Tim Schwanen. 2011. "Guest Editorial: The Space – Times of Decision Making." *Environment and Planning A* 43 (12): 2801–2818.
McKay, Deirdre. 2007. "'Sending Dollars Shows Feeling' – Emotions and Economies in Filipino Migration." *Mobilities* 2 (2): 175–194.
Nail, Thomas. 2015. *The Figure of the Migrant*. Stanford: Stanford University Press.
Ong, Aihwa. 2007. "Please Stay: Pied-a-Terre Subjects in the Megacity." *Citizenship Studies* 11 (1): 83–93.
O'Shea, Anthony. 2002. "Desiring Desire How Desire Makes Us Human, All Too Human." *Sociology* 36 (4): 925–940.
Papadopoulos, Dimitris, and Vassilis S. Tsianos. 2013. "After Citizenship: Autonomy of Migration, Organisational Ontology and Mobile Commons." *Citizenship Studies* 17 (2): 178–196.
Ravenstein, Ernest George. 1889. "The Laws of Migration." *Journal of the Royal Statistical Society* 52 (2): 241–301.
Robertson, Shanthi. 2013. *Transnational Student-Migrants and the State*. Houndmills: Palgrave Macmillan.
Rubinov, Igor. 2014. "Migrant Assemblages: Building Postsocialist Households with Kyrgyz Remittances." *Anthropological Quarterly* 87 (1): 183–215.
Shubin, Sergei. 2015. "Migration Timespaces: A Heideggerian Approach to Understanding the Mobile Being of Eastern Europeans in Scotland." *Transactions of the Institute of British Geographers* 40 (3): 350–361.
Simone, AbdouMaliq. 2010. *City Life from Jakarta to Dakar: Movements at the Crossroads*. London: Routledge.
Smith, Daniel W. 2007. "Deleuze and the Question of Desire: Toward an Immanent Theory of Ethics." *Parrhesia* 2: 66–78.
Tyner, James A. 2013. *Made in the Philippines*. London: Routledge.
Valentine, Gill, and Joanna Sadgrove. 2014. "Biographical Narratives of Encounter: The Significance of Mobility and Emplacement in Shaping Attitudes Towards Difference." *Urban Studies* 51 (9): 1979–1994.
Xiang, Biao, and Johan Lindquist. 2014. "Migration Infrastructure." *International Migration Review* 48 (1): S122–S148.

Forced to leave? The discursive and analytical significance of describing migration as forced and voluntary

Marta Bivand Erdal and Ceri Oeppen

ABSTRACT

This article examines voluntariness in migration decisions by promoting the acknowledgement of forced and voluntary migration as a continuum of experience, not a dichotomy. Studies on conflict-related migration and migration, in general, remain poorly connected, despite calls for interaction. This reflects the forced–voluntary dichotomy's stickiness within and beyond academia, which is closely connected to the political implications of unsettling it and potentially undermining migrants' protection rights. We delve into notions of the 'voluntariness' of migration and argue for the analytical need to relate evaluations of voluntariness to available alternatives. Drawing on qualitative research with people from Afghanistan and Pakistan coming to Europe, we hone in on three particular renderings of migration: migrants' own experiences, scholarly qualitative observations and labelling by immigration authorities. Analysing migration as stages in a process: leaving – journey (and transit) – arrival and settlement – return or onward migration, we highlight the specific effects of migration being described as being forced or voluntary. Labelling as 'forced' (or not) matters to migrants and states when asylum status is on the line. For migration scholars, it remains challenging to decouple these descriptions from state systems of migration management; though doing so enhances our understanding of the role voluntariness plays in migration decisions.

Introduction

Migration studies often utilises oppositional typologies to categorise different groups and experiences: skilled-unskilled; temporary-permanent; and, key to this article, forced–voluntary. However, the blurring of boundaries between categories is also regularly acknowledged, and most scholars prefer to think of such dichotomies as a spectrum of experiences (see Castles, De Haas, and Miller 2014; Fussell 2012; Richmond 1993).

Regarding the forced–voluntary distinction, whilst there may be identifiable extreme cases, most migrants' experiences of the degree of volition in their migration decisions means they fall somewhere in the blurry middle of the forced–voluntary spectrum. Even a cursory review of migrant experiences shows overlaps between migrants who are labelled as 'forced' or 'voluntary'. Fieldwork observations convince us of the impossibility of describing someone's decision to migrate as entirely voluntary or entirely forced. Making a clear-cut distinction between forced and voluntary migration is not acceptable from an empirical, and consequently, analytical, point of view, even if labelling for the sake of migration management upholds the notion (see also Carling 2017; Crawley and Skleparis 2017).

However, is it enough to point out the complexity and highlight the spectrum of experiences, before moving on? Can migration studies grapple with the drivers of migration and their connection to aspirations and desires (Carling and Collins 2018) without addressing the volition involved in migration? Whilst our fieldwork observations rightly encourage us to emphasise complexity, we, as migrations scholars, cannot – and should not – simply leave the discussion there. Because the distinction between forced and voluntary, as two very different forms of migration, has a tendency to stick around in academic work and policy, migration scholars must unpack the experienced, observed and labelled dimensions of this distinction. And we can do so by examining differing analytical and discursive constructions.

Firstly, if we as academics emphasise the 'mixed' nature of all migration, then what are the implications for those with particular protection needs and those with the right to refugee status under the 1951 Refugee Convention (Kumin 2014; Van Hear, Brubaker, and Bessa 2009; Van Heelsum 2016)? Secondly, migration management, as practised by many European countries, requires labelling migrants as forced or voluntary to sort them into bureaucratic categories such as asylum seeker, refugee, labour migrant, family reunification migrant and international student, amongst others; where the first two categories are seen as forced migrants and the latter three are seen as voluntary migrants.

Even if the particular terminology of forced and voluntary is not necessarily used in public discussions of migration, the academic categories of forced and voluntary can be mapped onto public categories of refugee/asylum seeker and economic migrant, respectively, at least in Europe. Bureaucratic distinctions and labels have discursive power, and the labelling of individuals as forced or voluntary impacts their migratory experiences.

We argue that it is not enough to simply point out that the distinction between forced and voluntary migration is complex. We propose that whilst migration scholars need to keep acknowledging the complexity of the degree and type of volition involved in migration decisions, we also need to further unpack the forced–voluntary spectrum. Our focus is thus on migration decisions, honing in on the question of when someone – in their own experience, via scholarly observations or through an immigration authority label – might be described as having been 'forced to leave', and how this matters analytically and discursively.

Our hope is to advance analytical discussion of voluntariness, choice and alternatives, whilst also seeking to tackle the stickiness of the forced–voluntary migration dichotomy from an analytical angle. Undertaking this is no simple task, and we aspire to encourage discussion, rather than to provide answers. Addressing the distinctions and similarities between forced and voluntary migration is fraught with dilemma. Unsettling the common understanding of a clear-cut 'forced migrant' may contribute to undermining the international refugee regime. However, it has also been argued that a presumed binary between forced and voluntary migrants has been instrumental in creating the figure of the 'illegal migrant' and 'bogus asylum seeker' – those *not deserving* of international protection (Casas-Cortes et al. 2015).

This article is positioned as a discussion piece with applications beyond any one migration context. That said, it is shaped by our longstanding ethnographic engagements with two migrant groups: one usually labelled as forced (Afghans) and one generally labelled as voluntary (Pakistanis). It is also shaped by the time of writing, as the 2015–2016 European 'crisis' over refugees and migration was unfolding. We start by investigating the effect of labelling and how labels can have discursive significance. We then discuss some of the ways the concept of volition has been addressed by scholars of migration and other disciplines. This is followed by a brief overview of Afghan and Pakistani migration, setting the stage to examine how voluntariness, choice and alternatives in migration decisions are experienced by migrants, observed by scholars and labelled by immigration authorities, as well as how they intersect and what their implications are.

The significance of labelling migration

Writing about conceptualising migration and displacement, Bakewell (2011) makes a strong case for unpicking the usage of 'migration' and 'displacement' as terms to describe a process, a condition and a category. This means that a migrant might be someone who is *doing* migration, who is *being* a migrant or someone who is being *described as* a migrant. Moreover, different actors may use the term 'migration' (or 'displacement') in these different ways without considering the implications of the different usages (2011).

Building on Bakewell's (2011) suggestions, we use analytical and discursive significance as a way to differentiate the implications of labelling migration as forced or voluntary. Following Foucault (1972 inter alia), discourse represents a way of thinking, which then has a significant effect on the social construction of 'reality' (e.g. through language). Crucially, discourse also checks the realms of possibility, what is and is not seen as acceptable (Butler 1997). In migration and refugee studies, the discourse and 'labels' (Zetter 1991, 2007) to describe migrants sway the selection of responses – which are 'acceptable' and which are even possible – to those migrants. Whether someone is discursively presented as an economic migrant or a refugee, for instance, majorly influences their treatment by immigration authorities and humanitarian actors. As Zetter (2007, 173) notes, labelling people as 'refugees' not only serves a descriptive purpose, but can also explain 'the complex and often disjunctive impacts of humanitarian intervention'. In other words, a key part of the discursive significance of identifying people as refugees, vis-à-vis other migrant categories, is how they will be treated.

If we accept the discursive (and normative, see Ottonelli and Torresi 2013) power of labelling someone as a forced or voluntary migrant, then we should also question those descriptions, especially being written, as they are, by powerful governments and international institutions. Are they accurate? Are they appropriate? As migration scholars, we should not just accept the discourses handed to us, but also recognise our own roles in creating, influencing and maintaining or disrupting them. In addition, we should question whether a discourse represents 'reality' as we see it through fieldwork observations and other research interactions. It is here that we get insight into migrants' experiences and their own interpretations of experiences, which are inevitably produced through migrants' execution of their agency in relation to prevailing constraints.

In referring to discursive and analytical significance, these are the dimensions we examine, including, on the one hand, the labelling of individuals into bureaucratic categories. On the other hand, there are the observed and experienced realities that are analytically produced through data collection and analysis. Encompassing migrants' lifeworlds and the role of agency, these dimensions necessarily become nuanced and complicated.

We acknowledge that by focusing on the forced–voluntary continuum, we run the risk of reifying extremes. To avoid doing so, we take a critical approach that questions not simply 'causes', but also responses, as they are mediated through migrants' agency and, in turn, do or do not trigger states' duties to protect individuals according to international obligations. The role of agency is crucial, as virtually no migration happens without a great deal of it in place. Nevertheless, migrant agency is often seen as suspect by restrictive immigration regimes, such as those seeking to control migration from Africa, the Middle East and Asia to Europe as well as from South America to North America. Following De Genova (2016), those labelled as refugees may be pitied as 'victims' of forced displacement whilst they reside in camps in neighbouring countries; yet, as soon as they show more 'entrepreneurial' agency by choosing to leave the camp and head farther afield, they become suspect, labelled as 'illegal migrants' or 'bogus asylum seekers', reflecting the discursive power of migrant labels and categories.

Despite their thematic dovetails, studies on conflict-related migration and migration, in general, remain poorly connected. Within the sub-discipline of forced migration studies, discussions about description – whether as forced migration studies, refugee studies or the study of conflict-related migration, war-time migration and war mobilities (see Harpviken 2009; Hathaway 2007; Lindley 2010; Lubkemann 2008a, 2008b) – reflect the definitional challenges of pinning down 'forced' migration as something analytically distinctive from 'voluntary' migration. What may be pinned down, though, is the usual context of violent conflict, which frequently proxies for a specification of which contexts are associated with forced migration and which are not. This has also been critiqued by scholars of such contexts, for example, Liberia (Lubkemann 2008a).

The literature in both migration studies and forced migration studies is somewhat limited in its analysis of the implications of volition on migration processes, despite forced–voluntary being a key dichotomy in typologies of migration (notable exceptions include Fussell 2012; Ottonelli and Torresi 2013). In forced migration studies, much of this debate has concerned the implications of expanding 'refugee studies' as a field focusing on those outside their country of origin due to a well-founded fear of persecution (as defined by the 1951 Refugee Convention), to 'forced migration studies' as a field that incorporates a much more diverse range of displaced people.[1] This has led to interesting discussions about the term 'forced', but the focus has been on the difference between being 'forced' by political factors recognisable under the 1951 Refugee Convention versus other factors (e.g. economic or environmental), and whether forced migration necessitates crossing an international border, or includes internal displacement.

Meanwhile, in mainstream migration studies, theorising around why people migrate has largely focussed on migrants assumed to be migrating voluntarily, rather than looking at the forced–voluntary spectrum as a whole. However, there is also an emerging limited body of work bringing to attention the counterpart to forced migration, namely 'involuntary immobility', where volition *is* a key concern (Carling 2002; Jónsson 2008; Lubkemann 2008b).

The difficulty in pinpointing whether someone's migration was entirely voluntary or entirely involuntary has led to a small, but compelling body of literature, which explores volition in more depth (see e.g. Bartram 2015; Long 2013; Ottonelli and Torresi 2013). In the following section, we draw on these studies as well as some non-migration research on the concept of voluntariness (see Colburn 2008; Olsaretti 2004) to examine current academic understandings of volition.

The role of volition in migration decisions and processes

'Voluntary' – meaning acted by choice, with free will and without compulsion – is a term regularly used to refer to migration types. However, there is a range of ways to understand it. Do we understand voluntary in terms of a totally free choice from a range of options? Or do we understand it as choosing the least worst choice from a limited or virtually non-existent range of options?

Whilst acknowledging that some people may migrate out of the 'joy' of mobility, for adventure and to see the world, the majority choose to migrate because they believe that physically moving to another place will lead to improvement in their and/or their family's living situation. 'Improvement' may take diverse forms (a better job, being closer to family, escaping a war zone, more pleasant weather, etc.). Consequently, a starting point for understanding volition in migration is the range and quality of alternatives available to potential migrants if they just stay where they are. In other words, to what extent will they be able to enjoy a reasonable quality of life without migrating? We might consider the migration less voluntary when the answer is 'not at all' rather than 'to some extent'. The perception of suitable options and necessity of alternatives – and the notion of a 'reasonable quality of life' – are subjective. Still, it is the premise of much conceptual literature, some of which we examine here, exploring voluntariness outside of migration studies.

For example, if we take a worker in a '3D' (dirty, dangerous and demeaning) job, we could argue that as long as they are not a slave then they are doing that job voluntarily. In neoclassical economics, a worker *voluntarily* gives labour in exchange for income because the alternative – no income – is worse. But is this acceptable? Is it enough to say that a worker in a 3D job is doing that work voluntarily because they are not enslaved, when the alternative to doing that job is perhaps destitution? For the libertarian philosopher Nozick (1974), voluntariness depends on non-infringement of rights. His case is that if another individual or the state's actions infringe on a person's rights, then we can consider their consequent choices coerced, rather than voluntary. Taking this approach, it is clear that the observer's view on what constitutes 'rights' will have an important bearing on whether they view actions to be coerced or voluntary.

To return to the example of the 3D worker, if we consider it the right of that worker to receive an income (for example in the form of welfare payments) by the state if they are unable to find acceptable non-demeaning work, then a lack of that alternative income might lead us to conclude that they were coerced into do that 3D job. This is a very different stance from Nozick (1974) whose view of rights minimised them to rights to life, liberty and property, and whose work suggests that he would have taken a dim view of the state taking such an expansive role as to provide welfare assistance (Kymlicka 2002). If we apply Nozick's (1974) understanding of voluntariness to migration, and if the potential migrant's rights to life, liberty and property were being infringed, then their migration would be non-voluntary. A case in point would involve the archetypal 'convention refugee', for example, an intellectual forced to leave Afghanistan in the late 1970s because the alternative was being imprisoned by the Communist government for their political views. This scenario does not portray a migrant leaving because they cannot find employment and, according to Nozick, they have no right to expect an external actor to provide employment in their current place of residence. The migration would thus be voluntary, even if the alternative was destitution, because the choice was made 'freely'.[2]

Like Long (2013, 160), we see Olsaretti's (1998, 2004) more expansive view of voluntariness as an improvement on Nozick's minimalist approach to rights. Whereas Nozick holds that someone who is 'free' (i.e. their rights to life, liberty and property are not being threatened) means their choices are voluntary, Olsaretti (1998) argues that freedom and voluntariness do not necessarily map onto each other. She illustrates this point through comparative examples, which we adapt here using migration-relevant scenarios.

> Example 1: Amira is an inhabitant of Syria, which she is free to leave. However, although she wants to leave, Amira knows that if she leaves she will not survive the hardship of the journey out of the country and she will die. Her choice to remain in Syria is *not* a voluntary one.
>
> Example 2: Bisrat is a national service conscript in Eritrea, meaning he is not free to leave the country. However, Eritrea has all Bisrat feels he needs and he does not want to leave, so he remains *voluntarily*. (after Olsaretti 1998, 71)

Olsaretti (1998) posits that a choice is voluntary when it is made in the context of acceptable alternatives *or* if the lack itself of alternatives is acceptable to the person making the choice. Bisrat does not make a choice based on a lack of alternatives because he is not concerned with the lack of alternatives; he is content with the alternatives he has – this determines whether or not his choice is voluntary. The above scenarios illustrate how freedom, the presence of acceptable alternatives and voluntariness do not necessarily coincide. Amira is free but staying involuntarily; Bisrat is not free but staying voluntarily. Both Nozick and Olsaretti take a philosophical approach to volition, aiming to demonstrate that a choice is *either* voluntary *or* involuntary. This contrasts to empirical research by migration scholars, which reinforces the difficulties in drawing such sharp distinctions. However, Olsaretti's (2004) argument – that choices must be made not only freely, but also in the context of acceptable alternatives – has been echoed by migration scholars (see Bartram 2015; Ottonelli and Torresi 2013).

To Olsaretti's work, Colburn (2008) makes an important addition: that the perception of acceptable alternatives is shaped by a person's beliefs and access to information. Acceptable alternatives are instrumental to whether a choice is voluntary or not (Bartram 2015). Migrants themselves, immigration authorities, migrant rights' activists (and other civil society, non-governmental organisations and UNHCR) also each have ideas of what is acceptable, as illustrated by the international refugee regime. The disjuncture between what is and is not acceptable is starkly illustrated by refugee status determination decisions that posit internal relocation to 'safe areas' as an acceptable alternative to asylum, thereby enabling the removal of rejected asylum seekers to insecure countries, such as Afghanistan.

This is the basic premise of Bartram's (2015) article, which points out that the majority of refugees are not physically forced to leave. Rather, finds Bartram, certain implications of staying (for example, being forced to change religion or being made a political prisoner) are recognised as an affront to human dignity and as unacceptable alternatives to fleeing, whereas other implications (for example, extreme poverty) are not seen in the same way. Thus, volition in relation to migration decisions is closely tied to available acceptable alternatives and the agency to act on those options. Whether someone's migration is labelled as voluntary or not, however, depends on the labellers' perception of what constitutes 'acceptable' alternatives. Ottonelli and Torresi's (2013) and Bartram's (2015) proposition of voluntariness results in many more of the worlds' migrants – international and internal – falling in the non-voluntary bracket than the 1951 Refugee Convention covers.

Another crucial insight from Olsaretti's (1998) work that has not yet been embraced by migration scholars is the distinction between primary and secondary choices. She argues that just because a choice is made voluntarily (or involuntarily) does not mean its subsequent related decisions are necessarily voluntary or involuntary. An example is given of a worker who might involuntarily work in an exploitative industry but might voluntarily choose to work for one employer over another; the voluntariness of the second-order choice does not prescribe the voluntariness of the original choice. Relating this to migrants, we may consider those who voluntarily leave their country of origin but then involuntarily put themselves in the hands of smugglers because there are no acceptable alternatives. Or, another example would be migrants who are forced to leave but then make voluntary choices about their mode of travel (Koser 2008). Such distinctions prove crucial because one of the main critiques of 'forced migration' is that all migrants exercise agency in their decision to migrate. However, following Olsaretti (2008), migrants exhibiting agency in their choices of how (or when or where) to migrate does not negate the possibility that they migrated involuntarily in the first place.

Afghan and Pakistani migration

The remainder of this article draws on our longstanding empirical engagement with Afghans and Pakistanis in Europe (specifically, the United Kingdom and Norway) (see Erdal 2012; Erdal and Oeppen 2017; Oeppen 2013). To reiterate, we endeavour to unpack where and how the distinction between forced and voluntary migration matters vis-à-vis migrant experiences, scholars' observations and labelling by immigration authorities. In this section, we outline our involvement in the field and briefly comment on the nature of Afghan and Pakistani international migration.

In the summer of 2001, as undergraduate students, we together conducted fieldwork among Afghan refugees in New Delhi (Bivand and Oeppen 2002). Our questioning in this article of categorising and labelling 'forced' and 'voluntary' migration was initially contextually and temporally informed by our studies: that fieldwork and a module called 'The Global Refugee Regime'. The urban refugees we engaged with in Delhi, mainly middle-class Afghans who fled Kabul after the toppling of the Soviet-backed regime in 1992 or during the ensuing civil war, were all seeking resettlement through UNCHR programmes. In striking contrast to media images of vulnerable fleeing masses, these individuals showed agency and were obviously on quests for a better life – not in India, which did not allow them to gain legal employment, but elsewhere, notably preferring North America, Scandinavia or Australia. Talking to our research participants about their future plans impressed upon us the need to examine migration as a process, a cycle or a trajectory, rather than a one-off event.

Broadly speaking, Afghan migration is often labelled as forced migration and Pakistani migration, as voluntary. These general categorisations stem from the region's recent history. Afghanistan has experienced war since 1979; against the Soviet Union in the 1980s, civil war in the early 1990s, followed by the Taliban regime until 2001 and the NATO-led military presence until 2014, and on-going insecurity. The number of casualties and level of displacement nationally and internationally concretely expose the high costs of these conflicts. For Afghan populations, these tolls provide the inevitable backdrop for the discursive use of the forced migration category and are a reminder of the undeniable persecution fears of many Afghans seeking asylum in Europe. Whilst the conflict dominates discussions around Afghan migration (Harpviken 2009), it is also predated by a historical culture of Afghan migration and mobility, largely connected to international trade networks (Marsden and Hopkins 2011).

By contrast, recent Pakistani migration has been dominated by regional male labour migration to the Gulf States, involving both short-term contracts and longer term migration. Pakistani migration has also included European and North American destination countries. That said, Pakistan is experiencing low-intensity conflict in several regions, most notably in Baluchistan and, since 2009, in the northwest. This violence along with the effects of the 'Global War on Terror', including drone attacks, have taken a heavy toll on civilian populations, resulting in deaths, injuries, disabilities and psychological harm.

The current situations in Afghanistan and Pakistan thus do not lend themselves to a simplistic divide in which migration from one is 'forced' and migration from the other, 'voluntary'. Rather, the categories must be unpacked, analysing degrees of volition in individual cases and how forced and voluntary are constructed. In the next section, we use a stylised migration trajectory as a framework to explore the analytical and discursive significance of describing migration as forced and voluntary at different stages. There are of course limitations to seeing migration as a trajectory (or cycle, Black and Koser 1999) with identifiable stages, rather than a more fluid on-going process. For the purposes of our analysis, however, we found it useful to break it down into stages.

Stages of the migration process

Examining the decision to leave on a forced–voluntary continuum, we consider stages of migration including leaving, the journey, entrance, settlement, return and remigration, onward migration. We explore where and when differing descriptions of volition matter for the individuals involved, as we observe them and how they themselves describe their experiences, but also in terms of categorisation by immigration authorities. Aiming to move beyond merely accepting that the distinction is complex, we note how and where the distinction is more or less relevant and where there are intersections of experiences, observations and labelling as forced or voluntary migrants.

Of course, there are plenty of Afghans in Pakistan and Iran, and migrant workers from both Afghanistan and Pakistan find their way to the Gulf States and farther afield in Asia.

Nevertheless, our fieldwork has been about migration to Europe, so we focus upon that trajectory here.

Leaving

As reflected in our title question, 'forced to leave?', it is the circumstances and reasons for leaving that unlock potential protection from the international refugee regime. This is a fact despite migrants'[3] trajectories being complex and migration reasons being likely to evolve in the run-up to, during and after the actual decision to leave, where the degree of volition and the alternatives available will vary, for the initial decision, as well as en route. Reasons to leave are always compound – comprising reasons that are experienced, observed and labelled – and result in varying analytical and discursive constructions. If a broad interpretation of voluntariness is applied – where a lack of alternatives is the criteria – a different discursive construction of what constitutes being 'forced to leave' emerges, than if it is the 1951 Refugee Convention criteria which are applied, or indeed broader 'humanitarian leave to remain' definitions.

Consider, for example, Amir,[4] a young Afghan going to Europe. His decision to leave, as he experiences it, may be forced on several levels: due to the on-going conflict and insecurity in Afghanistan, but the decision to leave might have been taken by his parents, thus adding to his experience of feeling forced and without alternatives.

However, because of that on-going conflict, millions of Afghans have been displaced to neighbouring countries, particularly Pakistan and Iran. Over 35 years of conflict means many Afghans have been born and brought up in these countries. Amir's family lives in Pakistan, where they experience insecurity due to discrimination and insufficient opportunities for livelihood (Human Rights Watch 2015). Thus, at least three reasons compel Amir to experience his leaving as forced: the conflict in Afghanistan; the decision being taken by his parents; his immediate insecurity in Pakistan.

Meanwhile, within Pakistan, albeit on a different scale than in Afghanistan, there is displacement due to insecurity, low-intensity conflicts, earthquakes and flooding. Thus, when Parvez leaves Pakistan, his experience is that he has no alternatives, other than to leave, due to insecurity, the misfortune of prematurely losing his father and lacking contacts who might have helped him secure a livelihood locally.

Amir's and Parvez's experiences of their decisions to leave focus on lacking alternatives, with conflict, family circumstances and livelihood opportunities playing a role. From our point of view, their decisions to leave might be analytically constructed as forced due to lacking alternatives. Yet, when it comes to their labelling within the international refugee regime, there are certain distinctions between the two cases. Labelling by immigration authorities in countries of asylum varies, as individual histories and experiences are scrutinised; an assessment may start from an assumption that Parvez's migration is not forced and Amir's is, based on their country of origin. Another difference in the circumstances that frame their departures is the hope of the migration being labelled 'forced' and so being able to apply for and possibly obtain asylum, which Amir nourishes, whilst Parvez sees as unattainable.

The decision to leave might be more or less forced depending on how we interpret available alternatives. Do we expect alternatives to exist at merely the level of survival, or beyond? Analytical and discursive constructions of leaving as forced depend not just on the experienced and observed levels of voluntariness, but also on *the anticipation of particular labelling* by immigration authorities in Europe. It is worth noting that many of our research participants, from both Afghanistan and Pakistan, felt forced – in some sense of the word – to leave.

The journey

For Afghans and Pakistanis able to obtain a visa, movement is relatively easy, usually involving flying to Europe, as for the small number who comprise resettlement quotas. For Amir and Parvez, unable to access means to travel and enter another country legally, the journey itself becomes a dangerous, clandestine endeavour (Koser 2008). The journey is where the differences between Afghan and Pakistani migrants are the smallest. Whether the decision to leave is constructed as forced or voluntary makes little difference at this stage. For those who have no legal means to enter Europe, differences in journey experiences are related to financial resources (and other forms of capital), rather than whether their decision to leave was more, less or not at all forced.

Attention has increasingly turned to the journey itself, including migration brokers and the migration 'industry' more broadly (Baird and van Liempt 2016; Gammeltoft-Hansen and Sorensen 2013; Xiang and Lindquist 2014). In our encounters with Afghans and Pakistanis, such as Amir and Parvez, we found little difference in modes of arranging mobility through migration brokers (see also Ahmad 2013). The business of 'fixing' migration enables people to obtain fake passports and visas and to use what are essentially travel agent services that organise physical transport, border-crossings and the circumvention of border controls. Using the services of 'fixers' and smugglers does not make the journey itself more or less forced by nature – it is simply the means to enter Europe (Koser 2008). For migrants who are trafficked, the issue of volition is to a greater extent taken out of their hands. However, none of our research participants were the victims of trafficking, so this particular issue falls outside the scope of this article.

The journey, usually interrupted along the way, constitutes instances of mobility and immobility (Collyer 2007; Crawley et al. 2016). Routes, like those followed by Amir and Parvez, would run through Turkey, into southern Europe and Greece, and an extended stay in Turkey or Greece would not be uncommon. On the Turkish side, most transit migrants would seek to cross the border and not make efforts to regularise their status. For the majority of migrants from Afghanistan and Pakistan, entering Europe happens without valid entry visas, making their journeys precarious. They tend to circumvent border controls, planning once in Europe to, as in Amir's case, apply for asylum or, as in the case of Parvez, who lacked clear *strategies* but had clear *aspirations*, become regularised (Abdin and Erdal 2016; Carling and Collins 2018).

Migrants' own experiences of a forced decision to leave remain significant during the journey, being tied in with hopes for eventually applying for asylum. During the journey, the degree of volition in the decision to leave is of little analytical significance. From the immigration authorities' point of view, it makes a potential difference, but only in relation to a future asylum claim, which may or may not be filed. We see therefore how during the journey, distinctions between forced and voluntary migration effectively become insignificant. This underscores how immigration controls in Europe have an overarching effect on *the discursive construction* and survival of these labels. Migrants' assessments – of their own experiences and, equally, their chance of convincing immigration authorities of the forced nature of their decision to leave – are salient for onward migration beyond transit. Thus demonstrated are the intersections of experienced, observed and labelled dimensions of volition in migration decisions.

Entrance and settlement

When Amir arrived in Sweden, he applied for asylum at the local police station. Entrance is where the distinction between those who do and do not stand a chance of being labelled as forced matters. Amir and Parvez were both in Greece for extended periods, but for Amir it was always a transit stay and for Parvez it became the destination. Both could seek asylum in Greece or pursue further travel and seek asylum elsewhere in Europe. For Amir, it was important to make sure he did not apply for asylum in Greece, in light of the Dublin Regulation (Koser and Kuschminder 2015).

Both men's stay in Greece was, in practice, similar. Their future prospects differed, however; Amir believed it possible to apply for asylum in Europe, but for Parvez, this was not relevant. Meanwhile, both felt a responsibility towards their family, wanting to remit money to settle the debt with their migration brokers. For Parvez, a future plan was to go to Spain, joining relatives who had regularised their status there. Parvez's cousin was a student in Norway, having obtained a scholarship to pursue a degree there, which sensitised Parvez to the existence of alternative routes to entry, although they were not accessible to him.

Thus, entrance is a relative construction. For Amir, formal entrance was in Sweden, where he applied for asylum. For Parvez, formal entrance might never happen or might be found in Spain in the future. In both cases, the location of existing social networks mattered. For many journeying Afghans, like Amir, the stages of transit and entrance become conflated, as there are multiple instances of 'entering' before the final 'entrance' and the filing of an asylum claim. Here, European migration management is crucial in shaping the migration process of individuals, often more so than whether or not the decision to leave was experienced – or observed – as forced or voluntary (Ghosh 2000).

Settlement is regularly conflated with the stages of transit and entrance as these actions occur repeatedly. Here, we focus on the process of settlement occurring when a destination, however it may be defined, has been reached. For Afghans who, like Amir, apply for asylum, the first period during which the asylum claim is being processed is one of uncertainty. The salience of state systems of evaluation of asylum claims is key to how experiences of being 'forced to leave' are performed (Kea and Roberts-Holmes 2013), in response to the understandings of persecution put forward by bureaucracies. This is a crucial intersection of experiencing, observing and labelling decisions to migrate as forced or not – in the outcome of an asylum claim, there is little room for debate: asylum is either granted or not. You are either defined as a 'forced migrant', or you are not.

For those who get asylum, settlement in many European countries follows a fixed strategy comprising language and skills-training programmes that aim to boost refugees' financial and social self-sufficiency over time. For the rejected, regardless of their experience of a migration decision as forced or not, return migration, onward migration and forced return are common. That is, provided they do not 'go underground'. For Pakistani migrants entering southern Europe, like Parvez, few roads lead to legal residency. Instead, migrants' own entrepreneurship and networks prove defining of settlement processes, determining how they find a way to earn a living and a place to stay (Ahmad 2013).

In practice, for Afghans with rejected asylum claims, strategies and experiences are similar to those of Pakistani migrants without a regular status in Europe. The analytical construction of migrants with rejected asylum claims being 'forced to leave' depends not only on the actual experienced or observed volition and available alternatives. To a great deal, it also depends on the interpreted legitimacy of immigration authorities' labelling of migrants as forced (with access to protection granted) or not. Meanwhile, migrants, like Parvez, are more often than not analytically constructed as voluntary; this is a direct result of being labelled as voluntary in migration management terms, rather than evaluating experiences and observations of available alternatives and thus a migrant's volition in deciding to leave. Authorities' power to label migrants, based on evaluations of the nature of their decision to leave, impacts analytical and discursive constructions. Bureaucratically, the frame of what is forced is relatively narrow and specific, leaving few descriptive shades between black and white. It is a stark contrast to any experienced and observed realities, which are far more nuanced.

Return or onward migration

For both Afghans and Pakistanis in Europe, the issue of return is less related to the voluntariness of their initial migration and more related to immigration status. With a time-restricted student visa in Norway, Parvez's cousin has a return for a specific date; if she does not respect it, her status will become irregular and she risks deportation. For Parvez, living as an irregular migrant, staying may be a question of how likely he is to be detected and deported, but it is also a question of family matters and how well he can cope. Many migrants do return to their origin country, at least temporarily, and some circulate between countries over time. For Amir, who was granted asylum, return or onward migration is a question of voluntariness, within some constraints, where the evaluation of his initial migration as forced proves instrumental, for if his asylum claim had been rejected he would have become deportable.

Experiences and observations of decisions to leave as more or less forced are relatively insignificant in the face of immigration authorities' return policies. For them, it is the evaluation of someone's decision to leave as forced, deemed valid according to set criteria, which makes a difference. However, analytical and discursive constructions as forced and voluntary may have an effect on public sympathy and support, as seen, for example, in anti-deportation campaigns (Gibney 2013).

On the whole, migrants like Parvez and his cousin would not be discursively constructed as deserving of public sympathy in the face of deportation. Meanwhile, migrants from Afghanistan, with its well-known insecurity, would likelier be seen as victims of incorrect evaluations concerning whether or not migration was forced. The distinction between forced or voluntary decisions to leave in the first place thus sticks throughout the asylum-determination process, and has a great impact on Afghans with rejected claims. Europe has also seen a rise in Pakistanis who file asylum claims, which frequently get rejected and lead to deportations, or who are intercepted as irregular migrants and become subjected to deportation.

Migration is neither a linear process nor, necessarily, a circular one (Harpviken 2014). Among those with refugee status in Europe or, more broadly, third-country nationals acquiring European citizenships, onward migration within Europe as well as to North America is relatively common. Amir contemplated the idea of one day joining relatives in California.

Meanwhile, onward migration regularly occurs among those without legal documents, sometimes seeking opportunities of legality. We see this among Pakistani migrants moving towards Spain or Afghans moving to Italy and applying for asylum there to access mobility within the rest of the Schengen Area.

For those migrants deported from European countries back to Afghanistan or Pakistan, onward migration might essentially be remigration to Europe. Often this involves migration between Afghanistan and Iran or Pakistan whilst preparing for remigration to destinations further afield (Majidi 2009). Among Pakistani migrants who are forcibly returned to Pakistan, remigration to Europe as well as labour migration to the Gulf States is common (Koser and Kuschminder 2015).

It is worth noting, too, that what might start as a voluntary migration could involve forced onward migration, or vice versa. For example, West African migrants arriving in Europe, having been forced to leave Libya in recent years, where their initial migration was more voluntary, but their secondary migration was shaped by the conflict in Libya. In such cases, the importance of countries of origin and nationality may be over-emphasised in labelling migrants as forced or voluntary, particularly for refugee status determination.

Conclusion

Embarking on this article, we stated that it is not enough to point out the complexity of the forced-voluntary continuum. Whilst many academics have rightly noted that defining an individual as a forced or a voluntary migrant is highly problematic (Castles, De Haas, and Miller 2014; DeWind 2007; Fussell 2012) – and even more so when describing migrant flows en masse – the distinction sticks in academic work and public discourse. Following Bakewell (2011) and Zetter (1991, 2007), we believe that semantics are relevant to consider, as are considerations of who is doing the labelling and what the discursive work of those labels entails. There are also important distinctions between self-identification and imposed labels; an analytical description of an individual's migration decisions along a forced-voluntary continuum is necessarily more reflective of the complexity of individual experiences, agency and contextual circumstances than a binary labelling of forced or not. Yet, analytical descriptions of the processes of migration decisions are part of a broader landscape, within which we must acknowledge that discursive constructions of migration, and the labels attached to them, carry a 'normative weight'. How a migrant is labelled may have significant implications on treatment from receiving states (see Ottonelli and Torresi 2013).

An analytical understanding indicates that by applying criteria of voluntariness and available alternatives, many migration decisions are not seen as entirely voluntary. A discursive construction of 'the migrant' or 'the refugee' veers away from the complexity of reality and reifies the binary of forced vs. voluntary; it turns it into two boxes between which migrant experience necessarily can and must be divided. The discursive significance of describing migration as forced or voluntary matters to states, as to whether or not individuals are seen as legitimate asylum seekers, with the right to international protection. Analytically, the salience of describing migration as forced and voluntary lies in the intellectual pursuit of better understanding the role of volition in migration decisions, under differing conditions. In analytical terms, resisting the dichotomy of forced vs. voluntary, which largely sticks for migration management reasons, should lead neither to using the nebulous 'mixed migration' term nor accepting the discursively constructed binary of 'forced' and 'voluntary'.

A state may have legitimate reasons for approaching border control, migration management and humanitarian protection as it does, and these may stray from an individual migrant's perspective. Forced and voluntary migration is also a distinction made by migrants themselves, whereby someone fleeing a violent conflict may be recognised by other migrants as having *no choice.* Despite feeling they had no other acceptable alternatives, but to migrate in pursuit of a life that could be lived, some migrants may effectively have had more of a choice. And here the significance of how migration is described returns: whether a migrant is labelled as forced or voluntary within an immigration system majorly impacts their access to protection.

We readily recognise that many migrants forced to flee the conflict in Afghanistan have legitimate needs for protection. We also acknowledge the unsettling idea that questioning migration categories may contribute to destabilising an already eroded refugee regime in Europe (Koser and Martin 2011). Yet, the discursive and analytical implications of describing migration as forced and voluntary need to be scrutinised. There must be better ways of safeguarding needs for protection than the world currently offers. One course of action might be for scholars to challenge the status quo more, not only by deconstructing government labelling, but also by further unpacking the assumed dichotomy between forced and voluntary migration, thereby examining voluntariness.

As Ottonelli and Torresi (2013) caution, discussions of the forced–voluntary migration continuum risk becoming circular if policy hinges on particular interpretations of volition in migration, whilst scholarly approaches to volition are also built on those very policy definitions. We therefore support the stance that '[i]f other principles than the recognition of migrants' agency must come into play, they need to do it openly, rather than under the guise of an unorthodox and inconsistent notion of voluntariness' (Ottonelli and Torresi 2013, 810).

The purpose of describing migrants as forced and voluntary analytically and discursively is different in intent, but it is also different according to scale. In migrants' experiences as well as scholars' qualitative, field-based observations, the analytical unit is often the individual or family. For the state, whilst protection is determined individually, the scale of the analytical unit is that of groups: be it of refugees from particular conflict areas or another mass of people feeding into the broader category of 'immigrants'. States' migration management efforts are not individual-level; they target collectively. Thus there is a discrepancy in the scales to which attention is being paid reflective of the primary interests of different actors: of controlling populations on the part of states; of finding safety and quality of life, on the part of migrants; and for scholars, analytically trying to understand what is going on and why.

The use of 'mixed migration' makes us, like many others who study migration, uncomfortable. What we see empirically is that people migrate from both Afghanistan and Pakistan for a diverse set of reasons. Different degrees of volition are involved, and in many cases across both countries no acceptable alternatives to migration can be found. If emphasising that mix means that migrants in need of protection are less likely to receive it, or must go through multiple stages of 'proving' that they need it, then emphasising the fluidity of the forced–voluntary continuum can have negative implications for our research participants (Bakewell 2011, 15).

However, as migration scholars we have an obligation to move beyond a statement acknowledging complexity. We must dare to grasp what has so far been analytically difficult, even if that means destabilising the fragile and dysfunctional refugee regime. The current need for humanitarian assistance and relief to people fleeing violent conflict in Europe's neighbouring areas is obvious. Meanwhile, enormous resources are invested in seeking to control Europe's borders, to limited avail. Yet, asking the obvious question – what if border control was not the primary focus, but rather the lives of those in desperate humanitarian circumstances? – is not politically permissible in the public debate in European countries.

Whilst states may have particular priorities relating to control and management, scholars of migration should be free to choose which perspectives are best to apply. A state-centred analysis is arguably no more valid, reasonable or scientific than one emphasising the experiences of migrants who are differently placed along the forced–voluntary continuum. Some are in need of protection; all are in search of a future in which life may be lived.

Notes

1. For a key discussion in this debate, see Hathaway (2007) and responses to that article in the same issue of the *Journal of Refugee Studies*.
2. For a similar discussion relating Nozick's ideas to the notion of voluntary repatriation, see Long (2013).
3. For ease of expression, in this section we use 'migrant' as an umbrella term to describe people moving (including refugees and others labelled as forced migrants).
4. Names used are pseudonyms, which were created for compound characters. We collated details of migration trajectories from several individuals in order to present 'typical' examples, where the point is not any one individual's story, but the fact that such trajectories are shared by many migrants. We chose to focus more on young male examples, reflective of current migration flows to Europe from Afghanistan and Pakistan.

Acknowledgements

The authors are indebted to our Afghan and Pakistani research participants in various locations over the years, for their trust and willingness to share experiences and stories. Also, to Khalid Koser and Tony O'Connor, who in their undergraduate lectures ignited an interest in questions of international migration and refugee protection, encouraged our first fieldwork plans, and provided analytical, as well as practical guidance. The authors are also grateful to the anonymous reviewers, and to the special issue editors Francis Collins and Jørgen Carling, for feedback which has helped develop our argument.

Disclosure statement

No potential conflict of interest was reported by the authors.

References

Abdin, Z., and M. B. Erdal. 2016. "Remittance-Sending among Pakistani Taxi-Drivers in Barcelona and Oslo: Implications of Migration-Trajectories and the Protracted Electricity Crisis in Pakistan." *Migration and Development* 5 (3): 378–393.

Ahmad, A. N. 2013. *Masculinity, Sexuality and Illegal Migration: Human Smuggling from Pakistan to Europe*. Farnham: Ashgate.

Baird, T., and I. van Liempt. 2016. "Scrutinising the Double Disadvantage: Knowledge Production in the Messy Field of Migrant Smuggling." *Journal of Ethnic and Migration Studies* 42 (3): 400–417.

Bakewell, O. 2011. "Conceptualising Displacement and Migration: Processes, Conditions, and Categories." In *The Migration-Displacement Nexus: Patterns, Processes, and Policies*, edited by K. Koser, and S. Martin, 14–28. Oxford: Berghahn Books.

Bartram, D. 2015. "Forced Migration and "Rejected Alternatives": A Conceptual Refinement." *Journal of Immigrant & Refugee Studies* 13 (4): 439–456.

Bivand, M., and C. Oeppen. 2002. "Resettlement: The Only Chance for Long-Term Security?" *Forced Migration Review* 13: 31.

Black, R., and K. Koser, eds. 1999. *The End of the Refugee Cycle? Refugee Repatriation and Reconstruction*. Oxford: Berghahn.

Butler, J. 1997. *Excitable Speech: A Politics of the Performative*. New York: Routledge.

Carling, J. 2002. "Migration in the Age of Involuntary Immobility: Theoretical Reflections and Cape Verdean Experiences." *Journal of Ethnic and Migration Studies* 28 (1): 5–42.

Carling, J. 2017. *Refugee Advocacy and the Meaning of 'Migrants'*. PRIO Policy Brief 2/2017. Oslo: PRIO.

Carling, J., and F. Collins. 2018. "Aspiration, Desire and Drivers of Migration." *Journal of Ethnic and Migration Studies* 44 (6): 909–926. doi:10.1080/1369183X.2017.1384134.

Casas-Cortes, M., S. Cobarrubias, N. De Genova, G. Garelli, G. Grappi, C. Heller, S. Hess, et al. 2015. "New Keywords: Migration and Borders." *Cultural Studies* 29 (1): 55–87.

Castles, S., H. De Haas, and M. J. Miller. 2014. *The Age of Migration*. Oxford: Macmillan.

Colburn, B. 2008. "Debate: The Concept of Voluntariness." *Journal of Political Philosophy* 16 (1): 101–111.

Collyer, M. 2007. "In-Between Places: Trans-Saharan Transit Migrants in Morocco and the Fragmented Journey to Europe." *Antipode* 39 (4): 668–690.

Crawley, H., F. Düvell, K. Jones, S. McMahon, and N. Sigona. 2016. Destination Europe? Understanding the Dynamics and Drivers of Mediterranean Migration in 2015. *MEDMIG Final report* www.medmig.info/research-brief-desination-europe.pdf.

Crawley, H., and D. Skleparis. 2017. "Refugees, Migrants, Neither or Both: Categorical Fetishism and the Politics of Bounding in Europe's 'Migration Crisis'." *Journal of Ethnic and Migration Studies*. doi:10.1080/1369183X.2017.1348224

De Genova, N. 2016. The "European" Question: Migration, Race, and Postcoloniality. *Symposium: The Refugee Crisis. Whose Crisis Is It? Where Is It?* 12 May 2016. Brighton: University of Brighton.

DeWind, J. 2007. "Response to Hathaway." *Journal of Refugee Studies* 20 (3): 381–385.

Erdal, M. B. 2012. "Who Is the Money for? Remittances Within and Beyond the Household in Pakistan." *Asian and Pacific Migration Journal* 21 (4): 437–457.

Erdal, M. B., and C. Oeppen. 2017. "Forced to Return? Agency and the Role of Post-Return Mobility for Psychological Wellbeing among Returnees to Afghanistan, Pakistan and Poland." In *Return Migration and Psychosocial Wellbeing: Discourses, Policy-Making and Outcomes for Migrants and their Families*, edited by Z. Vathi, and R. King, 39–55. London: Routledge.

Foucault, M. 1972. *The Archaeology of Knowledge*. Translated by A. M. Sheridan Smith. New York: Pantheon.

Fussell, E. 2012. "Space, Time, and Volition: Dimensions of Migration Theory." In *The Oxford Handbook of the Politics of International Migration*, edited by M. R. Rosenblum, and D. J. Tichenor, 25–52. New York: Oxford University Press.

Gammeltoft-Hansen, T., and N. N. Sorensen, eds. 2013. *The Migration Industry and the Commercialization of International Migration*. Abingdon: Routledge.

Ghosh, B., ed. 2000. *Managing Migration: Time for a New International Regime?* Oxford: Oxford University Press.

Gibney, M. 2013. "Deportation, Crime, and the Changing Character of Membership in the United Kingdom." In *The Borders of Punishment: Migration, Citizenship, and Social Exclusion*, edited by K. Franko Aas, and M. Bosworth, 218–236. Oxford: Oxford University Press.

Harpviken, K. B. 2009. *Social Networks and Migration in Wartime Afghanistan*. Basingstoke: Palgrave Macmillan.

Harpviken, K. 2014. "Split Return: Transnational Household Strategies in Afghan Repatriation." *International Migration* 52 (6): 57–71.

Hathaway, J. C. 2007. "Forced Migration Studies: Could We Agree Just to 'Date'?" *Journal of Refugee Studies* 20 (3): 349–369.

Human Rights Watch. 2015. What Are You Doing Here? Police Abuses Against Afghans in Pakistan. *Report*. New York: Human Rights Watch.

Jónsson, G. 2008. Migration Aspirations and Immobility in a Malian Soninke Village, *Working paper 10*, Oxford: International Migration Institute.

Kea, P. J., and G. Roberts-Holmes. 2013. "Producing Victim Identities: Female Genital Mutilation and the Politics of Asylum Claims in the United Kingdom." *Identities* 20 (1): 96–113.

Koser, K. 2008. "Why Migrant Smuggling Pays." *International Migration* 46 (2): 3–26.

Koser, K., and K. Kuschminder. 2015. *Comparative Research on the Assisted Voluntary Return and Reintegration of Migrants*. Geneva: IOM.

Koser, K., and S. Martin, eds. 2011. *The Migration-Displacement Nexus: Patterns, Processes, and Policies*. Oxford: Berghahn Books.

Kumin, J. 2014. "The Challenge of Mixed Migration by Sea." *Forced Migration Review*, 45: 49–51.

Kymlicka, W. 2002. *Contemporary Political Philosophy: An Introduction*. 2nd ed.Oxford: Oxford University Press.

Lindley, A. 2010. "Leaving Mogadishu: Towards a Sociology of Conflict-Related Mobility." *Journal of Refugee Studies* 23 (1): 2–22.

Long, K. 2013. *The Point of No Return: Refugees, Rights, and Repatriation*. Oxford: Oxford University Press.

Lubkemann, S. C. 2008a. "Involuntary Immobility: On a Theoretical Invisibility of Forced Migration Studies." *Journal of Refugee Studies* 21 (4): 454–475.

Lubkemann, S. C. 2008b. *Culture in Chaos: An Anthropology of the Social Condition in War*. Chicago: University of Chicago Press.

Majidi, N. 2009. *Understanding the Return and Reintegration Process of Afghan Returnees from the UK*. Kabul: Altai Consulting.

Marsden, M., and B. D. Hopkins. 2011. *Fragments of the Afghan Frontier*. London: Hurst.

Nozick, R. 1974. *Anarchy, State, and Utopia*. New York: Basic Books.

Oeppen, C. 2013. "A Stranger at 'Home': Interactions Between Transnational Return Visits and Integration for Afghan-American Professionals." *Global Networks* 13 (2): 261–278.

Olsaretti, S. 1998. "Freedom, Force and Choice: Against the Rights-Based Definition of Voluntariness." *Journal of Political Philosophy* 6 (1): 53–78.

Olsaretti, S. 2004. *Liberty, Desert and the Market: A Philosophical Study*. Cambridge: Cambridge University Press.

Ottonelli, V., and T. Torresi. 2013. "When is Migration Voluntary?" *International Migration Review* 47 (4): 783–813.

Richmond, A. H. 1993. "Reactive Migration: Sociological Perspectives on Refugee Movements." *Journal of Refugee Studies* 6 (1): 7–24.

Van Hear, N., R. Brubaker, and T. Bessa. 2009. *Managing Mobility for Human Development: The Growing Salience of Mixed Migration*. MPRA paper no. 19202. Oxford: UNDP.

Van Heelsum, A. 2016. "Why Migration Will Continue: Aspirations and Capabilities of Syrians and Ethiopians with Different Educational Backgrounds." *Ethnic and Racial Studies* 39 (8): 1301–1309.

Xiang, B., and J. Lindquist. 2014. "Migration Infrastructure." *International Migration Review* 48 (s1): S122–S148.

Zetter, R. 1991. "Labelling Refugees: Forming and Transforming a Bureaucratic Identity." *Journal of Refugee Studies* 4 (1): 39–62.

Zetter, R. 2007. "More Labels, Fewer Refugees: Remaking the Refugee Label in an Era of Globalization." *Journal of Refugee Studies* 20 (2): 172–192.

OPEN ACCESS

Shifting migration aspirations in second modernity

Elisabeth Scheibelhofer

ABSTRACT

This article explores the aspirations of Western European emigrants as part of wider processes of life course and self-development within what has been called 'second modernity'. Starting from the observation that migration often happens in stages, the article focuses on the changing meaning and content of aspirations within migratory projects. Furthermore, in order to understand the specific place chosen for migration, a multi-scalar approach is proposed. The analysis is based on two empirical studies addressing migration experiences of Austrians migrating to the United States during the 1990s and 2000s. The empirical material is drawn from qualitative interviews that explore the aspirations, realisations and evaluations of migrants after moving abroad. The article concludes by highlighting the importance of situating aspirations for migration to on-going broader societal changes by applying theoretical concepts such as second modernity and multi-scalar approaches. Migrants' experiences and meaning-making are shaped by these societal developments and contribute to them via their everyday activities.

Introduction

As this journal's special issue highlights, theoretically oriented research on aspiration and migration is scarce (Carling and Collins 2018). It is even rarer when we consider the aspirations of migrants from the so-called Western European countries. From a social scientific point of view, it is a rather neglected form of emigration compared with emigration from other world regions (Dijkstra, Garcilazo, and McCann 2015; Zamora-Kapoor and Coller 2014). Whenever typologies of migration include movements from the Western European countries, the studies are usually only of a few occupational groups, such as managers, diplomats, artists and scientists engaged abroad (Green and Weil 2007; Scheibelhofer 2006). A number of case studies, however, show that other groups of people – in this respect hitherto largely ignored – emigrate as well (Ackers and Stalford 2007; Breivik 2012; Hall and Hardill 2014). Still, the research carried out so far discusses the question of aspirations only within the framework of specific group motives studied, for example, diplomats (Niedner-Kalthoff 2006), international aid workers (Roth 2012) and individuals moving with religious congregations (Hüwelmeier 2010).

Yet, for European migrants, in general, aspirations are no trivial matter. This article, therefore, examines the changing aspirations of European migrants who have settled or are still settling in their new country of residence, rather than those with migration aspirations that are not (yet) realised (for individuals still at home who aspire to migrate, see e.g. Bal and Willems 2014).

Aspirations discussed in this article are perceived as hopes, plans, ambitions or goals that can be clearly formulated or kept rather vague (Gutman and Akerman 2008). In terms of temporality, aspirations are a two-sided coin as they simultaneously address the present and the future. These aspirations are also likely to be connected to social class and milieu (Lowe and Krahn 2000). Aspirations can be defined as the 'ability to identify and set goals for the future, while being inspired in the present to work toward those goals' (Quaglia and Cobb 1996). These abilities and consequent aspirations are perceived as embedded in a specific social context (Ray 2006). Within the context of migration, it is important to note that aspirations are rather enduring; however, they are not to be expected to stay entirely stable over time because they can also be shifted by biographical changes such as employment, migration, having children and retirement. Moreover, changes in social contexts, brought on by broader societal transformations, also change individuals' aspirations.

A biographical perspective helps us understand such changes in aspirations in that it can take multiple forms of knowledge into account.[1] Aspirations are part of our biographical stocks of knowledge, or *Wissensbestände* (Berger and Luckmann 1972), that are formed through individuals' everyday life experiences and the socially constructed interpretations connected to them (Wohlrab-Sahr 1997). In that sense, aspirations are an important part of our broader action orientations which are not situational but rather enduring through the life course, influencing how individuals act and react over longer periods of time (Scheibelhofer 2003).

Most studies on migrant aspirations focus on persons in or from economically deprived world regions (Carling 2002; Van Meeteren, Engbersen, and Van San 2009; Wissink, Düvell, and van Eerdewijk 2013). Instead, I concentrate on Austrians as a case study of Western Europeans who have already left Europe for the United States. While research on migrant aspirations has concentrated on social upward mobility and/or securing survival, my interviewees did not share comparable aspirations. It was, therefore, necessary to reconstruct the aspirations analytically and use apt theoretical frameworks for doing so. In this regard, the concept of second modernity was helpful (Beck and Grande 2010; Beck and Lau 2005) because it deals with the question of which life courses are most probable under given conditions and how they may emerge. The effects of individualisation tendencies prove to be of paramount importance here: neither corporatist orders nor social classes offer individuals social anchorage. Likewise, stable family relationships no longer last a lifetime, with individuals themselves becoming 'a life-world reproduction unit of social matters' (Beck 1986, 209). Despite constraints on directing one's own life plan, we also notice a growing consistency of individual biographies and positions. Institutions, such as the labour market, that produce differentiated living situations also bring about their uniformity. In an effort to lead a meaningful life, an individual must put more effort into planning life pursuits. Such plans must, however, be flexible enough and subject to continuous change so as to adapt to various conditions. The individual is thus conceived of as a 'quasi-subject' (Beck, Bonß, and Lau 2003, 25 f.), becoming both the product and the producer of his or her networks, living and working situations. To write, as it were, one's biography, socially acceptable parts of the past need to be communicatively ordered, eventually reordered and then contextualised in relation to the individual's will. Authors, such as Lash (2003, 51), have referred to tightrope biographies or identity bricolage, pointing out that biographies are characterised by fast choices and quick decisions (Roberts 2015).

In the context of second modernity, it is argued that social structures become fluid and unbounded. In the process of eliminating boundaries and undoing distinctions, many more delimitations and differences are thus created. The new boundaries are characterised as 'less final, more helpless, more provisional, and morally and legally more plural' (Beck and Lau 2005, 553). They are fluid themselves and open to change.

While the conceptual framework of second modernity is useful for understanding emigration outside situations of economic or other forms of deprivation, it does not indicate why migrants aspire to move to or stay in a *specific* place. In this respect, a multi-scalar approach seems promising. Rescaling is understood here as an analytical concept useful for studying current social transformations that emerge from late modern capitalism. It is the aim of rescaling research to study the effects of late capitalism on nation-state agency and urban and rural restructuring (Brenner 2004; Jessop, Brenner, and Jones 2008). In migration studies, Glick Schiller and Çağlar have shown how migration is embedded in multi-scalar conditions of cities that are smaller in scale and face difficult economic situations. They also emphasise how migrants are involved in the rescaling of cities (see Çağlar 2013; Çağlar and Glick Schiller 2015; Glick Schiller and Çağlar 2008, 2009, 2011; Glick Schiller and Çağlar 2016; Glick Schiller, Çağlar, and Guldbransen 2006). Introducing multi-scalar approaches into migration research is an on-going effort, and the conceptualisations of scaling vary significantly (Silvey 2004; Williamson 2015; Xiang 2013). Migrants are, at the same time, influenced by scalar processes and themselves influence scalar changes by the way of their activities (Scheibelhofer 2016).

In migration research, the focus has not yet been laid on the link between aspirations and scalar processes. The argument at hand is that a multi-scalar approach might be worthwhile when considering why individuals within second modernity aspire to migrate to *specific* places. The following examples from original empirical research, therefore, not only highlight how second modernity shapes aspirations of Austrian emigrants, but also how multi-scalar approaches help explain the choice of a specific place of migration.

Empirical findings on migrant aspirations within second modernity

The arguments developed here are based on two grounded theory research projects carried out between 1998 and 2002 (Scheibelhofer 2003, 2005). In total, 47 persons were interviewed, mostly in New York City. The research concentrated on biographical processes leading to migration, transnational lifestyles and/or short-term mobility. While the first project did not specify an occupational group, the second one zoomed in on the mobility aspirations of Austrian researchers who were at the time of the interview based in the US during early stages of their careers.

As a method, the qualitative problem-centred interview (Scheibelhofer 2004; Witzel 1985; Witzel and Reiter 2012) was chosen because it allows focus on biographical processes. At the beginning of the interviews, an open-ended prompt was given to encourage a biographical entry to the interview (Schütze 1980). Doing so ensured that the interviewees would have as much freedom as possible to structure accounts according to their own relevance systems.

The analysis of the material was based on constructivist grounded theory strategies (Charmaz 2006) combined with the examination of biographical phases (Scheibelhofer 2008). This analytical process involved the construction of a chronological order of the migration experience. Applied here was an analytical scheme (Witzel 1985, 2001) in which researchers go through the reconstructed phases of a migration biography establishing for each of these phases the relevant aspirations, realisations and evaluations of the interviewed persons (cf. Witzel 2001).

The interviewees did not make a decision to emigrate at any certain point in time prior to emigrating, which they then acted upon and which would have led to a linear migratory biography. Rather, the empirical research showed different stages in the process of arriving at this decision and settling in the new place. Reconstruction of biographical phases also reveals divergent episodes that might have led to different migratory outcomes in individual biographies.

Most interviews were carried out in New York City, a place attractive to many Austrians because it holds a sense of opportunity for greater personal development. Ethnographic work on Japanese artists in New York shows that this opinion is shared by others (Sooudi 2014). Moreover, the city is a global centre not only in terms of financial markets, but also as a hub for arts-related production and creation, the fashion industry and academia.

Changing one's aspirations during migration

Individuals in second modernity are increasingly required to tailor their own biographies from socially more or less predefined elements. This is due to detachment from social milieus and the fact that individual life courses have come to be much less determined by social conditions (Botterill 2014). Flexibility in the sense of an ability to change thus becomes a dominant factor in everyday reality. Individuals themselves are expected to deal with large and unforeseen changes, such as unemployment and divorce, and to incorporate such events productively in their life plans at least after some period of time. But to do so, they need to be able to reshape their aspirations, too, and quickly tailor them to new circumstances.

Observing emigrants through the lens of second modernity, we see how the pressure to assign meaning to their own actions might be even greater than that of other migrants who are in the process of making some all-encompassing, life-defining decision that can be easily recognised as such by outsiders. It is a typical experience among migrants to be constantly confronted with questions in everyday life concerning their origin and reasons for migrating. Migrants in second modernity are also forced to deal with an environment that questions, scrutinises and judges their communicated aspirations concerning mobility.

Max Gerber,[2] age 46, was managing an art gallery in Manhattan at the time of the interview. As he described it, his own self-reflexivity shaped his aspirations. He made clear that the demands that came with having to forge his own path were frightening when moving to New York, though overall he believed that living in the city offered him opportunities for personal development. Being in that situation would let him to get to know his skills and limitations. On arrival, his ambition was to be an artist, yet, after comparing himself to other artists, he decided to let go of the aspiration – though it remained an important part of his self-identity. In retrospect, Gerber could present his evolving aspirations as a success story: although unable to fulfil the dream to work as an artist himself, he revised his aspirations according to the possibilities of the place he emigrated to. This speaks directly to the Quaglia and Cobb (1996) understanding of aspirations as the 'ability to identify and set goals for the future, while being inspired in the present to work toward those goals', and fleshes out how modern individuals navigate confronting high levels of insecurity and competition. Interviewees like Gerber saw the need to revise rapidly. Part of his career evolution was the need to find a niche, one in which his ability to make quick decisions would allow him to exploit his knowhow and talent.

Gerber talked about strategies that he used to deal with the pressure of job-seeking in an unknown setting and without help from friends or relatives.

> Essentially, you arrive in America, you meet a few people, and you say, 'I need a job' [laughs].
> **Interviewer:** So you didn't know anyone, didn't have any contacts here in New York?
> **Gerber:** No, not a single contact – well, at the beginning that's a little scary, but it's good because you somehow have to get yourself moving. And I believe that this is a very interesting experience – you essentially need to be very visionary, very inventive. You need to make your own life plan and also see it through. And you also need to be careful that you don't get stuck anywhere, you have to see that you also change your job at the right time, to leave something behind at the right time, in order to be able to get involved in something else because if you don't do that, the working situation and the work ethic in New York are very demanding, essentially, and very strong, and there is always the tendency that you lose yourself in it because – it's very demanding – and that also applies to the job I have here now. I also have to be careful.[3]

This need to adapt to the exigencies of a new place in terms of work as well as 'life plan', in a broader sense, relate directly to the theory of second modernity, as I briefly described. Gerber's account can also be read as the experience of a migrant moving to a vibrant city where economic life constantly changes and demands much of its residents. He characterises just what kind of agency is necessary in a place that has been described as a nodal point of the world economy and a driving centre of global financial markets (Sassen [1991] 2013). What Gerber experiences is the need to compete as an individual in a complex setting. Applying a multi-scalar perspective, we observe a learning experience in a world centre not only of economic power, but also of hegemonic cultural production. In Gerber's account, the implicit basis of comparison is Austria: a highly industrialised country yet one with economic and political dependency on other nation-states. Austria, moreover, is not an international hub of contemporary creative output, although its artistic and cultural legacy has given it a lasting tourist appeal. We might conclude that a scalar comparison of cultural environments allowed Gerber to aspire to move to New York and stay even when his job aspirations changed. The final thoughts in the excerpt reveal how he still believes that his aspirations and work ambitions may need to evolve in order to remain competitive on the job market.

Self-determination seemed a key factor in Gerber's attempt to independently and capably exploit the various resources available to newcomers. How he chose to recount his migration story included a reinterpretation of former aspirations, having had to part with what he came to consider unrealistic future plans. The creativity to revise and reinterpret prior aspirations thus largely depends on migrants' own ability to adapt quickly to external influences. In doing so, they continually undergo learning processes in which they usually cannot rely upon the support of ethnic (or other) networks or contacts. Looking at Gerber's case, one might conclude that migration within second modernity emphasises tendencies towards individualisation.

Another way to deal with aspirations that might later be deemed unrealistic, in the face of actual circumstances, is exemplified in the case of Herbert Weger, age 36. In our first conversation, he introduced himself as a producer and cameraman for experimental films. He also stated that he was an artist with a university degree in his field, who had been living in New York City for five years. In the interview, Weger talked about his job as a software developer for a local company, where he had started to work soon after his arrival. The following excerpt shows how he managed to reconcile his aspiration of being an artist with his work at a nine-to-five job.

> It's a very small company, with four or five people – and I get along with them very well. I work there three or four days a week, or more if necessary, and ah – and, well, I like my work a lot, well – I'm learning a lot there and – [I] also have to travel and such once in a while – this would really be my job if I wasn't an artist because I can learn a lot [on the job] for my art, and I have never had technical difficulties in my projects. That's always the big problem, that many of these projects don't really turn out right because the artists don't have a clue, and don't have enough money to be able to afford a good technician. This means that many things are only half-finished and then it doesn't really work – in this case, I am lucky to get all the necessary practice in this job. I wouldn't have chosen to make my living that way if it didn't work.

Weger emphasised his employment-related advantage over other artists in his field, having accumulated at his day job the technical knowhow he also needed as an artist. He pointed out various characteristics about the job to show how attractive it was for an artist: working in a small, friendly environment, the opportunity to work on a part-time basis and the chance to travel for work. Weger chose to make software development seem like a secondary occupation: it was a side job because his main aspiration was to be an artist and he perceived himself as such. The aim of my analysis is not to determine whether Weger was being honest with himself, but rather to examine how aspirations are kept intact by letting them co-exist with the need to meet daily life's economic demands and pursue vocational ambitions. Focus here is on how viable forms of everyday life practices get constructed and integrated into a non-contradictory whole.

Revising aspirations during the course of migration was a result not so much of dissociation from original desires and expectations. Rather, my interviewees were adjusting to the conditions they encountered in New York and, specifically, the labour market, which is a crucial component to the following discussion.

Striving towards positive self-state as main action orientation

Since the mid-1970s, empirical studies carried out in Europe have indicated a significant shift from the traditional value of fulfilling family-related duties to striving for self-realisation (Garhammer 2000). That shift mainly stems from the fact that self-realisation as a key value has modified other orientations of migration (Benson and O'Reilly 2009; Crespi 2014; Sooudi 2014; Vonk 2007). By contrast, studies dealing with the motives of migrants from economically deprived regions have shown that everyday actions are largely determined by the wish for a better future, economic or otherwise, which is often connected with a sense of duty vis-à-vis family and communities. Schiffauer (1991) described how the meaning of the moral principle of duty changes with the migratory experience: within the context of migration, a distinction is drawn between performing one's self-duty and the duty to obey others (e.g. elders). While these aspirations do not get altogether replaced by some orientation towards self-realisation, they take on a certain degree of freedom. According to Schiffauer's study, someone in Turkey cannot know in what way his migrant relative can most effectively support the family; meanwhile, the migrant himself makes a decision – on the basis of his new environment and/or experiences – as to how this duty would be best executed. The significance of this modified sense of duty towards extended family in the country of origin can manifest in migrants' aspirations and social practices (Six-Hohenbalken 2001). Much current research interprets aspirations for the family's economic well-being as key, serving as the guiding motive in the lives of many first-generation migrants.

Diverging from this pattern, the migration movements prompted by the conditions of second modernity can often be described as positively aspiring self-states. Those states may range from personal development and self-determination to hedonistic orientations. Aspiration towards self-realisation also features in empirical case studies on recent migration movements, although the empirical data are not systematically analysed in this respect. Most frequently, aspirations towards self-realisation form part of the reconstructed biographies in these studies (Schondelmayer 2003; Weiss, Schnell, and Ates 2013), indicating that migration experiences are connected to the desire to achieve a positive self-state, thus differing considerably from labour migration research findings. In my studies on Austrians who migrated to New York, this difference became most apparent during analytical reconstructions of aspirations of self-realisation; the most salient reason to migrate was the desire for personal development.[4] While the second modernity framework helps us understand shifting aspirations towards self-fulfilment, it cannot explain why people choose a specific place to emigrate. From my interviews, it seemed that that New York City's uniqueness and the opportunities the setting offered for social networking were what compelled Austrians to go. There, in a different sphere, they could enjoy their freedom as individuals. The city's global prominence played a decisive role in this respect. From a social scientific point of view, the hegemonic powers within such a discourse add another dimension to the evaluations. Comparing Austrian ways of life to those of the US was typical for the interviewees, who usually characterised their place of origin as rigid and trapped in tradition.[5] If we look at this characterisation through rescaling, we see that Austria has been unable to transmit an image of innovation, appeal broadly to artists and researchers or show that it has a culturally vibrant life influential beyond its borders. In social scientific terms, what stands out are Austria's political and socioeconomic stability, high standards of social welfare and rather conservative way of life (in terms of gender norms, social reproduction and political landscape). Esping-Andersen's (1990) characterisation of the US as a liberal welfare state with its market logic and Austria as a conservative welfare state come to mind, despite criticisms of this simplistic conceptualisation in recent years.

My interviewees continuously placed their aspirations in perspective by describing their limited opportunities for self-realisation in Austria. When I spoke with Alexander Mittersill, he was 45 and had been living in New York for over 15 years. He had left his university studies in Austria and worked briefly in different jobs before coming to the city to visit a friend. It was not his plan to stay, yet on arrival, his aspirations quickly changed. Here, we see the important influence of biographical momentum, which was described earlier as being characteristic to the formation of aspirations. After finding work as help in a kitchen and later on as a cook, Mittersill extended his stay, for reasons stated as follows:

> The energy level here is just so much higher, and the people are so much more ambitious – and I like it that way. It is always – you are always with people who feel some kind of urge and who want to start something new, who are supported by their friends and families if they want to start something new. This is what has fascinated me so much here right from the beginning. The support system here is so strong – there is so much strength here. The people you talk to, if you say, 'I want to do this or I want to do that,' they always tell you, 'Go for it! Do it! You can do it!' – Ah, while in Austria it's always like [...] if you have some kind of idea, which doesn't fit in well with your environment or your friends – you always hear 'Oh, well.' 'Oh, well' – 'maybe' – and this is what makes the difference to me.

Supported by his friends and acquaintances in New York, Mittersill had enough courage to get involved in projects that were entirely new to him. At the time of the interview, he owned a well-established restaurant, which he had opened by taking out loans on several credit cards and balancing the debts. It had been his ambition to buy his own restaurant. He explained how in Austria, his creative aspirations had taken various promising directions, but his actual efforts had all been impeded. Yet in New York, his ideas garnered a lot of positive feedback and encouragement, which pushed him each step of the way to what he deemed a successful, fulfilling life. Mittersill found that placing himself in a positive environment, one that would support him and his high ambitions, was a way to boost his own creativity and sense of innovation. From a sociological point of view, these experiences can also be linked to broader societal traits. In Austria, being an untrained restaurant-owning cook would not have been possible because the labour market is strictly regulated; a year-long apprenticeship and completion of exams would be required before being able to cook in – and own – a restaurant. In New York, Mittersill received enough social support to make such a project possible and did so on a labour market that is far less regulated.

Balancing degrees of self-determination

Self-determination also carried tremendous weight in the second empirical study that forms the basis for this article. The interviewed researchers, who moved to the US (for a limited period, at least initially) despite not having a long-term work position, developed divergent aspirations in terms of their migration. The crucial question for them concerned how they could – under the differing circumstances of their disciplines[6] – reconcile their self-determination in work and private life.[7] My empirical study identified two antipodal ways in which individuals coped with these exigencies, as illuminated by the following two cases.

At the time of the interview, Erwin Schmied had spent seven years at different universities across the US. Shortly before our meeting, he was offered his first assistant professorship after obtaining a postdoc in a social scientific discipline focusing on computer-assisted innovative testing methods. This new development in his biography was, on the one hand, a big step forward in realising his professional aspirations – he was a dedicated researcher hoping to pursue a career in academia. On the other hand, during the interview, he spoke of a 'lose-lose' situation; he was about to move, yet again, to another state within the US and would be living not just far from his family in Austria, but also from the friends he made over the years in the US. Most of them were young researchers like him and some also had to move around for academic positions. Schmied described the advantages and disadvantages of pursuing his ambitions, as follows:

> So, studying [in the US] at one of the best universities with big-name professors still does not mean that you'll get a job afterwards. So – there is no job guarantee anymore. But still, the probability [...] to find a suitable position is much better than [in Austria]. The suitability is important. I'd rather live – in terms of life quality and where in fact I'd like to have my life – I'd very much in fact like to return to Austria or to Europe. This would be the ideal thing to do for me. So, I really would like to return and continue my research. But it is not valued [in Austria]. So, for example, if I had a position in Austria – that does not exist anyway – I'd never have a suitable position comparable to the one I was offered in California. So in California, I'll be my own master with this assistant professorship. And this is simply because it is acknowledged that you have pulled through the programme.

Schmied's aspirations thus pulled him in different directions and could hardly be reconciled with his view of the present-day circumstances in the life course of many researchers. Securing a job that met his expectations meant having to be more mobile than he would like to be. Returning to Austria was not an option. At best, it would force him to bow to the hierarchies of the Austrian university system – which was too risky, especially considering the job scarcity – and to give up a good share of the academic independence he could expect in the US. Schmied's accounts correspond with on-going shifts in the politics of education and science: while researchers face financial constraints in the US and in Europe, many of the elite global research institutions within the US (which Schmied refers to) rank higher than those in Continental Europe. This impacts job opportunities for younger researchers in especially vulnerable biographical situations (Ackers 2005). Comparing the circumstances of young researchers in the US and Austria, we see how differences in the university systems often compel European researchers like Schmied to migrate to the US. These individual decisions also contribute to a further upscaling of the US research competitiveness.

As conceptualised in this article, aspiration must also be perceived as being embedded in specific social environments. Schmied accepted the norms that govern academic work in his field and thus embraced the professional aspirations that come with embarking on a successful career. Thus, Schmied accepted having to move to yet another region of the US, where he had to build social ties anew and could not realise his wish to return to Austria. Under different circumstances, another researcher faced a similar problem and forged another strategy to deal with competing interests.

Before turning to the second case of Vera Jungwirth, I should stress the limits of comparability between the two interviewees, largely concerning costs involved in their research. While Schmied relied on expensive testing devices, Jungwirth worked in cultural science requiring, above all, brainpower and empirical research. Consequently, Jungwirth's research routines could be carried out independent of the office infrastructure, laboratory space and equipment that Schmied depended on.

Jungwirth was a 36-year-old political scientist who had been living in New York City for 10 years. After studying for two of them on an Austrian grant at a university in the city, she received her diploma and obtained a PhD fellowship at the same university. While doing her PhD, she cooperated with two scientist friends who, like her, lived partly in Austria and partly in New York. When we spoke, Jungwirth was teaching at two universities in New York and one in Austria. Additionally, she had won a grant for her research in Austria, thus stabilising her finances for another two years. She planned to secure research funds from the US, although up until then, her money mainly came from Austrian or European funding sources.

To reconstruct her aspirations was no easy task. From her own observations and descriptions of her past and present situations, one might derive that she strives for a high degree of independent work and personal living conditions. However, unlike Schmied, she plainly pointed out that she was not ready to follow the unwritten rule of taking up less attractive academic positions for the sake of being at a more renowned university or living in a better city. In other words, she did not believe in applying for university positions in places where she did not wish to live. Still, in her view, the path to full professorship in a highly popular city, such as New York, was first to take up a position at a less attractive university and then to work one's way up to better reputed places. Being a researcher with expectations beyond the job itself – that is, the wish to live in a certain place – Jungwirth found another way of financing her position as a scholar in a globalised academic arena. This strategy worked for her; yet looking only at her professional pathway it would not suffice to understand the complexity of her situation.

Jungwirth is part of a large social network whose members are used to moving back and forth between two places. The network contacts facilitated consultation between members about various difficulties arising from a common transnational lifestyle. Jungwirth emphasised the need to be highly organised when holding employment contracts in two countries. Having annual teaching duties in Austria and spending part of her summer holiday there, Jungwirth still rented an apartment in Vienna. Discussing the insecurities of her current situation as a researcher, Jungwirth was simultaneously forging strategies for how to cope with the field's demands and her work conditions. Exploiting resources (contacts, information, teaching opportunities and research funds) both in Europe and the US was necessary to meet her aspirations to live as a researcher in the place or places she chose. Jungwirth was actively engaged in constructing a social environment that was transnationally oriented and that, in turn, helped her achieve work goals and find satisfying living arrangements.

The interview also permitted a glimpse at aspirations-in-the-making. When we spoke, Jungwirth's economic circumstances implied potential precariousness in the future. But going back to work full time in Austria was ruled out as an option for personal reasons; her husband, an American, spoke no German and would struggle to find employment there. The couple discussed the possibility of moving to London or Berlin so that both would have a chance at finding professional positions in their respective fields. Yet also keeping Jungwirth from pursuing her aspirations was an awareness that she would immediately move back home, to the Austrian countryside, should her aging parents ever need care. As an only child, she saw no other solution to a problem, which she anticipated coming sooner or later. Although, in general, she avoided thinking about these uncertainties, she could not imagine how her professional and private life, with her husband still in the US, would evolve after returning to Austria at some point. Gender-specific norms and views on caring for parents or young children proved recurrent when talking to other female scientists about their future aspirations. While the issue of children and their education was brought up by male scientists who were also fathers, caring for the elderly did not come up in our interviews.[8]

Concluding discussion

Most studies on migration aspirations have centred on a particular type of connection between spatial and social mobility. They have examined how people in economically deprived and insecure places see migration as a pathway to a better future and a successful life. Also after having left home, the migratory projects under study are typically intertwined with striving for a better life in the face of adversities (Carling 2002; Van Meeteren, Engbersen, and Van San 2009; Wissink, Düvell, and van Eerdewijk 2013). A fuller understanding of aspirations in international migration requires attention to different types of contexts too, namely those in which individuals are not leaving their countries of origin to better their economic prospects or to secure a future not endangered by war or ecological crisis. My work on Austrians in New York City contributes to such an endeavour.

I have suggested here that the perspective of second modernity is a helpful theoretical venue for such cases. My respondents revised their aspirations once already living in the US, and this dynamism resonates with the continuous need within second modernity to be flexible in one's action orientations in order to accommodate changing circumstances. While studies on aspirations and migration have concentrated on emigration environments, looking more profoundly at the immigration context would enhance the already existing research. To appreciate how a migrant's biography develops, we need to appreciate shifting and changing aspirations in new environments. Meeting the demands of the new environment can lead to further migration or to revising aspirations. In the material presented here, such revision of aspirations was most prominent in the case of Gerber, the art gallery manager.

Analyses of aspirations should examine not only dynamism and revisions, but also explore prevailing trends in their direction. What I observed among Austrians in New York City was that they typically aspired to a positive self-state. This overriding action orientation means that migrants are not orienting themselves towards traditional values, such as performing one's family duty or attaining a higher standard of living, but rather that they are striving for self-realisation (Schondelmayer 2003; Weiss, Schnell, and Ates 2013). Researching the opportunities migrants have to realise their personal potential by trying out life elsewhere can contribute significantly to understanding migrants' aspirations in more general terms, especially when newcomers move to societies that can be analysed through the lens of second modernity.

Cases such as that of restaurant owner Mittersill are deeply embedded in an immigration context of a neoliberal economic market, which is linked to its own set of immigration and settlement laws. These political and economic circumstances lead to the scalar positioning of New York City, which is, in turn, very attractive for many international migrants.[9] In Austria, by contrast, economic markets are highly regulated: without a year-long training, Mittersill would not have gotten the necessary licenses to open a restaurant – and he likely would have struggled with the higher taxes and incidental wage costs financing the conservative Austrian social welfare state. Thus, research that takes the scalar positioning of emigration and immigration environments, both, into account is certainly also useful when discussing migrant aspirations.

A final theme that emerged from the interviews concerns migrants' balancing degrees of self-determination. Aspiring to high degrees of self-determination is a core mechanism within second modernity because the extenuating socioeconomic circumstances are not as decisive for the biography (Beck, Bonß, and Lau 2003). The problematic of balancing was especially salient with those interviewees who worked as junior researchers in the US. Most of them aimed at reconciling a career as a researcher with satisfying social relations with family members and friends. Schmied's and Jungwirth's cases exemplified how the meaning-making and strategies of migrants can vary. Although different aspirations shaped their migratory moves, both shared their ambition for high levels of self-determination in their biographies.

The concept of second modernity helps us see the individual work of bricolage in one's biography; it highlights the importance of interpreting and re-interpreting one's own life course. Individuals who move across international borders are thus engaged, as are those who stay, in bricolage work in order to build their own biography and interpret it according to their action orientations.

Whilst second modernity may explain the social phenomenon of emigration from countries, such as Austria, we still need to examine why the interviewees mostly chose the US, and specifically New York City. Here, a scalar approach reveals the aspirations for these specific locations. In these case studies, the migrants aspired to be in a place that influenced world economy, arts, research and academia as well as popular culture, in a broad sense. Conversely, the Austrian migrants themselves contributed to the upscaling of New York City and elsewhere through their own everyday activities, professions and financial investments in these places.

Notes

1. For a by now classic argumentation in favour of a biographical approach, see Halfacree and Boyle (1993).
2. All names, dates and specifics of empirical work presented here have been altered in order to maintain the anonymity of data. Half of the empirical work has been financed through a grant of the Jubilee Fund of the Austrian National Bank (grant number 9156, project name 'mobility perspectives of young Austrian researchers').
3. All interview excerpts were translated from German by the author.
4. The study on which these results are based had also endeavoured to reconstruct the main action orientations of migrants. Here, it was found that besides action orientation towards self-realisation, orientations towards personal realms such as family, career and work life were highly important. In many actual cases, these action orientations also overlapped in differing ways (Scheibelhofer 2009).
5. For further reflections on methodological nationalism in everyday life of migrants, see Scheibelhofer (2011).
6. Interviewees were selected from two disciplinary groups – life sciences and social science – in order to see how working in different subject matters create different research circumstances.
7. The divide between professional and private life spheres is applied cautiously here, keeping in mind feminist works on gender-specific inequalities hidden by such discourses (Acker 1990).
8. For further insights on gender issues in the mobility of female researchers, see Ackers (2004).
9. For an example of Japanese emigrants to New York City, see Sooudi (2014).

Disclosure statement

No potential conflict of interest was reported by the author.

References

Acker, Joan. 1990. "Hierarchies, Jobs, Bodies: A Theory of Gendered Organizations." *Gender & Society* 4 (2): 139–158.

Ackers, Louise. 2004. "Managing Relationships in Peripatic Careers: Scientific Mobility in the European Union." *Women's Studies International Forum* 27: 189–201.

Ackers, Louise. 2005. "Moving People and Knowledge: Scientific Mobility in the European Union." *International Migration* 43 (5): 99–131.

Ackers, Louise, and Helen Stalford. 2007. "Managing Multiple Life-Courses: The Influence of Children on Migration Processes in the European Union." In *Social Policy Review 19: Analysis and Debate in Social Policy*, edited by K. Clarke, T. Maltby, and P. Kennett, 321–342. Bristol: Policy Press.

Bal, Ellen, and Roos Willems. 2014. "Introduction: Aspiring Migrants, Local Crises and the Imagination of Futures 'Away from Home'." *Identities* 21 (3): 249–258.

Beck, Ulrich. 1986. *Risikogesellschaft: Auf dem Weg in eine andere Moderne*. Frankfurt am Main: Suhrkamp.

Beck, Ulrich, Wolfgang Bonß, and Christoph Lau. 2003. "The Theory of Reflexive Modernization Problematic, Hypotheses and Research Programme." *Theory, Culture & Society* 20 (2): 1–33.

Beck, Ulrich, and Edgar Grande. 2010. "Varieties of Second Modernity: The Cosmopolitan Turn in Social and Political Theory and Research." *The British Journal of Sociology* 61 (3): 409–443.

Beck, Ulrich, and Christoph Lau. 2005. "Second Modernity as a Research Agenda: Theoretical and Empirical Explorations in the "Meta-Change" of Modern Society." *The British Journal of Sociology* 56 (4): 525–557.

Benson, Michaela, and Karen O'Reilly. 2009. "Migration and the Search for a Better Way of Life: A Critical Exploration of Lifestyle Migration." *The Sociological Review* 57 (4): 608–625.

Berger, Peter, and Thomas Luckmann. 1972. *Die gesellschaftliche Konstruktion der Wirklichkeit. Eine Theorie der Wissenssoziologie*. Frankfurt am Main: Fischer.

Botterill, Katherine. 2014. "Family and Mobility in Second Modernity: Polish Migrant Narratives of Individualization and Family Life." *Sociology* 48 (2): 233–250.

Breivik, Jan-Kåre. 2012. "Health Migration from Norway to Spain – Ambiguous Belonging." *Ethnic and Racial Studies* 35 (9): 1634–1653.

Brenner, Neil. 2004. "Urban Governance and the Production of New State Spaces in Western Europe, 1960–2000." *Review of International Political Economy* 11 (3): 447–488.

Çağlar, Ayşe. 2013. "Turkey and Europe: Locating Homeland Ties and Re-Scaling Migration Scholarship." *European Review* 21 (03): 400–411.

Çaglar, Ayse, and Nina Glick Schiller. 2015. "A Multiscalar Perspective on Cities and Migration." *Sociologica Italian Journal of Sociology* online 2/2015. doi:10.2383/81432.

Carling, Jørgen. 2002. "Migration in the Age of Involuntary Immobility: Theoretical Reflections and Cape Verdean Experiences." *Journal of Ethnic and Migration Studies* 28 (1): 5–42.

Carling, Jørgen, and Francis Collins. 2018. "Aspiration, Desire and Drivers of Migration." *Journal of Ethnic and Migration Studies* 44 (6): 909–926. doi.org/10.1080/1369183X.2017.1384134.

Charmaz, Kathy. 2006. *Constructing Grounded Theory: A Practical Guide Through Qualitative Analysis*. London u.a.: Sage.

Crespi, Isabella. 2014. "Foreign Families in the Italian Context: Migration Processes and Strategies." *Journal of Comparative Family Studies* 45 (2): 249–260.

Dijkstra, Lewis, Enrique Garcilazo, and Philip McCann. 2015. "The Effects of the Global Financial Crisis on European Regions and Cities." *Journal of Economic Geography* 15 (5): 935–949.

Esping-Andersen, Gøsta. 1990. *The Three Worlds of Welfare Capitalism*. Cambridge: Polity Press.

Garhammer, Manfred. 2000. "Das Leben: eine Stilfrage – Lebensstilforschung hundert Jahre nach Simmels "Stil des Lebens"." *Soziologische Revue* 23: 296–312.

Glick Schiller, Nina, and Ayse Çaglar. 2008. "Migrant Incorporation and City Scale: Towards a Theory of Locality in Migration Studies." In *Willy Brandt Series Working Papers in International Migration and Ethnic Relations*, edited by Malmö University. Malmö: Malmö University.

Glick Schiller, Nina, and Ayşe Çağlar. 2009. "Towards a Comparative Theory of Locality in Migration Studies: Migrant Incorporation and City Scale." *Journal of Ethnic and Migration Studies* 35 (2): 177–202.

Glick Schiller, Nina, and Ayşe Çağlar. 2011. *Locating Migration. Rescaling Cities and Migrants.* London: Cornell University Press.

Glick Schiller, Nina, and Ayse Çağlar. 2016. "Displacement, Emplacement and Migrant Newcomers: Rethinking Urban Sociabilities Within Multiscalar Power." *Identities* 23 (1): 17–34.

Glick Schiller, Nina, Ayşe Çağlar, and Thaddeus C. Guldbransen. 2006. "Jenseits der "Ethnischen Gruppe" als Objekt des Wissens: Lokalität, Globalität und Inkorporationsmuster von Migranten." In *Die Macht des Lokalen in einer Welt ohne Grenzen*, edited by Helmuth Berking, 105–144. Frankfurt: Campus Verlag.

Green, Nancy L, and François Weil. 2007. *Citizenship and Those Who Leave: The Politics of Emigration and Expatriation.* Champaign: University of Illinois Press.

Gutman, Leslie, and Rodie Akerman. 2008. *Determinants of Aspirations [Wider Benefits of Learning Research Report No. 27].* Centre for Research on the Wider Benefits of Learning, Institute of Education, London: University of London.

Halfacree, Keith H, and Paul J Boyle. 1993. "The Challenge Facing Migration Research: The Case for a Biographical Approach." *Progress in Human Geography* 17 (3): 333–348.

Hall, Kelly, and Irene Hardill. 2014. "Retirement Migration, the 'Other' Story: Caring for Frail Elderly British Citizens in Spain." *Ageing and Society* 36: 562–585.

Hüwelmeier, Gertrud. 2010. "Moving East: Transnational Ties of Vietnamese Pentecostals." In *Traveling Spirits: Migrants, Markets and Mobilities*, edited by Gertrud Hüwelmeier, and Kristine Krause, 133–144. London: Routledge.

Jessop, Bob, Neil Brenner, and Martin Jones. 2008. "Theorizing Sociospatial Relations." *Environment and Planning D: Society and Space* 26: 389–401.

Lash, Scott. 2003. "Reflexivity as Non-Linearity." *Theory, Culture & Society* 20 (2): 49–57.

Lowe, Graham S, and Harvey Krahn. 2000. "Work Aspirations and Attitudes in an Era of Labour Market Restructuring: A Comparison of Two Canadian Youth Cohorts." *Work, Employment and Society* 14 (1): 1–22.

Niedner-Kalthoff, Ulrike. 2006. "Rotation und Objektivität. Diplomaten als transnationale Migranten." In *Transnationale Karrieren*, 83–99. Frankfurt: Springer.

Quaglia, Russell J., and Casey D Cobb. 1996. "Toward a Theory of Student Aspirations." *Journal of Research in Rural Education* 12 (3): 127–132.

Ray, Debraj. 2006. "Aspirations, Poverty, and Economic Change." *Understanding Poverty* 1: 409–421.

Roberts, Brian. 2015. "Biographical Research." In *Advances in Biographical Methods: Creative Applications*, edited by Neill Maggie,Roberts Brian,Sparkes Andrew11–29. London: Routledge.

Roth, Silke. 2012. "Professionalisation Trends and Inequality: Experiences and Practices in aid Relationships." *Third World Quarterly* 33 (8): 1459–1474.

Sassen, Saskia. [1991] 2013. *The Global City: New York, London, Tokyo.* Princeton, NJ: Princeton University Press.

Scheibelhofer, Elisabeth. 2003. *Migration und Individualisierung:Grundlegende Handlungsorientierungen bei Auswanderungen aus Westeuropa in die Vereinigten Staaten.* Frankfurt/M.: Peter Lang Verlag.

Scheibelhofer, Elisabeth. 2004. "Das Problemzentrierte Interview – Möglichkeiten und Grenzen eines Erhebungs- und Auswertungsinstruments." *Zeitschrift Sozialwissenschaften und Berufspraxis* 27 (1): 75–90.

Scheibelhofer, Elisabeth. 2005. "Mobilitätsperspektiven junger WissenschaftlerInnen im Ausland." *SWS Rundschau* 1 (1): 75–90.

Scheibelhofer, Elisabeth. 2006. "Wenn WissenschaftlerInnen im Ausland forschen. Transnationale Lebensstile zwischen selbstbestimmter Lebensführung und ungewollter Arbeitsmigration." In *Transnationale Karrieren: Biografien, Lebensführung und Mobilität*, edited by Florian Kreutzer, and Silke Roth, 122–140. Opladen: VS Verlag.

Scheibelhofer, Elisabeth. 2008. "Combining Narration-Based Interviews with Topical Interviews: Methodological Reflections on Research Practices." *International Journal of Social Research Methodology* 11 (5): 403–416.

Scheibelhofer, Elisabeth. 2009. "Understanding European Emigration in the Context of Modernization Processes." *Current Sociology* 57 (1): 5–25.

Scheibelhofer, Elisabeth. 2011. *Raumsensible Migrationsforschung. Methodologische Überlegungen und ihre empirische Relevanz für die Migrationssoziologie.* Wiesbaden: VS Verlag für Sozialwissenschaften/Springer Fachmedien Wiesbaden GmbH Wiesbaden.

Scheibelhofer, Elisabeth. 2016. "Reflecting on Spatiality in European Migration Research: From Methodological Nationalism to Space-Sensitive Observations of Social Transformations." In *An Anthology of Migration and Social Transformation*, edited by Anna Amelina, 73–86. Berlin: Springer.

Schiffauer, Werner. 1991. *Die Migranten aus Subay. Türken in Deutschland: eine Ethnographie.* Stuttgart: Klett-Cotta.

Schondelmayer, Anne-Christin. 2003. *Begegnung mit dem Fremden–eine qualitative Untersuchung zu Handlungspraktiken von Entwicklungshelfern.* Berlin: Freie Universität Berlin.

Schütze, Fritz. 1980. "Prozeßstrukturen des Lebenslauf." In *Biographie in handlungswissenschaftlicher Perspektive*, edited by J. Matthes, A. Pfeifenberger, and M. Stosberg, 67–156. Nürnberg: Verlag der Nürnberger Forschungsvereinigung.

Silvey, Rachel. 2004. "Power, Difference and Mobility: Feminist Advances in Migration Studies." *Progress in Human Geography* 28 (4): 490–506.

Six-Hohenbalken, Maria. 2001. "Migrantenfamilien aus der Türkei in Österreich. Wohnen, Verortung und Heimat." In *Mit einem Exkurs über die Wohnsituation im Aufnahmeland*, 1–78. Vienna: Österreichisches Institut für Familienforschung.

Sooudi, Olga Kanzaki. 2014. *Japanese New York: Self-Reinvention and Migrant Artists on the World Stage.* Honolulu: University of Hawai'I Press.

Van Meeteren, Masja, Godfried Engbersen, and Marion Van San. 2009. "Striving for a Better Position: Aspirations and the Role of Cultural, Economic, and Social Capital for Irregular Migrants in Belgium." *International Migration Review* 43 (4): 881–907.

Vonk, Esther. 2007. "Migration, Integration and Emancipation: Women's Positioning in the Debate in the Netherlands." In *Women Migrants From East to West: Gender, Mobility and Belonging in Contemporary Europe*, edited by Luisa Passerini, Dawn Lyon, Enrica Capussotti, and Ioanna Laliotou, 177–194. Oxford: Berghahn Books.

Weiss, Hilde, Philipp Schnell, and Gülay Ates. 2013. *Zwischen den Generationen, Transmissionsprozesse in Familien mit Migrationshintergrund.* Wiesbaden: Springer.

Williamson, Rebecca. 2015. "Towards a Multi-Scalar Methodology: The Challenges of Studying Social Transformation and International Migration." In *Social Transformation and Migration: National and Local Experiences in South Korea, Turkey, Mexico and Australia*, edited by Stephen Castles, Derya Ozkul, and Magdalena Cubas, 17–32. New York: Palgrave.

Wissink, Marieke, Franck Düvell, and Anouka van Eerdewijk. 2013. "Dynamic Migration Intentions and the Impact of Socio-Institutional Environments: A Transit Migration Hub in Turkey." *Journal of Ethnic and Migration Studies* 39 (7): 1087–1105.

Witzel, Andreas. 1985. "Das Problemzentrierte Interview." In *Qualitative Forschung in der Psychologie*, edited by Gerd Jüttemann, 227–256. Weinheim: Beltz.

Witzel, Andreas. 2001. "Prospektion und Retrospektion im Lebenslauf. Ein Konzept zur Rekonstruktion berufs-und bildungsbiographischer Orientierungen und Handlungen." *ZSE: Zeitschrift für Soziologie der Erziehung und Sozialisation* 21 (4): 339–355.

Witzel, Andreas, and Herwig Reiter. 2012. *The Problem-Centred Interview.* New York City: Sage.

Wohlrab-Sahr, M. 1997. "Individualisierung: Differenzierungsprozess und Zurechnungsmodus." In *Individualisierung und Integration: Neue Konfliktlinien und neuer Integrationsmodus?*, edited by U. und P. Sopp Beck, 24–36. Opladen: Leske und Budrich Verlag.
Xiang, Biao. 2013. "Multi-scalar Ethnography: An Approach for Critical Engagement with Migration and Social Change." *Ethnography* 14 (3): 282–299.
Zamora-Kapoor, Anna, and Xavier Coller. 2014. "The Effects of the Crisis: Why Southern Europe?" *The American Behavioral Scientist* 58 (12): 1511–1516.

Desiring 'foreign talent': lack and Lacan in anti-immigrant sentiments in Singapore

Peidong Yang

ABSTRACT

In recent years, the Singapore government's pro-immigration policy – specifically, its recruitment of so-called foreign talent – has caused a palpable rise in anti-immigrant sentiments and discourses amongst natives of the city-state. Drawing on Lacanian psychoanalysis, a perspective so far marginal in migration research, this article offers a provocative reading of Singapore's desire for foreign talent and the local society's reception of these subjects. The article focuses on the ways in which frustrated Singaporeans seem to find foreign talent immigrants, especially those from mainland China, to be lacking and undesirable. Lacan's theories enable the bold interpretations that: (1) foreign talent is not meant to fill a lack but precisely to produce it and (2) foreign talent stands for Singapore's and Singaporeans' unobtainable object of desire, which ultimately signifies the gaps and inconsistencies in the symbolic order confronting them. Moving away from existing conceptual frameworks and theoretical approaches, the article illustrates what a psychoanalytic lens of desire can contribute to migration and mobility research.

Introduction

We are yours, please make use of us! was the extraordinary plea voiced by a Singaporean chamber music quartet to the city-state's government, as reported in *The Straits Times* in the late 1990s (Li 1999). The quartet, which consisted entirely of *locally* born and bred members, felt strongly that the Singapore government favoured so-called *foreign* talent at the expense of local talents like themselves. They lamented how 'it seems that the authorities in Singapore are ashamed of us, ashamed of local talents. They seem to be afraid that we will disgrace them' (Li 1999). In the eyes of these disheartened local musicians, then, Singapore did not favour or love its own children, but instead invested its desire in foreigners. This desire for foreign talent was perceived to be an injustice or even a betrayal – something emotionally and psychologically unacceptable to native Singaporeans who believed they should be the favourite recipient of Singapore's love and attention.

Whilst this vignette may just be another expression of the tension Singapore's pro-immigration policy has caused in recent times (Vasu, Yeap, and Chan 2014), it is uniquely interesting in its accentuation of the psycho-emotional dimension of anti-immigrant sentiments, revealing the centrality of *desire*. Not only did the statement 'we are *yours*' sound somewhat submissive in its use of the possessive pronoun 'yours', furthermore, *please make use of us* leaves much room for interpretation. Although the quartet might dismiss such commentary as reading too much into the statement, psychoanalysis is precisely about reading into the unspoken, and sometimes unspeakable, sub-conscious and unconscious. Here we are appropriately reminded of one basic proposition of French psychoanalyst Jacques Lacan (1977, 264): 'man's [*sic*] desire is the desire of the Other'. Or, as one of Lacan's interpreters puts it, the subject's 'true aim was the Other's love' (Sheehan 2012, 19). In this case, the 'Other' is represented by the Singaporean state and the subject is the local quartet. The quartet supplicates to the Other, desperately needing the Other's attention and desire.

This article applies Lacanian psychoanalysis to the foreign talent situation in contemporary Singapore. For the present purpose, 'foreign talent' should be understood as a shorthand for immigration and immigrants. In Singapore, pro-immigration policy is justified by the state's rationale that certain types of foreigners are desirable because they possess specific talents and qualities that supplement the locals' lack thereof. However, Singaporean locals contest this rationale. As one often heard snub goes, 'FT' stands not for 'foreign talent' but for 'foreign trash'. Indeed, as I shall argue, anti-immigrant sentiments and discourses in Singapore frequently hinge on establishing the inadequacy of foreign talent. These subjects are persistently found to be lacking, undesirable and/or bogus. Ironically, this only makes 'perfect' and 'authentic' foreign talent something still desired, thus perpetuating the motion of desiring.

This seeming paradox about *lack* and *desire*, I argue, lies at the heart of the foreign talent situation in Singapore and demands closer examination and innovative analysis. To date, scholarly analyses of foreign talent-related issues in Singapore have not ventured beyond mostly descriptive accounts of locals' anxiety and resentment towards immigration (e.g. Koh 2003; Yeoh and Lin 2013; Gomes 2014; Vasu, Yeap, and Chan 2014; Yap, Koh, and Soon 2015) and/or ethnic, national and cultural identity politics (e.g. Liu 2014; Yang 2014a). These accounts may be regarded as more mainstream, with their conventional approach focusing on issues such as competition for economic and symbolic resources. Although undoubtedly useful, mainstream studies in this vein overlook the city-state's more elusive psycho-emotional undercurrents of trouble with foreign talent, this article's opening vignette being an example par excellence. Thus, my first objective is to fill the lacuna in existing scholarship by delving into the psychodynamics around lack and desire in Singaporean society's reception of foreign talent. Lacan's psychoanalysis is employed because of its pertinent theorisation of desire and lack.

Relatedly, and in line with the broader aim of this special issue focusing on 'aspiration, desire and the drivers of migration' (Carling and Collins 2018), my second objective is to explore how psychoanalysis can contribute to ethnic and migration studies in general. Scholars of these fields have in recent years begun to study the emotional and affective dimensions to human mobility. This concern with emotions may be further subsumed under the more general category of psychosocial research. Whilst this angle is relatively common and widely accepted, the *psychoanalytic* perspective – a distinct yet related approach – remains marginal. This article explains the distinction and is itself an attempt to illustrate what the much less common psychoanalytic lens can reveal about ethnicity and migration.

The next section elaborates my foregoing arguments before briefly introducing core ideas in Lacanian psychoanalysis. Following that is a background section on Singapore and its desire for foreign talent, touching on the historical, economic, sociocultural, linguistic and ethno-racial aspects to this desire. I then offer some notes on the methodology and data underpinning this study. Subsequently, the main analytical part unfolds in two thematic sections, each containing elaborations of Lacan's theories in conjunction with their application to the empirical case. Finally, the conclusion summarises the paper's main arguments and the relevance of a psychoanalytic approach to the broader field of migration studies.

Feeling ethnicity and migration: the emotional and affective, the psychosocial vs. the psychoanalytic, and Lacan

As Conradson and Mckay (2007, 172) noted, '[f]ar from being a secondary or unimportant dimension of mobility [...] affect and emotion are central aspects of international migration'. Indeed, in the decade since this statement, social research on migration has increasingly paid attention to emotion and affect (Svašek 2010).[1] A 2010 special issue in this journal entitled *On the Move: Emotion and Human Mobility* dealt with precisely this topic, defining emotions as 'dynamic processes through which individuals experience and interpret the changing world, position themselves vis-à-vis others, and shape their subjectivities' (Svašek 2010, 868). Using this definition, the special issue explored migrants' emotional experiences as well as emotive responses and reactions of migrant-receiving communities in various empirical contexts.

This inquiry into the emotional and affective aspects of migration and mobility can be viewed as a subset of the broader field of *psychosocial* research, which explores human psychic experiences in close conjunction with sociological analysis about social structure, power and inequalities. Reay (2008, 1075), who takes this approach when researching education in Britain, defines psychosocial studies as that which 'bring together the interior processes of the human mind, both individual and group emotions, with those that relate to the exterior, the public arenas of the social world, in order to examine structure and power'. Particularly concerned with the question of social class, Reay's (2005) work has explored the various psychic experiences and responses characteristic of distinct class positions. Although they do not fully overlap, the scholarship on migrant emotions shares with psychosocial studies the view that larger social forces (class structure, gender, geopolitical inequalities, power, etc.) are experienced as emotions and affects on the most intimate and subjective levels by human agents. The approach I take in this article is not unconnected to psychosocial studies; in fact, similar to Hall's (2010) and Wise's (2010) contributions to the 2010 *JEMS* special issue, this article largely also deals with the receiving society's reactions to immigrants. However, the article departs from the aforementioned studies in a notable way: my approach is explicitly psycho*analytic*.

A key distinction between psychoanalytic and psychosocial approaches is that the former entails the imaginative, perhaps provocative, use of theories rooted in the clinical psychoanalytic tradition.[2] This intervention of psychoanalytic theories can often seem metaphoric or highly abstract, sometimes demanding leaps of imagination from both researcher and reader. This is one possible reason why psychoanalysis has been scarcely applied in social science thus far. The leap of imagination, however, is essential because psychoanalysis is precisely about foraying into the sub-conscious and unconscious. By contrast, psychosocial studies appear more closely grounded in the empirical, using terminologies of emotions (anxiety, fear, desire, fantasy, etc.) in a more or less descriptive manner as they are used in everyday speech, without invoking the metaphoric or abstract concepts typical to psychoanalysis. One of Walkerdine's (2010) articles illustrates just this. In the same spirit as Reay's interest in the psychic experience of classed subjectivities, Walkerdine's study (2010) about a degenerating industrial town in Wales explores community members' senses of insecurity, loss and nostalgia following the closure of a steel plant. Studying these psycho-emotional experiences and linking them to a sociological analysis of neoliberal globalisation and local deindustrialisation, Walkerdine invokes the notion of 'psychic skin' – a concept borrowed from psychoanalysis' object relations theory. With it she argues that affective community relations provided a 'skin' to give people a sense of being held together, like the epidermis of the biological body. The case details are of less concern here; the point is that by bringing in a seemingly external psychoanalytic concept to the empirical case, Walkerdine offers an imaginative, insightful analysis of a sociological issue.

In this article, I similarly look through a psychoanalytic lens, focusing specifically on anti-immigrant sentiments, discourses and imaginations. Although a decade ago, Healy (2007) observed in the Irish context that receiving communities' anti-immigrant feelings and attitudes were under-researched due to misplaced political correctness, such studies have become more prevalent recently (e.g. Heizmann 2016; Hellwig and Sinno 2016). This article is unique by virtue of its psychoanalytic framing from the very outset. To date, psychoanalysis (though see Kuntsman 2009) and particularly its Lacanian strain have seldom been used in migration research (Shubin, Findlay, and McCollum 2014). One recent exception is a study by Shubin, Findlay, and McCollum (2014), which explored the identity production of migrant workers in Latvian labour recruitment agents' discourses and imaginaries. Specifically, Lacan's theories about the nature of lack, fantasy and subjectivity were used to explain the 'unachievable figure of the "ideal" worker' (Shubin, Findlay, and McCollum 2014, 466).

Parallels exist between Shubin et al.'s study and mine. I also examine how, in the Singaporean discourse and imagination, the *ideal* foreign talent never materialises; it remains desired yet its obtainment seems perpetually deferred. At the centre of Lacan's theory of desire is a *subject of lack* – a subject that 'in the process of acceding to meaning, [...] loses something of its being' (Shubin, Findlay, and McCollum 2014, 467). Here, 'meaning' refers to the realm of language and discourse or, in Lacanian terminology, the *symbolic*. Due to this loss, the subject of lack constantly desires *something*, but that *something* never seems to arrive because, as Shubin, Findlay, and McCollum (2014, 468) explain, '[t]he loss is anterior to what is lost: the power of coherent expression granted by the symbolic induces the very lack that it promises to make good'. In other words, when a pre-subject emerges as a subject through acceding to the symbolic, a loss or void is created. In short, for Lacan (2006), subjectivity and loss are two sides of the same coin, and the subject's desire is always directed at 'something else' (431). Thus, lack is perpetual and could even be said to be normal; it structures the desiring subject's relationship with social others.

This cursory look at Lacan will be elaborated and fleshed out in my empirical analysis. However, I must note that my reading of Lacan is necessarily partial and selective. Geared towards providing a provocative interpretation of an empirical social issue, my reading does not claim to be an exegesis of the Lacanian corpus, which is highly complex and wide-ranging. Arguably, there are as many ways to apply Lacan as there are interpreters and issues under interpretation. Bullock (2014), for instance, offered a rare analysis of the societal discourses surrounding the Singapore government's controversial decision to construct two casinos in early 2000s, using Lacan's concepts of 'the four discourses' and 'the mirror stage', neither of which I invoke here. Like Shubin, Findlay, and McCollum (2014) and Bullock (2014), I tend to rely more on Lacan's lucid contemporary interpreters (e.g. Žižek 1989; Sheehan 2012) than on his original texts.

Before applying Lacan to the analysis, however, it is necessary to lay some groundwork, accounting for why and how the Southeast Asian city-state Singapore has come to desire foreign talent – and foreign talent of specific kinds.

Background: Singapore and the desire for foreign talent

Modern Singapore was founded by the British in the early nineteenth century as a colonial trading post in the largely Malay-Islamic southeast Asia. However, significant inflows of sojourning labour from China throughout the nineteenth and early twentieth centuries meant that by the end of the Second World War, Singaporean society comprised a three-quarter ethnic Chinese majority, with Malays and Indians forming the main ethnic minorities. In 1965, due significantly to its 'Chineseness', Singapore was forced to leave the Federation of Malaysia, with which it had merged two years earlier, and became an independent state. As often said in the vernacular, Singapore was 'kicked out' of Malaysia. It could be said that a constitutive paranoia was germinated at this traumatic *birth-by-rejection*. This paranoia about its profound vulnerability and its *lack* of resources to survive on its own arguably became a defining trait of the government led by the People's Action Party (PAP).

After independence, the PAP state, headed by British-educated Straits Chinese of elite backgrounds, such as Lee Kuan Yew, pursued developmentalism based on attracting foreign investment and export-oriented manufacturing (Rodan 1989). The PAP put in place a 'soft authoritarian' (Roy 1994) political system to ensure general socio-political stability. Through suppressing the trade union movement and leftism in general, it kept down labour costs and created a favourable environment for foreign capital. As a result, Singapore's initial industrialisation was a success and, by the late 1970s, it was clear that the vulnerable independent island state had not only survived – it was on its way to becoming one of Asia's 'tiger economies'.

Towards the end of the 1970s, the PAP began to fear 'Western corruptive influences' on Singaporeans' moral values due to rising material affluence and increasing internationalisation (Kong 2000). In response, the pedagogical PAP state propagated a set of discourses organised around the notion of 'Confucian values' and 'Asian values' in the 1980s. This coincided with the launch of the Speak Mandarin Campaign – an official campaign rooted in the idea that for the majority Chinese Singaporeans, Mandarin, as their Chinese 'mother tongue', was the sub-conscious repository or source of their 'Confucian values' (Kuah 1990; Hill 2000; Thompson 2000). This was ironic because it was southern Chinese dialects such as Hokkien and Teochew, not Mandarin, that were the mother tongues spoken by most ethnic Chinese in Singapore up to that point. Put in simplistic terms, since the 1980s, Singaporeans were, on the one hand, expected to continue to be competent participants in an internationalising capitalist economy and, on the other hand, pressed by their state to stick to or reemphasise their putative 'Asian' (notably *Chinese*) roots and values. This latter expectation was to be institutionalised through bilingualism (Lee 2011) and moral-religious education introduced later into the school curricular (Kuo 1996).

Launched in 1979, the Speak Mandarin Campaign also coincided with China's momentous post-Mao 'reform and opening up' programme. China's then paramount leader Deng Xiaoping, credited to be the 'chief architect' of the reform, was said to have sought inspiration and advice from Lee Kuan Yew during a visit to Singapore late in 1978. Thus, one might view the Singapore state's abrupt favourable turn towards Mandarin as a pragmatic response to changing external geopolitico-economic circumstances. China presented great investment opportunities for Singapore and subsequently provided a huge market and a deep pool of human resources. Meanwhile, as the motherland of Confucianism and the 'middle kingdom' where Mandarin originated, China (or 'the PRC' as referred to in local parlance) started to loom culturally and symbolically large over Singapore. Whether Singapore's interest in China was utilitarian or otherwise, some scholars (e.g. Lai 1995, 142; Tan 2003; Teng 2005) have observed how Singapore since the 1980s began to be 'Sinicised'. Goh (2014) argued that China's ascendance has exerted reorienting influences over Singapore's governing elites' imaginaries of the island state's cultural and political self-identity.

Also during the 1980s, as local wage levels and living standards rose dramatically, the ever paranoid Singapore government began feeling pressure with regard to the country's economic competitiveness. It was imperative to develop a more skilled workforce compatible with the dawning knowledge-based global economy (Low 2002). Furthermore, rapid industrialisation had led to declining fertility rates (Hudson 2013) and 'brain drain' due to emigration (Tan 2005), both of which threatened to undermine Singapore's talent pool. Facing these challenges, the state responded by attracting foreign talent, seen as indispensable to the country's continuous economic prosperity and fundamental long-term demographic survival.

Since state-initiated foreign talent scouting first began in 1980 (Quah 1984), and particularly in the 1990s and the following decade, various policy measures were implemented to ease the path for skilled foreigners to work, study and settle in Singapore. These included general, passive measures such as liberal immigration and visa rules and low barriers for local employers to recruit foreign personnel (Yeoh 2013), as well as more specific, proactive measures such as state-sponsored programmes to recruit foreign sports talent (Yang 2014a) and tertiary science and engineering students (Yang 2014b, 2016). These skilled foreign subjects are generally considered as desirable candidates for naturalisation. They come in sharp contrast with the 'undesirable' foreign workers of lower skill and/or education level that Singapore nevertheless relies upon heavily (Montsion 2012). This division led Yeoh (2006) to characterise Singapore's foreign labour regime as 'bifurcated'. From inflows of both kinds, Singapore's population increased from the 1990 level of three million – 90% of whom were citizens – to the mid-2016 level of 5.53 million, less than 61% of whom were citizens (Singapore Department of Statistics 2016). Not all foreigners in Singapore are 'foreign talent' per se, yet the term has nevertheless become a catchall.

The recent rise of local 'anxiety', 'resentment' and 'xenophobia' towards foreign talent has been well documented (Leong 2011; Gomes 2014; Yap, Koh, and Soon 2015), with several accounts (Yeoh and Lin 2013; Liu 2014; Yang 2014a) specifically noting the ways in which immigrants from the PRC have figured centrally in these contentions. Although official statistics are lacking, PRC citizens no doubt make up one of the largest immigrant groups in Singapore, possibly the largest (Yim 2011). Since the Chinese are the local ethnic/racial group with the lowest reproductive rates, foreign talent from China is desirable because such subjects help shore up the status quo ethnic composition in Singapore (Yim 2011; Yeoh and Lin 2013). In addition, the Singapore state's self-consciousness as an Asian society with Confucian values and Chinese language forming the 'cultural ballast' to its Western facade puts ethnically Chinese immigrants in a uniquely favoured position. Foreign talent from China thus provides arguably the most productive case for analysing – and psychoanalysing – anti-immigrant sentiments and discourses in Singapore, which are indeed often directed at PRC immigrants.

Notes on data and methodological approach

The data underpinning this study comes from (1) secondary sources drawn from existing literature, (2) information gathered from official sources, such as ministerial speeches and government websites and (3) qualitative content collected from the mass media, especially that which is available on the Internet. Concerning the third type of data, as Gomes (2014) has pointed out, xenophobia in Singapore is found predominantly online due to the Internet's accessibility and anonymity. Thus, online content uniquely records psychic and emotional outbursts concerning foreign talent, which often contain discourses, narratives and imaginations not given outlet and/or deemed unacceptable in mainstream media channels.[3] The discursive content found on the Internet may not be statistically 'representative', but this does not undermine this article's objective of providing a fresh and provocative psychoanalytic reading of Singapore's foreign talent situation.

Consequently, instead of a more conventional approach to content extraction and analysis, my data collection was carried out in a purposive rather than systematic manner, which is above all informed and directed by theory. The Lacanian psychoanalytic lens helped filter and single out certain facts and discursive events about foreign talent as particularly relevant; conversely, specific events or discursive materials suggestive of desire – of the psychic – pushed me further in thinking about the relevance of Lacan's theories. Such an iterative process took place over a period of several years, during which I observed Singapore society online and offline in the dual capacity as a scholar and a student-turned-foreign-talent-migrant in the city-state. In fact, I do not deny that I occupied a particular position within the social field that is my object of study. This positionality, I believe, has been a significant strength, if not an indispensable element, to this study.

Of mainland Chinese background and having received a tertiary scholarship carrying a service bond from the Singapore government a decade-and-a-half ago, I may be regarded as a beneficiary of Singapore's foreign talent policy, in particular via the student recruitment route (e.g. Yang 2014b, 2016). For the same reason, however, as immigration became increasingly controversial and scandals specifically surrounding 'PRC foreign talent' drew online flak from time to time (Yeoh and Lin 2013; Yang 2014a), it was hard for me to remain unaffected. How PRC foreign talent and foreign talent in general, were talked about and imagined in Singapore held my attention, leaving me to mull over these observations regularly. As such, my analyses below have been informed by the knowledge I gathered organically as well as with the psycho-emotional experiences, observations and insights I collected over a long period of time.

Foreign talent as the production of lack

In official discourse as well as general knowledge, foreign talent is said to be injected into Singapore by the state to fill a lack – the lack of human capital. It has also become common to say that the arrival of foreign talent engenders *anxiety* amongst Singaporeans, which, in turn, accounts for the increasingly prevalent anti-immigrant discourses and behaviours in Singaporean life online and offline. However, these notions could be radically rethought in light of Lacan's counterintuitive insight: 'Anxiety is an affect ... that appears when there is no possibility of desire, when there is a "lack of a lack"' (Seshadri-Crooks 2000, 45). In Lacan's own words:

> I would just like to point out to you that many things can appear which are anomalous, that is not what makes us anxious. But if all of a sudden all norms are lacking, namely what constitutes the lack – because the *norm is correlative to the idea of lack* – if all of a sudden it is not lacking – and believe me try to apply that to a lot of things – it is at that moment that anxiety begins. (Lacan, quoted in Seshadri-Crooks 2000, 37, emphases added)

Lacan suggests that anxiety does not arise from lack because lack is the condition for desiring, and to be desiring is normal; instead, anxiety arises precisely when there is a lack of a lack, whereby it becomes impossible to desire and normality is disrupted as a consequence.

In Singapore, it can be argued that the resentment towards foreign talent is in fact not often about *anxiety*. Rather, revealing feelings of victimhood, a superiority complex or, at worst, visceral hostility, this resentment seems to be more accurately characterised by self-righteous indignation and egotism.[4] Such affective states differ from anxiety in that they involve a degree of aggression and certainty, which are not typical of anxiety. To the extent that these affective responses often appear to be very powerful, they might be regarded as the outward manifestations of a certain *desire* incited by the presence of foreign talent. Recalling Deleuze and Guattari's (2004, 29–30) pithy remark that 'Lack is created, planned, and organized in and through social production', it may be similarly argued that foreign talent in Singapore really serves to *produce and reproduce a sense of lack* at the core of the nation-state's psyche. Compared to this function, its ostensible role to supplement local manpower is secondary. The sense of lack, renewed and heightened each time foreign talent is desired and invited in by the state, reproduces a local desiring; and desiring, as Lyotard (1993) points out, is nothing short of the core ingredient to the competitive capitalist economy.

This logic is in fact somewhat openly acknowledged by the Singapore state itself. One of the declared objectives for importing foreign talent – students, professionals or entrepreneurs – is precisely to prevent local students and workforce from becoming 'complacent' by introducing competitive pressure (Fahey and Kenway 2010, 53, 54). In other words, foreign talent makes the locals desire more for themselves, from themselves.

In his first National Day Rally speech as Singapore's Prime Minister in 2004, Lee Hsien Loong (quoted in Oswin and Yeoh 2010, 170) spelt out what 'we' envisioned for the city-state, stating: 'I think this will always be work-in-progress because we will never be satisfied. We always want to move on, do better!' Foreign talent is revealed here as a concept conjured up by the state to serves as evidence and a reminder that Singapore is always 'not there yet' and should 'never be satisfied', which means it needs even more foreign talent. In short, foreign talent is desired so that Singapore can keep desiring.

Foreign talent as Singapore's *objet a*, or the unobtainable object of desire

As touched on in this article's introduction, in Lacanian theory, the subject is characterised by a loss that results from its accession to meaning, to language, namely, to the *symbolic order*. This symbolic order – 'the fabric of socially defined knowledge and the set of rules governing our behaviour and speech' (Sheehan 2012, 16) – is also known in Lacanian terms as the 'big Other'. Subjects are supposed to fill subject positions within the symbolic order; in other words, the big Other casts a demanding gaze of expectation at the subject. However, the Lacanian subject is never fully at ease with the symbolic position it has been assigned; it feels a loss. The process of loss is what Lacan calls a 'symbolic castration', performed by the big Other, subsequent to which the subject is always a subject of lack, incessantly desiring *something*. This something, in Lacanian terminology, is the *objet petit autre* (meaning 'little other object', henceforth *objet a*). Because the desiring subject came into being precisely through loss, the true attainment of *objet a* is impossible, for that would spell the dissolution of the subject altogether. The *objet a* is thus continuously desired but never attained. This paradox lies at the heart of Lacan's theory of desire. As Sheehan (2012, 21) explicates this unattainable *objet a*:

> It is a fantasy object that fills out the fissure in our sense of being, arising from the way our libidinal investment gives it a sublimity that it does not and cannot possess. An abiding attractiveness is attached to the object because it represents something that is felt to have been lost and which will bring closure if only it can be found.

But, as just explained, it can never be found. This *objet a* is not really the *object of desire*, but rather the *object cause of desire* (Fink [1995] 1997). In other words, *objet a* is that on account of which one desires, not that which one desires in the simple sense of possessing or consuming it.

I propose that foreign talent is Singapore's *objet a*. In the foreign talent situation, two distinct yet interrelated scenes can be identified, each involving a specific big Other and a correlative moment of symbolic castration; in both scenes, foreign talent embodies the void or loss and assumes the place of the *objet a*.

Scene 1: foreign talent as the Singaporean state's objet a

The first scene involves Singapore's accession into the post-Fordist global knowledge economy, whereby the big Other is the globalised economic system of financial capital, knowledge-intensive industries and digitalised production and consumption. This system involves a new set of game rules or a new grammar – a new symbolic order. It is *symbolic* in a double sense: firstly, it was the emerging big Other confronting nation-states worldwide, demanding they play by its new rules to stay afloat; at the same time, as Reich (1992) pointed out, the current global knowledge economy is literally *symbolic* because value is created largely through the manipulation of symbols (digital signals, computing codes, etc.) to be carried out by what he calls 'symbolic analysts', i.e. knowledge workers.

Eager to be fully compatible with this new economic mode – in other words, to accede to this emerging symbolic order – the Singaporean state suffers a symbolic castration, traumatically realising its lack of *something*. Foreign talent was identified as that something, the *objet a*, that will do the magic *if only* it could be found and brought to the city-state. Recall that Singapore's economy in the 1980s still largely consisted of low-value-adding manufacturing industries. As recently as his 2015 Labour Day speech, Prime Minister Lee Hsien Loong identified low productivity as a major threat to Singapore's future economic health (Prime Minister's Office 2015). The local workforce's skill level is identified as the main problem and foreign talent as the solution.

For some two decades now, Singapore has operated what is very much an open-door policy to foreigners deemed talented and of added value to the city-state. In the first years of the 2000s especially, official rhetoric about foreign talent became ubiquitous, being reflected in the rise of granting permanent residence statuses, which peaked at close to 80,000 in 2008 (population.sg 2015). No doubt the foreign talent policy proved effective in generating economic prosperity, and it was set to continue. Only in response to growing popular dissatisfaction – evidenced in the PAP's poor performance in the 2011 general election and a rare popular protest in 2013 following a whitepaper about population (population.sg 2013) – did the PAP state most recently start to tone down its rhetoric and slow down the admission of foreign talent. However, it is crucial to realise that this by no means indicated a policy U-turn, and there is no evidence that the government has stopped desiring foreign talent. In fact, the governing elites in Singapore continue to persuade the public, if only in a more subdued fashion, that highly skilled immigration is necessary for the greater good. For instance, although it was barely one year after the 'watershed' general election in 2011, as it had since come to be known, Prime Minister Lee Hsiang Loong addressed the Singapore Manufacturing Federation in 2012, remarking 'of course we need to continue to welcome foreign talent' (Prime Minister's Office 2012). Clearly, for Singapore, foreign talent remains highly desirable, and the endeavour to recruit such subjects remains a work-in-progress – a mission that is unlikely to be declared 'accomplished'.

If for the Singapore state, desiring foreign talent is an on-going concern and having enough foreign talent an as yet unachievable objective, it is even more apparent that from the perspective of the Singaporean public, the 'right' foreign talent had never been obtainable. Recall, *objet a* is 'a fantasy object … [that] does not have the quality attributed to it' (Sheehan 2012, 21). Indeed, there is abundant empirical evidence that the Singaporean public has been vociferously trying to establish the defects and undesirability of concrete foreign talent subjects found in their midst. In local social media and online tabloids of various kinds, foreign talent subjects have been portrayed as, amongst other things, too inadequate (therefore 'foreign trash'), too 'talented' (therefore clever by half and devious) or deficient in one way or another, such as lacking moral fibres or cosmopolitan sociability and sensibility.

For example, foreign students receiving Singapore-funded scholarships but not performing academically well and foreign professionals doing medium- and low-pay work are seen as proof that much foreign talent is mediocre or downright bogus (Yang

2014a). For some locals, this perception was so disturbing that expressions such as 'third-rate foreigners' (Wong 2001) and 'liabilities, not assets' (Wee 2001) were used to describe inferior 'foreign talent'. Even for those who are credited as being truly talented, there remain constant suspicions from Singaporeans that these foreign talents possess neither gratitude nor loyalty to Singapore (e.g. He 2008), and merely use it as a 'stepping stone' (Chong 2015) or treats it as a 'hotel'. Furthermore, scandalous cases such as those of Ma Chi,[5] Anton Casey[6] and Sun Xu,[7] all seem to illustrate how arrogant and obnoxious some foreign talent might be. Above all, such individuals are often perceived to lack the will or ability to integrate into the local society, as shown from the momentum gathered by the 'Cook a pot of curry' Facebook event in 2011.[8]

It is crucial to realise that whenever anti-foreign talent sentiments and discourses have been expressed by the Singaporean public, rarely at issue was the abstract idea of foreign talent, but rather human beings in flesh and blood. It is not so much a question of foreign talent being undesirable, but rather that the real foreign talent Singapore desires has yet to materialise. In this scene at least, the Singaporean public and state seem remarkably aligned: foreign talent as an *ideal* remains desirable and thus must continue to be desired because the concrete talent thus far imported is unsatisfactory.

Scene 2: PRC foreign talent as Chinese Singaporeans' **objet a**

In the second scene, the subject is the native Singaporean, and his big Other is the Singapore state. The state is an appropriate figuration of this, for it is the author of laws and rules – the symbolic order – as well as the paternalistic and pedagogical authority who never tires of telling its children-citizens how to behave and how to desire (Heng and Devan 1995). The Singapore state demands that its citizen-subjects embody certain qualities that define the subject position within the symbolic order. In acceding to this demand and trying to fill the position, the Singaporean subject undergoes a symbolic castration, thus acknowledging a lack, which then gives rise to the *objet a* of foreign talent.

Consider foreign talent from China – and these subjects' highly ambivalent significations for the majority Chinese Singaporeans – against the backdrop of the Singapore state's enduring valorisation of 'Chineseness' through the emphasis of Chinese language and the inculcation of so-called Confucian values. Apart from English, the Singaporean education system requires all students to learn a 'mother tongue' which correlates to a student's officially registered 'racial' identity, regardless of whether the student actually identifies with that language and/or race. Chinese Singaporeans' mother tongue is officially designated to be Mandarin. However, with English increasingly becoming the de facto native tongue spoken by younger generations (Lu 2013), many Chinese Singaporean students today struggle with learning a language, and its accompanying culture, which little interests them. Students who excel in their mother tongue are regarded – unfairly, some argue – as more talented; those who do not are often forced by their parents to get private tutoring because it is a prerequisite to have a certain proficiency level in one's mother tongue to qualify for government-subsidised local university education. It is not unheard of for Singaporean students to opt for more expensive higher education overseas because they have failed their 'mother tongue' subject in school. Thus, to some Singaporeans, the so-called mother tongue is anything but maternal or intimate, becoming an '(m)other tongue'. This irony – of having to actively learn a mother tongue – is a telling aspect of Singaporeans' experience of symbolic castration as they comply, willingly or by force, with their Sinicised (or self-consciously 'Asian') state, the big Other.

In this vein, PRC foreign talent becomes Chinese Singaporeans' object of envy and desire for being able to speak 'proper' Mandarin – the '(m)other tongue' which Chinese Singaporeans are expected to be competent at but have lost grip of. (One might add: this loss is an imagined loss founded on a fantasised possession that never really was.) Revealingly, a notable number of '(m)other tongue' Mandarin language teachers in Singaporean schools nowadays are foreign talent from mainland China. To share more auto-ethnographic evidence, I have regularly heard in my own interactions with Chinese Singaporeans that they believed their Chinese would never be as 'natural' or 'fluent' as mine and that their vocabulary would always be limited in comparison. Broadly speaking, the PRC Chinese supposedly embody more authentic Chinese values and culture, which Chinese Singaporeans have supposedly lost due to Westernisation and colonialisation and are now enjoined to rediscover by their big Other state. In this fashion, in a Singapore state-orchestrated symbolic order where Chineseness is extolled, PRC foreign talent is desirable because ideally it represents for the Chinese Singaporean 'some missing component of the subject's self', which is how Silverman (1983, 156) explains the abiding pull of the Lacanian *objet a*.

However, *objet a* is by definition unattainable. Parallel to how foreign talent in general fails to materialise in scene 1, the truly desirable ideal PRC foreign talent also dramatically fails to materialise; in fact, it oftentimes ends up in real life as an undesirable, even detestable, figure for Singaporeans. In Singapore, the mainland Chinese have acquired a reputation for being loud-mouthed and woefully uncivilised. In certain ethnic enclaves, such as Chinatown and Geylang, the Chinese spoken by the migrant workers of rural or urban working-class backgrounds and by those hard-working but suspected-to-be-cunning small business owners from China is emphatically not the pristine or stilted Mandarin that Singaporeans are accustomed to hearing through classroom learning. Instead, it sounds 'strange' and unsettling (Tan 2011) due to the regional accents and slang.

Even more prominently, despite hailing from the homeland of sage Confucius, the mainland Chinese are often seen by Singaporeans as the epitome of moral degeneration and behavioural indiscipline. Falling under this theme are more examples than space allows me to detail here. For instance, the image of the female Chinese gold digger who uses sexual allure to gain material advantages, wrecking local families, is deeply entrenched in Singaporean imagination, be it about those bogus student visa holders (*xiao long nü*) or 'study mamas' (Huang and Yeoh 2005). A recent high-profile case in the gold digger genre involved a male tour guide from China who manipulated an elderly Singaporean woman to get his hands on her substantial fortune. Over the years, numerous cases of rude or uncivilised public behaviour by PRC nationals have been recorded on people's mobile phones, with the images/videos subsequently going viral and generating many heated emotional exchanges.

One such instance in 2015 involved a Chinese woman who was filmed acting aggressively in an argument with a Singaporean man.[9] What was most intriguing about this case, however, was that soon after, on the same tabloid website that first carried the video, a post appeared under the sensational title '7 reasons why PRC women are better than Sg women'.[10] The seventh reason states: 'PRC women are good in bed. If they decide to play nice for the day and take a shower, they do offer more than the tame Singapore girl.' Here, the implicit correlation was between PRC women's stereotypically aggressive, loud behaviour and superior sexual energy and performance. For Singaporeans, an ambivalent calculus of PRC immigrants' desirability and undesirability is revealed here through imagining the figure of 'the PRC woman': she has more to offer, but it is contingent on her compliance with Singaporean morals and hygiene practices ('play nice for the day and take a shower'). In other words, she is potentially desirable, but always marred by a certain *excess* or *deficit*. This example, I argue, captures again how for Singapore and Singaporeans, the desired PRC foreign talent and foreign talent in general, are never quite 'right' when they actually arrive. This only makes the fantasied, ideal foreign talent yet more desirable, albeit perpetually unattainable.

Conclusion

In this article, I presented a psychoanalytic reading of Singapore's recent immigration tensions by applying Lacan to the local society's discourses and imaginations about foreign talent. Drawing particularly on Lacan's ideas that lack is normal and fundamental to a desiring subjectivity and that desire revolves around a paradoxically unobtainable object (*objet a*), I suggested that foreign talent mainly serves the function of producing lack and stands in as the *objet a* of both the Singaporean state's and Singaporeans' desires. As Žižek (1989, 158) has put it, *objet a* is 'the original lost object which in a way coincides with its own loss, [it is] precisely the embodiment of this void'. For a Singapore state inevitably confronted with the global knowledge economy – a symbolic order, 'foreign talent' stands for the structural void or loss in the symbolic order. This void or loss is structural to the extent that the capitalist knowledge economy can see no limit to value/wealth generation through creativity and innovation by talented knowledge workers. In other words, there is always a lack of knowledge workers; and for the Singapore state, such knowledge workers take the shape of 'foreign talent'. Secondly, for Singaporeans unavoidably interpellated into an impossibly ideal subjecthood by their paternalistic and pedagogic state, foreign talent stands for whatever qualities the local citizens are supposed to lack. In both scenarios, the actual foreign talent subjects arrive as disappointments, unable to satisfy the desire that Singapore and Singaporeans have invested in this object. As something that Singapore can never have enough of and yet always finds wanting when it actually obtains it, foreign talent shows itself to be the sublime object of Singapore's ideology (Žižek 1989) – a fantasy object impossible to materialise. Thus, the arrival of foreign talent in flesh and blood does not make Singapore somehow complete, wholesome or perfect, but only serves to make it even more of a work-in-progress and desiring-in-process.

In arriving at this reading, I mostly relied on PRC foreign talent in the city-state because this group seems to provide the most fertile analytical case. Nevertheless, this is not meant to be a reductionist reading of foreign talent, which is a necessarily disaggregated and unstable figure. Foreign talent of other ethnic or cultural backgrounds may have different significations for Singapore/Singaporeans, but similar arguments could be made, though this lies beyond the scope of this article.[11] Recognising the complexity and variability in Singapore's desire for foreign talent further helps highlight the inconsistencies in the big Other's demand and the unobtainability of the Lacanian *objet a*.

Finally and more broadly, in this article I have sought to contribute to and advocate a diversification of ways to approach migration and mobility research. Mainstream migration studies have been dominated by a governmental approach that accentuates state and state regulations (de Jong 2016) and a 'rationalistic' approach (see Carling and Collins 2018) rooted in neoclassical theories. Whilst the subjective and humanistic experiences in migration, such as affect and emotion, have received increasing attention as of late, this effort still remains limited. By prying open the black box of 'desire' with the theoretical tool of Lacanian psychoanalysis, this article shows that much more can be said about migration and mobility than merely policy and push–pull factors. It shows that novel and provocative explanations about mobility-related social phenomena can be made when migration scholars seriously consider fantasy, desire and emotion.

Notes

1. Following Svašek, I use 'affect' and 'emotion' interchangeably, although I acknowledge that in other contexts the distinction between the two is crucial (see Pile 2009).
2. It is worth recalling that psychoanalytic thinkers such as Freud and Lacan regarded themselves primarily as clinical practitioners.
3. In Singapore, the state retains strong influence, arguably ultimate control, over the press and media through state-owned holding companies.
4. Various examples could be found on prominent websites carrying dissenting opinions in Singapore, such as The Real Singapore (now defunct), All Singapore Stuff (http://www.allsingaporestuff.com) and States Times Review (http://statestimesreview.com).
5. Millionaire Chinese national Ma Chi's reckless driving (of a red Ferrari) cost him his own life and those of a Singaporean taxi driver and a Japanese visitor. The Singaporean public's reactions to this accident, however, seemed notably inflected by Ma's wealth and nationality (see Yeoh and Lin 2013).
6. In 2014, wealthy British businessman Anton Casey ridiculed the less well-to-do in Singapore, causing a public furore (http://www.independent.co.uk/news/business/news/anton-casey-fired-and-flees-singapore-in-economy-class-over-poor-people-comments-9088199.html).
7. Sun Xu, a student from China on a Singapore government-funded tertiary scholarship, offended the local public by making a statement of ill judgement and poor taste, saying that 'there are more dogs than human in Singapore' (see Yang 2016, p. 1).
8. In 2011, Singaporean netizens initiated a Facebook event called 'Cook a pot of curry' to protest the fact that a migrant family from China had requested their local Indian neighbour limit the cooking of curry and obtained favourable mediation from the housing estate council.
9. http://www.allsingaporestuff.com/article/prc-women-who-spit-and-hit-sg-man-aremenace-society (last accessed 9 May, 2015).
10. http://www.allsingaporestuff.com/article/7-reasons-why-prc-women-are-bettersg-women (last accessed 9 May, 2015).
11. For instance, Western and/or white foreign talent in the Singaporean schema of desire is often taken to signify creativity, entrepreneurship and individualism, which is in some ways the obverse of Confucian and Asian values but still highly desired.

Disclosure statement

No potential conflict of interest was reported by the author.

References

Bullock, Nathan F. 2014. "Lacan on Urban Development and National Identity in a Global City: Integrated Resorts in Singapore." *Singapore Journal of Tropical Geography* 35 (2): 213–227. 10.1111/sjtg.12062.

Carling, J., and F. Collins. 2018. "Aspiration, Desire and Drivers of Migration." *Journal of Ethnic and Migration Studies* 44 (6): 909–926. doi:10.1080/1369183X.2017.1384134.

Chong, Terence. 2015. "Stepping Stone Singapore: The Cultural Politics of Anti-Immigrant Anxieties." In *Migration and Integration in Singapore: Policies and Practice*, edited by M. T. Yap, G. Koh, and D. Soon, 214–229. London: Routledge.

Conradson, David, and Deirdre Mckay. 2007. "Translocal Subjectivities: Mobility, Connection, Emotion." *Mobilities* 2 (2): 167–174. doi:10.1080/17450100701381524.

de Jong, Sara. 2016. "Converging Logics? Managing Migration and Managing Diversity." *Journal of Ethnic and Migration Studies* 42 (3): 341–358. doi:10.1080/1369183X.2015.1074857.

Deleuze, Gilles, and Félix Guattari. 2004. *Anti-Oedipus*. London: Continuum.

Fahey, Johannah, and Jane Kenway. 2010. "The Ethics of National Hospitality and Globally Mobile Researchers." In *The Routledge International Handbook of the Sociology of Education*, edited by M. W. Apple, S. J. Ball, and L. A. Gandin, 48–57. Abingdon: Routledge.

Fink, Bruce. (1995) 1997. *The Lacanian Subject: Between Language and Jouissance*. Princeton, NJ: Princeton University Press.

Goh, Daniel P. S. 2014. "Elite Schools, Postcolonial Chineseness and Hegemonic Masculinity in Singapore." *British Journal of Sociology of Education* 36 (1): 137–155.

Gomes, Catherine. 2014. "Xenophobia Online: Unmasking Singaporean Attitudes Towards 'Foreign Talent' Migrants." *Asian Ethnicity* 15 (1): 21–40. doi:10.1080/14631369.2013.784511.

Hall, Alexandra. 2010. "'These People Could Be Anyone': Fear, Contempt (and Empathy) in a British Immigration Removal Centre." *Journal of Ethnic and Migration Studies* 36 (6): 881–898. doi:10.1080/13691831003643330.

He, Yanying. 2008. "Give Scholarships to Foreigners with Care." *The Straits Times*, August 15.

Healy, Claire. 2007. "A Nation of Emigrants or Immigrants? The Challenge of Integration in Ireland and Portugal." *Irish Migration Studies in Latin America* 5 (2): 117–120.

Heizmann, Boris. 2016. "Symbolic Boundaries, Incorporation Policies, and Anti-Immigrant Attitudes: What Drives Exclusionary Policy Preferences?" *Ethnic and Racial Studies* 39 (10): 1791–1811. doi:10.1080/01419870.2015.1124128.

Hellwig, Timothy, and Abdulkader Sinno. 2016. "Different Groups, Different Threats: Public Attitudes Towards Immigrants." *Journal of Ethnic and Migration Studies*, 1–20. doi:10.1080/1369183X.2016.1202749.

Heng, Geraldine, and Janadas Devan. 1995. "State Fatherhood: The Politics of Nationalism, Sexuality, and Race in Singapore." In *Bewitching Women, Pious Men: Gender and Body Politics in Southeast Asia*, edited by M. G. Peletz and A. Ong, 343–364. Berkeley: University of California Press.

Hill, Michael. 2000. "'Asian Values' as Reverse Orientalism: Singapore." *Asia Pacific Viewpoint* 41 (2): 177–190. doi:10.1111/1467-8373.00114.

Huang, Shirlena, and Brenda S. A. Yeoh. 2005. "Transnational Families and Their Children's Education: China's 'Study Mothers' in Singapore." *Global Networks* 5 (4): 379–400. doi:10.1111/j.1471-0374.2005.00125.x.

Hudson, Chris. 2013. *Beyond the Singapore Girl: Discourses of Gender and Nation in Singapore*. Copenhagen: NIAS Press.

Koh, Aaron. 2003. "Global Flows of Foreign Talent: Identity Anxieties in Singapore's Ethnoscape." *Journal of Social Issues in Southeast Asia* 18 (2): 230–256. doi:10.1355/SJ18-2C.

Kong, Lily. 2000. "Cultural Policy in Singapore: Negotiating Economic and Socio-cultural Agendas." *Geoforum* 31 (4): 409–424. doi:10.1016/S0016-7185(00)00006-3.

Kuah, Khun Eng. 1990. "Confucian Ideology and Social Engineering in Singapore." *Journal of Contemporary Asia* 20 (3): 371–383. doi:10.1080/00472339080000381.

Kuntsman, Adi. 2009. "The Currency of Victimhood in Uncanny Homes: Queer Immigrants' Claims for Home and Belonging Through Anti-Homophobic Organising." *Journal of Ethnic and Migration Studies* 35 (1): 133–149. doi:10.1080/13691830802489291.

Kuo, Eddie. 1996. "Confucianism as Political Discourse in Singapore." In *Confucian Tradition in East Asian Modernity: Moral Education and Economic Culture in Japan and the Four Mini-Dragon*, edited by W.-M. Tu, 294–310. Cambridge, MA: Harvard University Press.

Lacan, Jacques. 1977. *Ecrits: A Selection*. Translated by A. Sheridan. New York: Norton.

Lacan, Jacques. 2006. *Ecrits*. Translated by B. Fink. New York: Praeger Publishers.

Lai, Ah Eng. 1995. *Meanings of Multiethnicity: A Case-study of Ethnicity and Ethnic Relations in Singapore*. Kuala Lumpur: Oxford University Press.

Lee, Kuan Yew. 2011. *My Lifelong Challenge: Singapore's Bilingual Journey*. Singapore: Straits Times Press.

Leong, Susan. 2011. "No Longer Singaporean." *Continuum: Journal of Media & Cultural Studies* 25 (4): 559–572. doi:10.1080/10304312.2011.575215.

Li, Xueying. 1999. "We Are Yours, Please Make Use of Us." *The Straits Times*, December 8.

Liu, Hong. 2014. "Beyond Co-Ethnicity: The Politics of Differentiating and Integrating New Immigrants in Singapore." *Ethnic and Racial Studies* 37 (7): 1225–1238. doi:10.1080/01419870.2014.892630.

Low, Linda. 2002. "Globalisation and the Political Economy of Singapore's Policy on Foreign Talent and High Skills." *Journal of Education and Work* 15 (4): 409–425. doi:10.1080/1363908022000023551.

Lu, Luke. 2013. "Can English be a Singaporean Mother Tongue?" Accessed May 11, 2015. http://www.todayonline.com/commentary/can-english-be-singaporean-mother-tongue.

Lyotard, Jean-François. 1993. *Libidinal Economy*. Translated by I. H. Grant. Bloomington: Indianna University Press.

Montsion, Jean Michel. 2012. "When Talent Meets Mobility: Un/Desirability in Singapore's New Citizenship Project." *Citizenship Studies* 16 (3–4): 469–482. doi:10.1080/13621025.2012.683259.

Oswin, Natalie, and Brenda S. A. Yeoh. 2010. "Introduction: Mobile City Singapore." *Mobilities* 5 (2): 167–175. doi:10.1080/17450101003665002.

Pile, Steve. 2009. "Emotions and Affect in Recent Human Geography." *Transactions of the Institute of British Geographers* 35 (1): 5–20. doi:10.1111/j.5661.2009.00368.x.

population.sg. 2013. "A Sustainable Population for a Dynamic Singapore: Population White Paper." Accessed June 24, 2016. http://population.sg/whitepaper/resource-files/population-white-paper.pdf.

population.sg. 2015. "Population in Brief 2015." Accessed June 24, 2016. http://population.sg/population-in-brief/files/population-in-brief-2015.pdf.

Prime Minister's Office. 2012. "Speech by Prime Minister Lee Hsien Loong at Singapore Manufacturers' Federation 80th Anniversary Dinner." Accessed July 24, 2016. http://www.pmo.gov.sg/mediacentre/speech-prime-minister-lee-hsien-loong-singapore-manufacturers-federation-80th.

Prime Minister's Office. 2015. "Transcript of Prime Minister Lee Hsien Loong's May Day Rally speech on 1 May 2015." Accessed July 24, 2016. http://www.pmo.gov.sg/mediacentre/transcript-prime-minister-lee-hsien-loong-may-day-rally-speech-1-may-2015.

Quah, Jon S. T. 1984. "Singapore in 1983: The Continuing Search for Talent." *Asian Survey* 24 (2): 178–186. doi:10.1525/as.1984.24.2.01p0130q.

Reay, Diane. 2005. "Beyond Consciousness? The Psychic Landscape of Social Class." *Sociology* 39 (5): 911–928. doi:10.1177/0038038505058372.

Reay, Diane. 2008. "Psychosocial Aspects of White Middle-class Identities: Desiring and Defending Against the Class and Ethnic 'Other' in Urban Multi-ethnic Schooling." *Sociology* 42 (6): 1072–1088. doi:10.1177/0038038508096934.

Reich, Robert. 1992. *The Work of Nations*. New York: Vintage Books.

Rodan, Garry. 1989. *The Political Economy of Singapore's Industrialization: National State and International Capital*. London: Macmillan Press.

Roy, Denny. 1994. "Singapore, China, and the 'Soft Authoritarian' Challenge." *Asian Survey* 34 (3): 231–242. doi:10.2307/2644982.

Seshadri-Crooks, Kalpana. 2000. *Desiring Whiteness: A Lacanian Analysis of Race*. London: Routledge.

Sheehan, Sean. 2012. *Žižek: A Guide for the Perplexed*. London: Continuum.

Shubin, Sergei, Allan Findlay, and David McCollum. 2014. "Imaginaries of the Ideal Migrant Worker: A Lacanian Interpretation." *Environment and Planning D: Society and Space* 32 (3): 466–483. doi:10.1068/d22212.

Silverman, Kaja. 1983. *The Subject of Semiotics*. New York: Oxford University Press.

Singapore Department of Statistics. 2016. "Latest Data." Accessed July 15, 2016. http://www.singstat.gov.sg/statistics/latest-data - 17.

Svašek, Maruška. 2010. "On the Move: Emotions and Human Mobility." *Journal of Ethnic and Migration Studies* 36 (6): 865–880. doi:10.1080/13691831003643322.

Tan, Eugene K. B. 2003. "Re-Engaging Chineseness: Political, Economic and Cultural Imperatives of Nation-Building in Singapore." *The China Quarterly* 175: 751–774.

Tan, Ern Ser. 2005. "Globalization, Nation-Building and Emigration: The Singapore Case." In *Asian Migrations: Sojourning, Displacement, Homecoming and Other Travels*, edited by B. P. Lorente, N. Piper, H.-H. Shen, and B. S. A. Yeoh, 87–98. Singapore: Asia Research Institute.

Tan, Sumiko. 2011. "I Felt Like a Stranger in My Own Country." *Sunday Times*, July 10.

Teng, Siao See. 2005. "What 'Chineseness', Whose 'Chineseness?' A Preliminary Assessment of 'Sinicisation' in the Discussion of Culture and Ethnicity in Postcolonial Singapore." *Department of Sociology Graduate Journal*. http://www.essex.ac.uk/sociology/documents/pdf/graduate_journal/5_teng.pdf.

Thompson, Mark R. 2000. "The Survival of 'Asian Values' as 'Zivilisationskritik'." *Theory and Society* 29 (5): 651–686. doi:10.1023/A:1026550721141.

Vasu, Norman, Su Yin Yeap, and Wen Ling Chan, eds. 2014. *Immigration in Singapore*. Amsterdam: Amsterdam University Press.

Walkerdine, Valerie. 2010. "Communal Beingness and Affect: An Exploration of Trauma in an Ex-Industrial Community." *Body & Society* 16 (1): 91–116. doi:10.1177/1357034X09354127.

Wee, Ka Min Andrew. 2001. "Foreign-talent Contribution Report Flawed." *The Straits Times*, November 7.

Wise, Amanda. 2010. "Sensuous Multiculturalism: Emotional Landscapes of Inter-Ethnic Living in Australian Suburbia." *Journal of Ethnic and Migration Studies* 36 (6): 917–937. doi:10.1080/13691831003643355.

Wong, Seow Choon George. 2001. "Guard Against Hiring Inferior Foreign Talent." *The Straits Times*, August 21.

Yang, Peidong. 2014a. "'Authenticity' and 'Foreign Talent' in Singapore: The Relative and Negative Logic of National Identity." *SOJOURN: Journal of Social Issues in Southeast Asia* 29 (2): 408–437. doi:10.1355/sj29-2f.

Yang, Peidong. 2014b. "Privilege, Prejudice, Predicament: The 'PRC Scholars' in Singapore – An Overview." *Frontiers of Education in China* 9 (3): 350–376.

Yang, Peidong. 2016. *International Mobility and Educational Desire: Chinese Foreign Talent Students in Singapore*. New York: Palgrave Macmillan.

Yap, Mui Teng, Koh, Gillian, and Soon, Debbie, eds. 2015. *Migration and Integration in Singapore: Policies and Practice*. London: Routledge.

Yeoh, Brenda S. A. 2006. "Bifurcated Labour: The Unequal Incorporation of Transmigrants in Singapore." *Tijdschrift voor Economische en Sociale Geografie* 97 (1): 26–37. doi:10.1111/j.1467-9663.2006.00493.x.

Yeoh, Brenda S. A. 2013. "'Upwards' or 'Sideways' Cosmopolitanism? Talent/Labour/Marriage Migrations in the Globalising City-State of Singapore." *Migration Studies* 1 (1): 96–116. doi:10.1093/migration/mns037.

Yeoh, Brenda S. A., and Weiqiang Lin. 2013. "Chinese Migration to Singapore: Discourses and Discontents in a Globalizing Nation-State." *Asian and Pacific Migration Journal* 22 (1): 31–54. doi:10.1177/011719681302200103.

Yim, Ching-Ching. 2011. "*Transnational Social Spaces and Transnationalism: A Study on the new Chinese Migrant Community in Singapore*." *PhD*, University of Hong Kong.

Žižek, Slavoj. 1989. *The Sublime Object of Ideology*. London: Verso.

Navigating aspirations and expectations: adolescents' considerations of outmigration from rural eastern Germany

Frank Meyer

ABSTRACT

From the perspective of policymakers, young people are often regarded as the most important group for the future development of rural regions experiencing socioeconomic polarisation. They, in turn, usually see themselves and their desire to migrate not as the driving force of population decline, but as a symptom of it. Although politicians urge adolescents to not leave rural regions despite the hard times, adolescents expressly do so because of the socioeconomic conditions and limited local opportunities. Drawing on a case study of Altenburger Land – a rural district in eastern Germany suffering from limited job opportunities for adolescents, outmigration and negative depictions in the media – this article aims to explain the conditions of migration and their impact on adolescent migratory decision-making. In sum, adolescents' choices happen in a nexus of social relations, emotions and political programmes. Besides their own attempts of becoming, these contested fields of expectations from different entities create a norm-driven array of discourses permeating many aspects of their lives. Therefore, migration in this context can be considered as a product of spatial and spatialised discourses through which a subject must navigate.

Introduction

Since Germany's reunification, rural regions in the east of the country have struggled with outmigration, unemployment and poor economic performance, particularly when compared with urban regions. Under such conditions of socioeconomic polarisation, adolescents are often considered as the most important group for development of the rural from the perspective of policymakers. Although politicians urge them not to leave rural regions despite the hard times, adolescents do so expressly because of the socioeconomic conditions and limited local opportunities.

Migration seems to be a contested field with various entities ascribing meaning to it, beyond mere movement of people. Given the political impact of adolescent outmigration, it is even more pressing to acknowledge that 'experiences of migration are socially constructed and politically contested rather than the product of the "natural" evolution of demographic and economic processes' (White and Jackson 1995, 115). Adolescents do not choose in a vacuum; their choices happen within a nexus of social relations, emotions and political programmes. For some, 'the intention to migrate or not, then, is not simply a matter of comparing expected personal gain or place utility, but of taking a stance with ethical implications' (Carling 2002, 17). As such, understanding migration and its relation to concepts such as aspiration and desire must entail understanding its discursive dimension for those involved (Carling and Collins 2018).

This article presents three key arguments. (1) Adolescence in the context of rural outmigration becomes a contested field of expectations from different entities besides the adolescents' own attempts of becoming. (2) From the point of view of the adolescents, these divergent expectations create a norm-driven array of discourses permeating many aspects of their lives. (3) Migration therefore emerges from a subject navigating spatial and spatialised discourses. The paper is situated at the juncture of migration theory, critical geographies of childhood and youth and rural geography. It contributes to contemporary debates on rural outmigration of adolescents by highlighting how discursive ramifications of socioeconomic hardship exert social pressure and conditions the adolescents' migratory considerations and their aspirations. This complex realm is explored through empirical examples from the rural German district of Altenburger Land. I use the case study to show how the local situation is subjectively negotiated and thus shapes rural outmigration. In the article, I share detailed perspectives on outmigration from those who deal with it in their professional capacities. And I relay the adolescents' own perspectives – their process of reasoning through the various aspects of migration – as a way to elaborate on the discursive field of migration prevalent in the region.

Conceptualising adolescent migration from rural regions

Based on a conceptual framework for adolescents' migratory considerations and their conditions on the verge of transitioning from school into tertiary education or the labour market, my article presents an empirical analysis of rural outmigration of adolescents at the intersection of two key premises. First, adolescence is 'a shifting social and historical construction' (see James and Prout 1997, 245). Second, migration is not an individual's isolated action but happens in 'discursive fields that push migrants to develop specific views of themselves' (Silvey 2004, 498).

This paper contributes to understandings of rural outmigration by linking these two assertions with a recognition that young people must actively negotiate the discursive and social fields they encounter. This can involve not only an accommodation to local expectations and constraints but also reveals the ways in which young people actively participate in the reproduction and remaking of local expectations. Put another way, the subject, as Butler (1997) argues, has a dual nature. It is simultaneously the instance from which discursive effects originate and the instance that is affected by them. As a consequence, those discursive and social fields in which migration happens are social arrangements consisting of subjective acts of ascribing meaning (to staying, to leaving), of interpreting perceptions (of acts of staying, leaving, pondering migration) and communicating about both. Such a perspective highlights the complexity of social processes and stresses the need to investigate their subjective foundations, e.g. the adolescents' reasoning, their perceptions and their considerations.

Migration may occur at any time in childhood, often depending on a child's dependence on his or her parents (Horton, Kraftl, and Tucker 2010). The point at which such changes occur may have crucial impact on the development from childhood to adulthood. This transition is doubted to be a single instance, but rather seen as 'a series of small transition points' (James and Prout 1997, 246). However gradual, this development may appear from the adult's perspective, 'for children themselves these points of partial transition, such as their moves through the schooling system [...], can take on quite intense meaning' (James and Prout 1997, 246).

Whereas migration sometimes coincides with such developmental transitions, the question of whether or not to migrate is usually connected to concerns about changing social ties. Thus, it may be accompanied by emotional reactions, regardless of how labour migration 'is considered to be a typical and acceptable practice for the transition period between the end of schooling and becoming an adult' (Horváth 2008, 781). Deciding which path to take often involves adolescents navigating 'multiple and competing demands', pondering 'attachments and perceptions of home' and weighing future prospects (Drozdzewski 2008, 160). Symptomatic of that, migratory expressions are 'complex and do not follow simple, linear expectations', as Drozdewski (Drozdzewski 2008, 160) reported of her respondents. Adolescent migration may satisfy needs and aspirations that have been forged in the life course. They may go hand in hand with attempts to balance them with normative expectations often perceived to originate from entities other than the subject himself or herself (see Horváth 2008, 783).

Given the limited work opportunities, the transition between the local school and the workplace is a key concern for adolescents in rural regions (see Nugin 2014, 52f.). Thus, adolescent decision-making in the context of rural outmigration has become the focal point of several studies, many elaborating on specific regional conditions and arguments for leaving and staying from the migrants' perspective. For example, Punch (2002) identifies several structural constraints shaping migratory considerations such as education opportunities, social networks, economic resources and parental attitudes. Moreover, several studies highlight intra-family interactions as being key influences for rural outmigration. For instance, researching former German Democratic Republic (GDR) territories, Leibert (2016, 277) states that 'the cohorts born in the 1980s and in the 1990s have witnessed the (failed or successful) adaption strategies of their parents which have shaped their own life plans, values and norms'. Some scholars stress that peer group discourses in rural areas may also be influential in shaping migratory considerations (e.g. Azaola 2012). This is in line with claims that migratory considerations may happen under the impression of more general regionalised discourses, for example, concerning poverty (Carling 2002).

In essence, migration, as most scholars on rural migration highlight, is embedded in 'complex discursive fields' (Nugin 2014, 51) that must be considered in analysis. On a micro scale, they may comprise peers, family members, neighbours and friends. However, there may also be other narratives in effect which are not specific to the prospective migrant's everyday life, but instead refer to more general conditions. These can involve the discursive normalisation of outmigration 'by conceptualising leaving as moving forward rather than moving away' (Nugin 2014, 51). Wiest (2016) emphasises that fears of 'being left behind' often play important roles in shaping adolescent migratory considerations. These emotions seem to be triggered by meanings migration has acquired in its particular regions (e.g. with regard to self-fulfilment).

Therefore, some researchers have taken up the concept of a 'culture of migration' to label circumstances where outmigration is socially negotiated as an inevitable step in one's life. Horváth (2008, 773f.) highlights three different uses of this term. The first presupposes a factual existence of such a lived pattern of behaviour. The second is concerned with an array of norms and ideas organising the discussion of migration. The third highlights the possibility that migration may have acquired some symbolic functions. 'From a possible, optional or desirable practice, migration can turn into a crucial and necessary social act, that is quasi-compulsory for certain social categories', writes Horváth (2008, 774). What these approaches share, he finds, is their claim to identify structures that are common in decision-making. Easthope and Gabriel (2008, 173) specifically state that the term may not ultimately involve actual people moving, 'but rather the ideas that people share about these movements'.

While the normalisation of migration has already been shown in transnational contexts (e.g. Collins 2014), the presence of a culture of migration in rural areas has special significance for regions suffering from economic decline. While the term itself may be contested for its metaphorical nature and essentialist undertone, several scholars have empirically observed the implications of a culture of migration. Wiest (2016, 289) notes the pressure her respondents felt in knowing that friends planned to leave their rural home region because they were worried about their educations. Easthope and Gabriel (2008, 177) reveal how for some of their respondents, leaving was undoubtedly the 'default position'.

Besides such accounts of 'culture', the discursivity of migration has also been covered under various terms. The concept of 'emigration environment' is used by Carling (2002, 17) to refer to 'discourses about emigration, place and poverty' and the 'social, economic and political context which is largely common to all members of the community'. Carling (2002, 13) specifically stresses that actual migration may be a 'demographic event', yet 'people who consider it as an option relate to migration through the meanings with which it is embedded'. While most researchers note that the demographics of migration can be quantitatively approached, the subjective evaluation of migration-related opportunities seems important enough in the process of decision-making to require qualitative inquiry.

From a discourse-analytical point of view, such cultures of migration may be conceptualised as regional (they are performed in the region) and/or regionalised discourses (they involve articulations about the region, e.g. as stigmata). In this regard, I use the term 'discourse' as a differential and structured system of positions of 'very diverse material elements' (Laclau and Mouffe 2001, 79). However theoretical such an understanding may appear, it rejects linguistic restrictions and encompasses any social phenomena (e.g. documents, practices and institutions) that may be of significance for the subjects involved. Regionalised discourses may then be seen as dynamic sets consisting of semantics, actions, objects, etc., that ascribe meanings to regions using specific signifiers (e.g. unemployment and poverty) and have a certain relevance for the subjects' process of reasoning (see also Meyer and Miggelbrink 2013). From a governmental perspective, the subject can be seen as a manifestation of multiple attempts and offers of structuration, eventually taking up a subject position as discursive identity (see Davies and Harré 1990). Consequentially, subjects are always exposed to the discourse as well as the entities (re-) producing it (see Butler 1997). Regional and regionalised discourses, then, are systems of articulation in and/or about a region that organise knowledge in and/or about the region in specific ways and are of relevance for those subjects involved.

Furthermore, the specific discursive fields in which migratory considerations of adolescents happen are not neutral, but rather dynamic, being subject to normative influences from numerous sources. James and James (2004, 7) argue that the structural factors that may construct and shape childhood include, for example, 'family structure, the nature of kin and gender relations, the structure of the school system; conceptions of the educational process and of the child's health and welfare [...] and the economic and political conditions which underpin such discourses'. Like politics seeking to shape adolescents' decision-making (e.g. Brown 2011), migration as such is also subject to numerous determining factors, such as laws, economic conditions and societal norms (e.g. MacKenzie and Forde 2009).

While some of these factors may emerge from everyday interactions, others are specifically intended to shape their respective fields. Kraftl, Horton, and Tucker (2012, 2–9) analyse the 'youth policy-making' that took place in the UK between 2000 and 2010, which political programmes relied on as a way to intervene in young people's lives and shape the spaces essential to them. In the context of rural outmigration and in times in which mobility is considered normal, adolescents are often seen as human capital for the future development of the region (see Stockdale 2006). Unfortunately, such external perspectives from the political realm often fail to grasp the complexity of the decision-making process, the complexity of adolescents' 'social and psychological outlooks', the social relations within their communities as well as the relations towards their hometowns – all of which compete to shape their considerations (Gibson and Argent 2008, 136). Moreover, adolescents do not only value their immediate social field, but also notice how migration is evaluated in the media. For instance, Easthope and Gabriel (2008, 178) describe how Tasmanian outmigration has been shaped by 'powerful narratives about those who leave and those who stay', sometimes labelling this move as a loss, sometimes hailing outmigration as a symptom of Tasmania's ability to 'compete on a world stage'.

In sum, adolescent outmigration from rural regions is a product of subjective evaluations at various levels including individual (e.g. family relations), socio structural (e.g. local economic conditions), legal (e.g. incentives supporting labour migration) and political (e.g. programmes promoting certain adolescent behaviour). These levels are dynamic in the way they change over time and, from the perspective of the potential migrant, their conditions may overlap. They are multifaceted in their ability to affect different aspects of life. And they are specific in that they only possess significance from the individual migrant's perspective. However, this complexity intensifies when taking discourse into account: the circumstances discussed above not only affect the migrant's movement itself, but also his or her orientation towards migration and its underlying conditions.

The aforementioned body of literature specific to rural outmigration and childhood already encourages research to take a very open stance. However, I want to modulate its conceptual cornerstones by making two additional conceptual points.

First, numerous scholars stress that investigating migration cannot rely on focusing solely on the migrants or their institutional, discursive or social context. There are, however, myriad approaches. Findlay et al. (2013, 146) criticise prevalent micro-scale accounts of individual motivations with regard to the 'insufficient attention given to the economic, social and cultural structures that shape the context within which people move'. Consequently, Findlay *et al.* analyse prevalent images of migrant workers. In contrast, Easthope and Gabriel (2008, 180) argue for taking the perspective of the prospective migrants themselves, noting that 'migration was an important part of the lives of the young people we spoke with and that it had strong influences on the transformation of their own identities'. A common thread in all these approaches is found in the claim that 'relationships, rules and conflicts relating to spaces can reveal contemporary social norms and structures' (Kraftl, Horton, and Tucker 2012, 8f.). Elaborating on the perspective of the adolescents implies 'remaining sensitive to how people imagine themselves, how they see their identities as belonging or being constrained in particular places' (Gibson and Argent 2008, 137).

Second, it is worthwhile to elaborate on the emotional dimension of migratory decision-making (see Mai and King 2009) as the migrants' relationship to their home place is often 'emotionally charged, representing ambivalent feelings' (Wiborg 2004, 427). Some scholars accordingly utilise conceptualisations of the human subconscious that may augment our understanding of the process of reasoning. Examining migration related to higher education within South East Asia, Collins (2014) contributes an understanding of the role of desire within the process of generating a subject's wish to migrate. Detailing the case of Singapore, Collins et al. (2014) specifically dissect the political practice of promoting academic excellence to generate students' mobility aspirations for transnationally enlisting in universities. Methodologically, some scholars have analysed drawings of their respondents (e.g. Findlay et al. 2013; Shubin, Findlay, and McCollum 2014), often relying on Lacan's teachings in psychoanalysis, yet also attempting to apply methods other than interviews and focus groups (on questions of method, see Bondi 2014).

That said, my analysis does use focus groups. It begins with an elaboration of the region's socioeconomic, institutional and legislative conditions, which are the backdrop to adolescent outmigration in Altenburger Land. Next, I detail the point of view of Altenburger Land professionals concerned with adolescent outmigration. I then contrast these descriptions with the adolescents' migratory considerations, elaborating on how several aspects of their lives are permeated by these different discourses.

Methodology

Beginning in 2013, I conducted fieldwork in Altenburger Land under the auspices of the research project 'Discourse and practices in shrinking regions'. In the following sections, I present empirical findings from a sample of 53 conversations with Altenburger Land inhabitants, 32 of whom were professionals in the political and administrative realm. All of them were at least partially responsible for youth-related policies and initiatives (such as labour market, education and culture). Of those 53 conversations, 21 were focus groups of varying sizes and involving respondents between ages 14 and 19. Fifteen of the groups were convened at local secondary schools, four at sports clubs and two at groups preparing for the Protestant sacrament of confirmation. Given the rich empirical data, I chose to just summarise the professionals' statements and give the adolescents' own accounts in detail.

The conversations were audio recorded. After transcription and anonymisation, the conversations were codified using the MAXQDA software so as to inductively elaborate central concepts. In accordance with the method of qualitative content analysis (Mayring 2014), this article summarises and structures the topics emerging across the different focus groups.

From a methodological perspective, it was important to bear the possible impact of researchers interviewing subjects in regions suffering from severe population decline in mind. Therefore, the goal of investigating migration in specific was never revealed to my respondents. Instead, they were asked to detail their feelings towards home and how they imagined their future. The early stages of these conversations were characterised by repeated complaints about a lack of career opportunities within the district's towns and rural areas, yet the more time my respondents were given to flesh out their stories, the more they dwelled on the complex conditions of attempting to choose to stay in or leave the region, how they perceived themselves and their future as well as how they felt towards their home region.

Case study: Altenburger Land

Although more than 25 years have passed since German reunification, economic deprivation caused by deindustrialisation and continued age- and sex-selective outmigration still pose significant challenges for rural regions in eastern Germany (see Leibert 2016). According to officials from the regional public employment service in Altenburger Land, population losses and rampant unemployment were the main reason for actually having *suggested* outmigration to adolescents since the 1990s. Despite the simultaneous factors of an ageing population, outmigration and low birth rates after reunification (e.g. Klemm 2012), outmigration was initially not seen as an important problem because the local companies' need for skilled trainees was still being met.

However, between 2000 and 2010, youth between ages 10 and 19 declined by over 56% in the district several rural settlements and towns (Thuringian State Office for Statistics 2015). Local companies thus struggled more and more to find qualified employees. Because the allocation of tax revenues to German territorial entities depends on for one thing population figures, there was a risk that the local situation would worsen. Minds changed around 2005 and local companies were urged by the district administration to provide more traineeships to keep adolescents from leaving the region. Although such efforts were unique across rural eastern Germany, they were contradicted by continued media coverage about Altenburger Land's poor performance in regional rankings (e.g. INSM 2009). The reports highlighted a worrying socioeconomic situation, earning considerable attention from regional politicians and triggering new calls for economic, demographically oriented measures.

Adolescent outmigration in Altenburger Land: the professionals' perspective

Professionals dealing with the on-going outmigration of Altenburger Land adolescents can be found working in public administration, local and regional politics, local and regional public employment services and other initiatives concerning the local and regional economic development. From their perspective, the outmigration can be blamed on a socioeconomic triad of doom, leaving the region no chance for salvation. First, Altenburger Land is known for its low-wage levels compared with regions in western Germany. Second, having no university and no schools that train students in high-level technical skills in the region, adolescents who reject what is locally available – social, agricultural and health sector traineeships – seemingly have no option but to leave. Third, given the broader patterns of Germany's ageing populations and rural exodus, the local administration is said to struggle with regional finances, which compels decisions on whether to concentrate on cultural, leisure or infrastructural needs (Meyer and Miggelbrink 2015).

Local programmes have long tried to tackle adolescent outmigration. They have applied various measures to foster career opportunities in the region. For instance, secondary regional school students get mandatory counselling on regional career opportunities. Often, they are obliged to do annual internships with local companies starting from the age of 13. Contests, such as the youth science and technology competitions known as *Jugend forscht*, endeavour to have highly skilled adolescents come into contact with local companies. So-called girls days try to demonstrate the various regional opportunities for girls in what were once considered men's jobs.

Moreover, political articulations about the region's future often stress the need to sustain its demographic potential and highlight regional job opportunities when addressing adolescents. In many rural areas, the public administration is highly concerned with preventing the adolescent population from even considering outmigration. For instance, in March 2015, the head of Altenburger Land's administration addressed highly skilled pupils who had just completed small research projects in cooperation with local companies:

> Dear pupils, your scientific curiosity gives me confidence in the future of our district because you are the qualified employees of tomorrow and you are urgently needed in Altenburger Land. Learn, study, gather knowledge, travel the world – but do not forget your home. Come back. You are needed here.

Such articulations attempt to establish a discursive point of reference – home – against the alleged adolescent bias towards outmigration. This is just one of many examples that illustrate the political importance adolescents and their migratory behaviour have in a region that lacks a university and job opportunities, not to mention is surrounded by Leipzig, Chemnitz and Gera. Although Altenburger Land residents often commute to these large cities, Leipzig's increasing economic power, its renowned university, vibrant cultural community and job market drain Altenburger Land – it is often the rule, not the exception, for adolescents to at least consider a move to Leipzig.

A somewhat transformative power has been attributed to these adolescents, so it is unsurprising that they have become focal points of demographically oriented politics. However, despite numerous measures to increase the adolescents' consideration of local and regional career opportunities within Altenburger Land, outmigration has not stopped. There looms a common irritation about the region's inability to keep hold of its adolescents despite various political and administrative efforts over the past years. During our conversations, professionals frequently complained about the lack of adolescents' interest in regional career opportunities. Exerting more pressure on the adolescents to acknowledge local opportunities was seen as one way to go, as the head of an organisation devoted to promoting the regional labour market admitted: 'You have to make the best of it and transform your frustration into positive energy, and do more!' Accusations of adolescents having a somewhat restricted worldview and selective perception – being mainly externally focused rather than considering regional opportunities – were made, off the record. Some interviewees insinuated a prevalent childishness with 'the youth today'.

To migrate or not to migrate? Adolescence in Altenburger Land

For my adolescent respondents, adolescence revolved around high-pressure decisions. The transition between school and the labour market necessitated considerations of whether to migrate or not. This meant contemplating leaving home and family and ultimately completing the transition between childhood and adulthood. Some stressed their determination to choose for themselves, while others revealed an inner strife about what to do and all that would influence the decision. Yet, common to all were the institutional and social contexts in which these reflections were. The question of migration filled three key aspects of their lives: how they saw their abilities to fulfil education and labour market demands, their relationship with their family and reflections on their own needs and aspirations.

Abilities, career demands and regional opportunities

How an adolescent performs at school affects expectations of how he or she can meet job market demands. Having no university or other tertiary educational opportunities nearby, most pupils who obtain their Abitur (a qualification equivalent to A-level exams or Matura) consider leaving Altenburger Land to pursue a university degree or an advanced traineeship. However, it is not always up to the applicant to decide whether to move or not. For example, a 10th grader at a rural secondary school who wanted to move to western Germany to become a chemical lab technician described how she experienced the pressure to migrate. The boss at her internship outside the region had said that 'I would have to relocate – they said they would not take someone who has to commute for hours each day.'

The cap on employment opportunities found in rural regions is a complex topic. Adolescents often complained that jobs were only available in the industrial, agricultural and health sectors, while work in advanced industries (chemical, biology) and the creative sector would require leaving Altenburger Land. But even when young people are interested in – and have good academic qualifications for – a particular field, such as the regional IT sector, they experience obstacles because such few jobs are available. For instance, a boy from a small town, in his final year in a secondary school, went on about the fact that although interesting jobs in IT were available, 'it's hard to get an internship within IT. Everything gets rejected. I only get offers within sales. But I am not interested in sales'.

In view of these struggles and the importance of the decision whether to migrate itself, some pupils receive remarkable support from parents in their pursuit of traineeships across different parts of Germany. This is something they often do during their holidays and for which they usually temporarily relocate, in some instances accompanied by the parents who themselves must use vacation days for the time away from their own work. The complaints of several employment professionals about adolescents not making use of the region's job offerings came in sharp contrast to the tremendous career support some parents provided for their children. Indeed, school performance is not the only asset a future jobseeker can rely on – it must be supplemented.

Yet from a formal perspective, school grades persist to possess a special significance. For prospective trainees without an Abitur, local employers often expect certain grade minimums in German language and mathematics. Others rely on the pupils' performance in internships and dismiss the school grades' relevance. However, enrolment in a vocational school requires certain minimum grade averages, depending on the trainee programme. This aspect – such as in the case of a boy in ninth grade at a rural secondary school – is connected to migratory considerations.

> It is all about the grades. If I had good grades, I'd leave this place, taking up a job in automobile mechanics. If I had bad grades, I'd change to something in metal engineering or something, somewhere within the region.

This interview excerpt references a common conception about the region's capacity to attract those performing considerably well in school. Given the narrow availability of employers and positions, school and internship performances, from as early as age 13, are crucial to determining one's ability to pursue a career in Altenburger Land – from the adolescents' as well as the employers' perspective. This structural connection between career, school performance and migration regularly came up. Underperforming at school was thus unanimously seen as falling short – it meant lacking merits and precluding the possibility to leave the region. I frequently heard a local idiom that epitomised this shared notion: those who stay are not 'capable of finding the train station'.

That school performance is a condition for one's career and potential to migrate, yet it does not determine one's migratory considerations, is exacerbated by a common insecurity. That is, how to assess one's own abilities in view of the demands a particular career path will entail. Furthermore, pupils usually seem to evaluate their own abilities against anticipated demands. For instance, a young girl in 10th grade at a rural school described the luxury of being guaranteed a traineeship at a local hotel following her internship. However, the hotel was quite small, so she wondered whether she should relocate to find a larger company that would give her better work experience. Yet, she was hesitant to make that choice since she had heard that bigger employers allegedly place higher demands later on: 'Sometimes you have to go to university after your traineeship. Will I make it? Won't it be too much?' Many teachers complained about their pupils' unrealistic expectations and self-assessments. However, in the course of our conversations, the pupils reflected on how their performance was valued, the opportunities their performance would yield and which circumstances conditioned their choice to migrate or not.

Adding to the complex interplay between school performance, future professional demands and self-assessments were gender stereotypes, which were said to still possess potency in the local industrial and agricultural sectors. Several female pupils of regional vocational schools described experiences of trying to pursue 'men's work' that ultimately led to abandoning those plans despite the sustained interest and qualifying school performance: 'I applied for a traineeship as a machine operator. This one company told me it was not for me. [...] It is always harder for women in men's jobs.' In rural areas, with few employees per company, certain costs are seen as getting in the way of providing gender-specific workplace infrastructure: 'All those bosses are against females in industrial jobs, because these women would also have to go to the toilets, would have to change clothes – they are seen as unnecessary costs.'

The transition between school and the labour market entails a transition between two different systems of evaluation, and it is seen as a highly complicated one. Our discussions were seldom about school grades themselves, but rather the correlation between grades, job opportunities, the luck involved in finding a position and how all that affected the decision to broaden one's opportunities by relocating.

Family dynamics and regional opportunities

During the empirical fieldwork it quickly became obvious that neither professional demands from educational facilities nor the job market alone affects the adolescents' process of reasoning. Instead, the realm of the family features as a key site where migratory considerations are negotiated against the background of subjectively perceived career demands. Peers have considerable impact on the decision-making process, often even being the only source for leaning about the multitude of opportunities. Though they may inspire or, following negative experiences, deter specific decisions, the opinions and choices of friends, siblings and cousins have relatively minor influence on adolescents compared to those of other relatives.

Parents and grandparents were seen as the major influencers. However, while parents were commonly accepted as allies in my respondents' evaluation of migratory options, grandparents were considered more invasive. Parents usually seemed to encourage the adolescents to leave the region for their own good. For example, a pupil just one year before obtaining his Abitur described how his father, biased by his own history, encouraged, though did not order him, to leave the region:

> My father told me, no matter what I wanted to do, I definitely should leave. Sounds tough, but he said that – here – I weren't able to pursue a career. He says, go, go somewhere where you are drawn to, where you feel comfortable, but not here. That I could make big money in another city, he says. He once wanted to do it, but he couldn't, because of his father who said he should stay.

An observation emerging from all the conversations was that parents by and large were advising their children to pursue jobs that would satisfy them rather than pushing them to a specific position or location. Grandparents, by contrast, were commonly described as being more dominant, attempting to exert more influence on their kin's choices. Many respondents felt pressured by them to go in a particular direction, occasionally to the point where relations between grandchild and grandparents soured. This was apparent in the case of a girl determined to obtain her Abitur from a Gymnasium and then leave the region:

> [My grandparents] demand that I have a somewhat real profession, or study in order to secure a living financially. Instead, I'd like to do something in the arts, but often I am told that it's not profitable, that I should get something secure.

The parents' concern that their children's chances are severely constrained by the region contrasts with the grandparents' fixation more on jobs than geography. Nonetheless, this causes a considerable amount of dissent within families. For instance, a girl's choice to enter a police traineeship after completing the 10th grade at a rural school reveals some of her family's dynamics:

> My grandparents demanded that I complete my Abitur and enter university – in a field such as social work or teaching. But I was able to withstand their pressure. My parents supported me. They also would have favoured me studying, taking up a traineeship and then getting my Abitur. But they [still] stuck with me.

This kind of dissent is sometimes embedded in and informed by extenuating intra-family conflicts. I could trace one girl's decision shortly after finishing 10th grade back to the relationship between herself, her parents, her father's parents and her boyfriend. She was determined move in with her boyfriend, yet staying in the region. Conflict ensued, worsening her relation with her parents and father's parents. This has led her to develop a closer relation to her mother's father who informed her decision to pursue a public service career near their hometown:

> [My grandfather] was particularly interested in me and my career. [...] He asked about my interests and suggested where to look for jobs. He provided me with information on salaries. He searched the internet. Ultimately, I had to make the decision on my own. [...] But he provided me with the facts, and told me what I would have to do in the different jobs. It was pretty awesome, all this effort.

However complex their relations may be, the discussions among family members surrounding the transition between school and labour market showed considerable consistency. Most of my respondents stressed that their parents refrained from pushing them towards a specific job and restricted themselves to providing advice (often to leave the region, no matter which career path was pursued). However, in cases when my respondents were brought by their parents to the focus groups, short conversations on the adolescents' aspirations to migrate unfolded and each time, the parents showed signs of grief that leaving the region was considered a mandatory move for adolescents. Migration was obviously a common, frequent point of discussion at home. Furthermore, how my respondents' parents had made choices for themselves and how my respondents judged those choices severely shaped the pupils' considerations.

Emotions and imaginations as regional and regionalised discourses

The prospect of leaving a familiar context was emotionally challenging. Giving up the chance to spend time with peers in person was one concern, but sometimes it also had to do with appreciating one's old, simple life in a small town. A common topic of discussion was how it would be to substitute direct daily communication with email, telephone and Skype calls.

However, quite commonly, my respondents felt that leaving their parents would be a major obstacle. Several pupils enthused over the many opportunities of big cities, such as Leipzig, though they reigned in those feelings when reflecting on leaving behind what had been the centre of their existence. For instance, one ninth grader, having lived in a town of about 2000 inhabitants for all of her life, described fears of alienation:

> I'm afraid that – after going away and then returning back home – that I wouldn't just return. Instead, I would return as a guest and not as a family member. [...] Usually, the living room is quite messy when I come back from school. But if I return after half a year, everything will

> have been cleaned up by my parents in order to feel, kind of, comfortable. But I do feel comfortable – when it's messy, like always.

Besides fears of leaving something behind, the pressure to get accustomed to new surroundings was intimidating. One young girl in her final year at a rural secondary school relayed the struggle of accepting the social challenges that came with her decision to move to Leipzig to become a veterinary assistant:

> I am really not doing well with new people that I don't know yet. [...] just to achieve that, to get something permanent somewhere, and to have everything be really nice and have the people be nice to you, that's quite difficult for me.

Both excerpts reveal my respondents' ties to others and the nature and implications of their considerations. Although these interviews provide insights into the relational dimensions of social becoming and belonging, other discursive aspects added to the complexity of considering migration when on the verge of transitioning from school to labour market. My respondents linked their own personal experiences and aspirations to more normative imaginations about having a full life.

One common point of reference, for example, was the need to relocate for career reasons to an education-oriented and urbanised society, rather than stay in an environment where unemployment and rurality were often correlated with specific lifestyles and identities. Staying in the region, in this regard, was linked to underachievement: 'If I returned to this place, I would have failed a bit.' The notion of accomplishing something seemed to correspond with leaving the region, given its poor economic performance and sustained social problems related to an ageing population and severe outmigration. The opposite of leaving is often considered a personal defeat.

A second recurring observation from my respondents' concerning what they would get out of a full life was that their deliberation about a job and relocation would be a onetime decision. Despite numerous examples of relatives' meandering career paths, including changes in profession and location, the pupils attributed a sense of finality to their decision; they understood their transition as a form of self-fulfilment. One girl in her final year at a rural secondary school expressed being torn between all he different options for her future.

> I don't want to come to work one day and realise: 'No, that's not what I wanted, it's not satisfying.' Instead, I want to be happy with my decision. You don't want to get up every day, thinking: 'Shit, another day of work.' I don't want that. Nobody wants that!

For this girl, a suitable job is simply part of the larger life plan of finding personal satisfaction. However, her considerations are not positive, instead focused on self-distancing from the possibility of failing to achieve happiness. Linked thus are the region's inability to satisfy pupils' interests and the adolescents' perception that not acquiring a traineeship or a job will doom their employment chances. The existential worries the girl expressed as a result of the circumstances were clear.

> It is a fear, a fear of not being able to find the right job, to realise that I may have made the wrong decision, a fear of standing still, getting nothing, waiting another year, of being already too late.

The gravity of these decisions became even weightier after 2002s German labour market reforms, which exacerbated the situation for the unemployed and low-wage workers.

Pejorative depictions of unemployed and rural populations in the media contributed to a shared notion that making a job decision mistake is simply unacceptable.

In sum, the question of whether or not to migrate was entangled in my respondents' approach to their educational and professional paths, relationships with their family as well as their personal needs and what they perceived as a full life. In this context, Altenburger Land frequently served as regionalised marker for failure. Those from the rural parts of my case study region and those not pursuing an Abitur, in particular, experienced the transition from school to labour market as stressful. It was filled with expectations and demands, which exerted major pressure on them. To my astonishment, I hardly found wide-eyed and ambitious individuals looking forward to adulthood but rather worried adolescents, caught between conflicting paths, feeling obligated to make a decision and hardly able to escape this conundrum.

Discussion

In the course of my empirical work, it became apparent that many of my respondents' had developed a predominantly negative opinion about their home region and therefore tended to offer negative statements about the restrictions in Altenburger Land. The hegemony of this perspective proved resistant to intervention by the moderator (see Meyer, Miggelbrink, and Schwarzenberg 2016). Although there were occasional statements about positive aspects of their home (e.g. nature and quietude), no equally discernible pattern advocating for staying in the region could be identified – even despite the earlier cited political endeavours to do so. The presence of negative orientations towards staying in a rural region suffering from economic decline is nothing surprising (see, e.g. Nugin 2014). However, its persistence must be considered with respect to the dual nature of subjects (see Butler 1997) as (1) the outcome of its repeated usage and (2) the grounds on which future generations may build their own considerations.

Despite the volatile nature of adolescent orientation in the life course, significant conformity could be witnessed between them with regard to how my respondents' evaluated their future in Altenburger Land. The transitions between school and labour market and between living with one's parents and leaving home were conflated with obligatory considerations of migration. Yet, most of the time, the conversations seemed to serve as a valve to release the frustration of having to juggle so many factors. Some accommodated to this situation and presented themselves as rational beings doing what has to be done, only to later reveal significant uncertainty. The uncertainty seems to contradict the pattern of leaving being presented as the default option (see also Easthope and Gabriel 2008). Yet, this uncertainty must be seen less as an artefact and more as an integral part of migratory decision-making (see, e.g. Collins 2014), which has – in my case study – been intensified by the transition between school and work, between being home and being. In fact, the transition has felt a very severe and forced one.

However, there were few exceptions. Of the over 300 adolescents I spoke to, I met one girl who avidly shared her dreams and aspirations. She was determined to leave her home in a small town in Altenburger Land and relocate to a foreign country. While her friends smilingly affirmed her unswerving nature, she spoke emotionally, detailing her plans.

> *A:* I am interested in the prisoners – [...] Not [to be] in a cell [with them], but as an employee.
>
> *Moderator:* So, a policewoman, a prison guard?
>
> *A:* Yeah, [...] I don't want to have a well-behaved job, sitting all day at the computer and doing some shit [...] I am not like that, I need something practical. I need something where I can push my own boundaries. [...] And then – along the way – as a hobby, something with dancing, dancing instructor and stuff. I couldn't live without dancing.

These expressions might be seen by some as the result of fantasy (see Shubin, Findlay, and McCollum 2014), incomplete information (see Leibert 2016) or the girl's desire to liberate herself from rural restrictedness (see Wiest 2016), yet they provide – in their contrast to other prevalent notions – the grounds for further extrapolations. From an analytical point of view, one could argue that, under the weight of a region suffering from economic precarity and population decline, the majority of my respondents suppressed their interests and were conditioned to connect their aspirations to the various demands of various entities: their family, the local job market, general assumptions about the quality of life (see also Wiest 2016). With respect to life in a district continuously called a 'shrinking' region because of population decline (see Meyer and Miggelbrink 2015), my respondents were constantly having to accommodate their desires to their surroundings: to the fact that their actions were politicised and their individual choices imbued with major implications, which became open to family debate, school discussions and the public's attention. Hence, a migration discourse within the region had emerged, and it was exerting social pressure. Given this discursive context, the adolescents' becoming had to involve navigating a path through the instances shaping their lives, their region, their societal context and their peers' life experiences. They were not simply prone to their discursive environment, they were part of its making (see Meyer and Miggelbrink 2013).

Three specific conditions are crucial for understanding the context of migration with respect to my case study: (1) migratory considerations are a common topic of public and private reference; (2) a transition between childhood and adulthood is further conflated with other aspects of human life courses and (3) migration affects many aspects of adolescent life. As a consequence, my respondents adopted a norm-driven perspective on migration, while altogether locking the topic out of some of their social interactions (e.g. with friends).

While the specific choice to be made was highly subjective and related to personal preferences, influences from school experiences, family interactions and imaginations about a full life, it was not solely the choice of an individual; it was a product of the individuals' embeddedness in wider social and discursive contexts. This conclusion shifts the perspective away from the notion that intentional and intelligible decisions and actions form possible entities of explanation of migration. A more accurate abstraction, it would seem, is that of a subject torn between perceptions of what one wants, what one has to want and what is wanted from oneself.

This perspective is compatible with prevalent analyses of the role of aspirations as drivers for migration (see Carling and Collins 2018), discursive conditions for outmigration (e.g. Carling 2002; Nugin 2014), the subjective perceptions involved in pondering migration (e.g. Wiest 2016) as well as more interpretative contributions to an understanding of a possible culture of migration (see Horváth 2008). However, there is a peculiarity in – specifically – adolescents' outmigration from rural areas: The empirical data illuminate the social pressures linked to socioeconomic decline and prevalent outmigration that permeate the social bonds in such regions. The adolescents' becoming, their socialisation, their aspirations of life in and beyond their home has been profoundly shaped by these social pressures. Under such conditions, political attempts to counter the adolescents' flight have proven to be unsuccessful as they have failed to address the very subjectivity of migration.

Acknowledgements

Thanks to Jørgen Carling and Francis Collins and the reviewers of *JEMS* for their thorough, critical and, above all, useful comments on this manuscript. I also thank Judith Miggelbrink for her continued support and supervision and Tom Schwarzenberg for his highly useful comments.

Disclosure statement

No potential conflict of interest was reported by the author.

References

Azaola, M. C. 2012. "Becoming a Migrant: Aspirations of Youth During their Transition to Adulthood in Rural Mexico." *Journal of Youth Studies* 15 (7): 875–889. doi:10.1080/13676261.2012.677813.

Bondi, L. 2014. "A Liminal Practice? Making Interdisciplinary Spaces for Psychoanalysis." In *Making Spaces. Putting Psychoanalytic Thinking to Work*, edited by K. Cullen, L. Bondi, J. Fewell, E. Francis, and M. Ludlam, 37–54. London: Karnac Books.

Brown, G. 2011. "Emotional Geographies of Young People's Aspirations for Adult Life." *Children's Geographies* 9 (1): 7–22. doi:10.1080/14733285.2011.540435.

Butler, J. 1997. *The Psychic Life of Power: Theories in Subjection*. Stanford: Stanford University Press.

Carling, J. 2002. "Migration in the Age of Involuntary Immobility: Theoretical Reflections and Cape Verdean Experiences." *Journal of Ethnic and Migration Studies* 28 (1): 5–42. doi:10.1080/13691830120103912.

Carling, J., and F. Collins. 2018. "Aspiration, Desire and Drivers of Migration." *Journal of Ethnic and Migration Studies* 44 (6): 909–926. doi:10.1080/1369183X.2017.1384134.

Collins, F. L. 2014. "Teaching English in South Korea: Mobility Norms and Higher Education Outcomes in Youth Migration." *Children's Geographies* 12 (1): 40–55. doi:10.1080/14733285.2013.851064.

Collins, F. L., R. Sidhu, N. Lewis, and B. S. A. Yeoh. 2014. "Mobility and Desire: International Students and Asian Regionalism in Aspirational Singapore." *Discourse: Studies in the Cultural Politics of Education* 35 (5): 661–676. doi:10.1080/01596306.2014.921996.

Davies, B., and R. Harré. 1990. "Positioning: The Discursive Production of Selves." *Journal for the Theory of Social Behavior* 20 (1): 43–63.

Drozdzewski, D. 2008. "'We're Moving Out': Youth Out-Migration Intentions in Coastal Non-Metropolitan New South Wales." *Geographical Research* 46 (2): 153–161. doi:10.1111/j.1745-5871.2008.00506.x.

Easthope, H., and M. Gabriel. 2008. "Turbulent Lives: Exploring the Cultural Meaning of Regional Youth Migration." *Geographical Research* 46 (2): 172–182. doi:10.1111/j.1745-5871.2008.00508.x.

Findlay, A., D. McCollum, S. Shubin, E. Apsite, and Z. Krisjane. 2013. "The Role of Recruitment Agencies in Imagining and Producing the 'Good' Migrant." *Social & Cultural Geography* 14 (2): 145–167. doi:10.1080/14649365.2012.737008.

Gibson, C., and N. Argent. 2008. "Getting On, Getting Up and Getting Out? Broadening Perspectives on Rural Youth Migration." *Geographical Research* 46 (2): 135–138. doi:10.1111/j.1745-5871.2008.00504.x.

Horton, J., P. Kraftl, and F. Tucker. 2010. "Spaces-in-the-Making, Childhoods-on-the-Move." In *Children and Young People's Spaces. Developing Practice*, edited by P. Foley, and S. Leverett, 40–57. Basingstoke: Palgrave Macmillan.

Horváth, I. 2008. "The Culture of Migration of Rural Romanian Youth." *Journal of Ethnic and Migration Studies* 34 (5): 771–786. doi:10.1080/13691830802106036.

INSM (Initiative Neue Soziale Markwirtschaft). 2009. "Regionalranking 2009." Accessed December 10, 2015. http://www.insm-regionalranking.de/fs_index.html.

James, A., and A. L. James. 2004. *Constructing Childhood: Theory, Policy and Practice*. Basingstoke: Palgrave Macmillan.

James, A., and A. Prout. 1997. "Re-Presenting Childhood: Time and Transition in the Study of Childhood." In *Constructing and Reconstructing Childhood. Contemporary Issues in the Sociological Study of Childhood*, edited by A. James, and A. Prout, 230–250. London: The Falmer Press.

Klemm, M. 2012. *Job Security and Fertility: Evidence from German Reunification*. Bochum: Ruhr-Universität Bochum.

Kraftl, P., J. Horton, and F. Tucker. 2012. "Editors' Introduction: Critical Geographies of Childhood and Youth." In *Critical Geographies of Childhood and Youth. Policy and Practice*, edited by P. Kraftl, J. Horton, and F. Tucker, 1–24. Bristol: The Policy Press.

Laclau, E., and C. Mouffe. 2001. "Hegemony. The Genealogy of a Concept." In *The new Social Theory Reader*, edited by S. Seidman, and J. C. Alexander, 76–86. London: Routledge.

Leibert, T. 2016. "She Leaves, He Stays? Sex-selective Migration in Rural East Germany." *Journal of Rural Studies* 43: 267–279. doi:10.1016/j.jrurstud.2015.06.004.

MacKenzie, R., and C. Forde. 2009. "The Rhetoric of the 'Good Worker' Versus the Realities of Employers' Use and the Experiences of Migrant Workers." *Work, Employment and Society* 23 (1): 142–159. doi:10.1177/0950017008099783.

Mai, N., and R. King. 2009. "Love, Sexuality and Migration: Mapping the Issue(s)." *Mobilities* 4 (3): 295–307. doi:10.1080/17450100903195318.

Mayring, P. 2014. *Qualitative Content Analysis. Theoretical Foundation, Basic Procedures and Software Solution*. Klagenfurt: Beltz Juventa.

Meyer, F., and J. Miggelbrink. 2013. "The Subject and the Periphery: About Discourses, Loopings and Ascriptions." In *Peripheralization: The Making of Spatial Dependencies and Social Injustice*, edited by A. Fischer-Tahir, and M. Naumann, 207–223. Wiesbaden: Springer VS.

Meyer, F., and J. Miggelbrink. 2015. "Subjektivität und Kausalität in der Migration(sforschung): Annäherungen an Rationalisierungen von Migrationsentscheidungen in schrumpfenden Regionen[Subjectivity and Causality in (the Study of) Migration: Approaches to Rationalizations of Migration-related Decisions in Shrinking Regions]." *Raumforschung und Raumordnung* 73 (1): 17–30. doi:10.1007/s13147-014-0319-2.

Meyer, F., J. Miggelbrink, and T. Schwarzenberg. 2016. "Reflecting on the Margins: Socio-Spatial Stigmatisation among Adolescents in a Peripheralised Region." *Comparative Population Studies* (Preprint – Date of release: 23.11.2016). doi:10.12765/CPoS-2016-10en.

Nugin, R. 2014. "'I Think That They Should go. Let Them see Something'. The Context of Rural Youth's Out-migration in Post-socialist Estonia." *Journal of Rural Studies* 34: 51–64. doi:10.1016/j.jrurstud.2014.01.003.

Punch, S. 2002. "Youth Transitions and Interdependent Adult-child Relations in Rural Bolivia." *Journal of Rural Studies* 18 (2): 123–133. doi:10.1016/S0743-0167(01)00034-1.

Shubin, S., A. Findlay, and D. McCollum. 2014. "Imaginaries of the Ideal Migrant Worker: A Lacanian Interpretation." *Environment and Planning D: Society and Space* 32 (3): 466–483. doi:10.1068/d22212.

Silvey, R. 2004. "Power, Difference and Mobility: Feminist Advances in Migration Studies." *Progress in Human Geography* 28 (4): 490–506. doi:10.1191/0309132504ph490oa.

Stockdale, A. 2006. "Migration: Pre-requisite for Rural Economic Regeneration?" *Journal of Rural Studies* 22: 354–366. doi:10.1016/j.jrurstud.2005.11.001.
Thuringian State Office for Statistics. 2015. "Population development 2000–2010 ABGL". unpublished original data.
White, P., and P. Jackson. 1995. "(Re)theorising Population Geography." *International Journal of Population Geography* 1: 111–123. doi:10.1002/ijpg.6060010202.
Wiborg, A. 2004. "Place, Nature and Migration: Students' Attachment to Their Rural Home Places." *Sociologia Ruralis* 44 (4): 416–432. doi:10.1111/j.1467-9523.2004.00284.x.
Wiest, K. 2016. "Migration and Everyday Discourses: Peripheralisation in Rural Saxony-Anhalt from a Gender Perspective." *Journal of Rural Studies* 43: 280–290. doi:10.1016/j.jrurstud.2015.03.003.

Index

Note: Page numbers in **bold** type refer to tables
Page numbers in *italic* type refer to figures
Page numbers followed by 'n' refer to notes